Illuminating Dance:
Philosophical Explorations

Illuminating Dance: Philosophical Explorations

Edited by
Maxine Sheets-Johnstone

Lewisburg
Bucknell University Press
London and Toronto: Associated University Presses

Associated University Presses
440 Forsgate Drive
Cranbury, NJ 08512

Associated University Presses
25 Sicilian Avenue
London WC1A 2QH, England

Associated University Presses
2133 Royal Windsor Drive
Unit 1
Mississauga, Ontario
Canada L5J 1K5

Library of Congress Cataloging in Publication Data
Main entry under title:

Illuminating dance: philosophical explorations.

Includes bibliographical references.
1. Dancing—Philosophy—Addresses, essays, lectures.
I. Sheets—Johnstone, Maxine.
GV1588.3.I45   1984   793.3'01   83-45958
ISBN 0-8387-5063-X

Printed in the United States of America

To an ever-widening community of scholars
in the aesthetics of dance

Contents

Notes on Contributors

ADINA ARMELAGOS, doctoral candidate at New York University in the Department of Performance Studies; currently working on problems in dance theory.

JOHN E. ATWELL, Department of Philosophy, Temple University; areas of special interest are nineteenth century German philosophy from Kant to Nietzsche, existential phenomenology, and theoretical and applied ethics.

MONROE C. BEARDSLEY, Department of Philosophy, Temple University; author of numerous articles and books on aesthetics, including *Aesthetics: Problems in the Philosophy of Criticism* (1958) and *The Aesthetic Point of View* (1982).

SIBYL S. COHEN, Department of Philosophy, Rutgers University; special interests are literature and art.

ALBERT A. JOHNSTONE, recent doctoral graduate of the University of Waterloo; areas of special interest are skepticism, rationalized epistemology, and foundational phenomenology.

JOSEPH MARGOLIS, Department of Philosophy, Temple University; most recent publications include: *Art and Philosophy* (rev. ed., 1978), *Philosophy of Psychology* (1984), and *Culture and Cultural Entities* (1983).

DAVID B. RICHARDSON, Department of Philosophy, Edinboro University of Pennsylvania; author of *Berdyaev's Philosophy of History* (1969); special interests are studies in comparative civilizations and the philosophy of history.

MAXINE SHEETS-JOHNSTONE, author of *The Phenomenology of Dance* (1980) and essays treating philosophical issues in dance; most recent research is in philosophical anthropology.

9

MARY SIRRIDGE, Department of Philosophy, Louisiana State University; research and writings have centered mainly on the areas of aesthetics and medieval philosophy.

FRANCIS SPARSHOTT, Department of Philosophy, University of Toronto; books include *The Structure of Aesthetics* (1963) and *The Theory of the Arts* (1983).

SUZANNE YOUNGERMAN, recent doctoral graduate in anthropology at Columbia University; faculty member of Laban Institute of Movement Studies; publications in anthropology, dance history, and Laban Movement Analysis.

Preface

Given the unprecedented interest in and enthusiasm for dance in the United States over the past several years, it is surprising that philosophical inquiry into dance lags so far behind. The thrust of this book is to inaugurate formally the field of dance aesthetics, thereby expanding and at the same time focusing more finely the dialogue between dancers and philosophers. A major purpose of the dialogue is to encourage people to participate in a lively discussion of dance: to become aware of aesthetic issues within dance, to be caught up in different and differing viewpoints, and to explore a range of connections between dance and philosophy. While the present dialogue may be weighted more on the side of the philosopher, it is hoped that in the future more dancers will literally rise to the aesthetic occasion and come to share in the illumination of dance.

In his essay, "The Significance of Dance in Nietzsche's Thought," John Atwell reminds us that dance may be considered in other ways than as a performing art; that dance may be *conceived,* as well as appear in many guises. For Nietzsche, for example, dance is more than meets the eye: it is a potent concept for a full, yea-saying life, a power of being. One might wonder whether dance, so conceived, is a metaphor for life or whether one might affirm with Wittgenstein that where what is expressed cannot be said in any other way, the expression is not metaphorical at all. The question of metaphor aside, Atwell shows us that thoughts about dance can be stretched in many new ways: whether dancer or philosopher, we can, for example, reexamine such familiar notions and experiences as gravity and find open spaces in which to discover new meanings, just as

11

we might in a more practical vein reexamine our notion of "elective" courses and perhaps find new values.

Monroe Beardsley's essay, "What Is Going on in a Dance?" converges upon the question, What makes movement dance? or more specifically, What turns motion into aesthetic movings? Beardsley's quest is to find a way of taking into account actual physical movement and the aesthetic reality of a dance at a single conceptual stroke. He does so by examining the possibility of utilizing a basic concept from philosophical action theory, a quite novel and refreshing approach to dance. In the process of examining dance from the viewpoint of action theory, he offers a tentative definition of dance that is rooted in the volitional qualities of actions and characterizable as a surplus of expression. In a larger sense, what is particularly interesting about this essay is its exploration of the relationship of a concept to a phenomenon outside its original area of application— a testing out of the limits of a conceptual domain, as it were.

In "Dance, Whitehead, and Faustian II Themes," David. B. Richardson and I suggest that we can deepen our knowledge of contemporary Western dance by viewing it both as an embodiment of a Faustian II world view and as a reflection of Alfred North Whitehead's process philosophy. The methodology is in part hermeneutical, insofar as the analysis of dance is based upon critical writings, particularly those of dance critic Arlene Croce. Set in the perspective of a civilizational *Weltanschauung,* the phenomenon of dance becomes a new and rich subject for examination; at the same time, the hermeneutical uses of dance criticism suggest a way of penetrating to the aesthetic core of critical writings on dance and thus to highly specified aesthetic standards. But if dance may be seen as an expression of a Faustian II world view, Whitehead's process philosophy may be no less so. It is thus not surprising that a striking accord is to be found between a twentieth-century Western philosophy and a twentieth-century Western dance. To do full justice to the hermeneutical nature of the study, one would, on the one hand, need to take up and analyze a range of critical appraisals of dance, weighing their accord with the regnant ideas of a Faustian II world; on the other hand, one would need to explore at deeper levels the remarkable and provocative affinities noticed here between Whitehead's process philosophy and twentieth-century Western dance.

With the essays by Joseph Margolis, Adina Armelagos and

Mary Sirridge, and Suzanne Youngerman, inquiry shifts to questions about the dancer and the dance. In these essays are probings, parryings, and counterparryings centering on the question of whether, in terms of expression and style, and in the moment of performance, the dancer makes the dance or the dance makes the dancer. Margolis in "The Autographic Nature of the Dance," argues strongly for the view that expressive style is part of the authority of the dancer rather than the correlate of correct movement, and he centers his thoughts on the consequent autographic nature of dance. Armelagos and Sirridge in their essay, "Personal Style and Performance Prerogatives," are equally convinced that expressive style is a matter of the dance itself. Their central concern is less with the allographic or autographic nature of dance than with the separation of movement in a dance from any particular body; that is, they want to say that the movements of a dance manifest a particular style and expressiveness apart from any individual actualization of it. The intricacies permeating the issue extend all the way from ontological concerns—e.g., Which qualities belong to the dancer and which to the dance—to the question, What exactly does dance notation notate? Youngerman's essay, "Movement Notation Systems as Conceptual Frameworks: The Laban System," provides anchor points for understanding and dealing with some of the notational problems and questions involved. In the course of providing an exposition of Labananalysis and an account of Laban's life work as well, Youngerman offers ample ground for appreciating the enormous complexity of human body movement, and she writes persuasively of the need to acknowledge and understand this complexity in assessing the nature of dance or particular aspects of dance such as expression and style.

With my essay, "Phenomenology as a Way of Illuminating Dance," the focus temporarily shifts from particular ontological, definitional, or hermeneutical concerns to more general philosophical and methodological ones. The aim of the essay is to make dancers and dance scholars more aware of the benefits of a philosophically enlightened perspective upon dance, and to make philosophers of art more aware of the benefits of a studio/theater perspective upon dance. A summary exposition of phenomenology is presented together with remarks on the nature, value of, and research possibilities within a phenomenological approach to dance. The exposition is substantially fleshed out by a description of critical issues that often surface in discussions of phenomenology.

The next two essays illustrate in different ways the actual practice of phenomenology. Sibyl Cohen's paper, "Ingarden's Aesthetics and Dance," while not itself a phenomenological analysis, is indirectly suggestive of one insofar as it explores the applicability to dance of phenomenologically derived insights into another art form, i.e., literature. The essay might thus be viewed as methodologically parallel to Monroe Beardsley's: an attempt, in this case, to test out essential rather than conceptual domains. To assay the ultimate validity of Cohen's account, it would, of course, be necessary to do a phenomenological analysis of dance directly and then proceed to a comparative study of the two analyses in order to determine whether the essential structures of literature say all there is to say about dance, whether strata that would otherwise be found in a descriptive account of dance are being omitted, or whether one would find strata at all in a phenomenological analysis of dance. Beyond this, the question of whether distinct phenomenological accounts of the various arts are generalizable, that is, the question of whether, where, and how such accounts converge, constitutes a worthy and provocative, if far-in-the-future, question for study.

Albert Johnstone's essay, "Languages and Non-Languages of Dance," invites us, on the other hand, to turn our attention directly to the complexities of dance itself and to the hazards of making too quick or too generalized declarations about dance. Again, the essay is not strictly a phenomenological study, since it is "goal-directed": it seeks to clear out the unexamined and overgrown underbrush of beliefs about dance being symbolic and to discover instead, on the basis of experience, the ways in which dance may be said to be and not to be a language. The essay thus provides a preliminary phenomenological view of the terrain and, in the process, opens up a new vantage point upon movement: an aesthetic classification of different kinds of *movement* in dance, in contrast to the more customary (and usually perfunctory) subsumption of movement *in toto* under aesthetic classifications of different kinds of *dance*. While students and teachers of dance composition and dance critics might find this new vantage point particularly worthwhile in their evaluations and discussions of choreography, it might also be of special interest to people in dance notation, insofar as it allows one to separate out differing strands of movement, as it were, which are woven into the same dance.

Francis Sparshott's initial concern in the final essay of the book, "The Dancing Body," is to discover the kind of dance possible to each of three Sartrian dimensions of bodily presence. But a consideration of dance on the Sartrian ground of bodily presence leads not only to a consideration of the possibility of certain kinds of dance; it leads also to a good many issues. To begin with, a consideration of dance as bodily presence gives way to a consideration of dance as movement; a consideration of dance as movement gives way to questions concerning the difference between dances in which the dancer's body is said to "disappear" into the movement and dances in which the dancer's body is seen to retain its very individual and human character; these concerns give way to the question of whether dance is a matter of artistically disciplined bodies trained within a certain movement system or whether any body movement is potentially dance; the latter possibility leads to the question of whether "free-movement" dance is less notatable than formally structured dance. Within the context of these dichotomies, questions of expression, of style, of what is seen in a dance, and of what constitutes a dance are raised. Precisely to the extent that they are raised for the purpose of clarifying and putting in manageable order the complex terrain of certain attitudes and beliefs about dance, their probing rather than conclusive air provides a fitting ending upon which to begin.

In reflecting upon the contents of the book as a whole, I have been consistently struck by the intertwining threads that connect the various essays, despite their intrinsic diversity. For example, while Beardsley contends that dance is a surplus of expression, or of emotive action, Johnstone holds that expressive movement is only one possible kind of movement in dance; while Cohen and Margolis share a similar concern with the body as a natural power of expression and would agree, albeit in two different senses, that the dancer does not function like marks on a page, Youngerman, though not wishing to deny that the body is a natural power of expression, would not agree that the "lived body" cannot be notated. In short, a web of issues becomes discernible within the text of the book: the notatability of the lived body, the human body as a natural power of expression, the relationship of dance to the human life-world, differing descriptive classifications or categoriza-

tions of dance, the distinction between mere movment and
dance, and the distinction among different kinds of movement
in dance.

Body, movement, expression—these are pivotal issues
throughout the book. Their recurrence within a diversity of
thoughts about and approaches to dance seems to emphasize
how much we do not know about dance, rather than how much
we do, i.e., these issues are clearly central to an understanding
of dance and cannot be taken for granted, assumed as completely transparent, or presumed to be already accounted for.
In this sense, the book offers no sudden or total illumination of
dance, but rather beacons along the way—beacons marking
paths traveled and paths yet to be explored in the process of
shedding light upon dance. Clearly many paths exist, and more
will come to exist. Some will undoubtedly prove more
profitable, viable, or enduring; others more transient and narrow. The vitality and open future of dance would lead us to
expect as much. Nevertheless we may hope that the vistas
opened up by this book prove to be substantially enlightening
ones.

I would like gratefully to acknowledge the following pub-
lishers for permission to reprint material:

The Midwest Quarterly for permission to reprint John Atwell's
essay, "The Significance of Dance in Nietzsche's Thought,"
which appeared in vol. 25, no. 2 (Winter 1984): 129–47.

Dance Research Journal for permission to reprint Monroe
Beardsley's essay, "What Is Going on in a Dance?," which appeared in vol. 15, no. 1 (Fall 1982): 331–36.

Alfred A. Knopf, Inc. for the quotations from *Afterimages,* by
Arlene Croce. Copyright © 1977 by Arlene Croce. Reprinted
by permission of Alfred A. Knopf, Inc. and for the quotations
from *Going to the Dance,* by Arlene Croce. Copyright © 1982 by
Arlene Croce. Reprinted by permission of Alfred A. Knopf,
Inc.

Journal of Aesthetics and Art Criticism for permission to reprint
Joseph Margolis's essay, "The Autographic Nature of the Dance,"
which appeared in vol. 39 (Summer 1981): 419–27.

Houghton Mifflin Company for the quotation from *The
Shapes of Change,* by Marcia Siegel. Copyright © 1979 by Mar-
cia B. Siegel. Reprinted by permission of Houghton Mifflin
Company.

Illuminating Dance:
Philosophical Explorations

The Significance of Dance
in Nietzsche's Thought

John E. Atwell

Watching Zorba dance, I understood
for the first time the fantastic
efforts of man to overcome his weight—

Nikos Kazantzakis, *Zorba the Greek*

Very few philosophers in the Western world have thought of
dance as significant to their metaphysical, ethical, or even aesthetic theories. But there are exceptions: there is Plato, for
example, and twenty-three centuries later, there is Friedrich
Nietzsche. Plato viewed dance as an integral part of *mousiké,*
"the art of the muses," hence as one facet of a triad that includes music and poetry. Dance, for him, was to be an essential
part of the young person's education, and as such it was meant
to help inculcate into the future citizen a rhythm and harmony
which, once developed and augmented by other studies, would
amount to justice. Plato did not think of dance as an optional
course of instruction, as an "elective," but as a required disci-
plining of the physical movement so natural to young children.
And, he would insist, any dancing—like any music playing or
poetry reciting or storytelling—that failed to contribute to a
harmonious psyche in the individual and thus to a well-
organized community would be disallowed in a proper polis. In
sum, Plato conceived of dance as a highly important formative
element in early education, hence as an element that ought to
be controlled so as to help produce ethically good citizens and,

19

ultimately, a just society. As much as anyone in the entire history of Western civilization, Plato recognized the influence of
"the arts" on young people's subsequent ethical and civil behavior; and among these arts he numbered dance.[1]

As one would expect, Nietzsche viewed dance in a very different way; but no more than Plato did he approach dance as
primarily a performing art to which one might apply standards
of aesthetic evaluation. Nor did he speak of an individual dance
or rather dance-type (say *Swan Lake*) as a peculiarly intractable
"art object" whose identity through time and performance is
extremely difficult to fix or account for. He did not write anything about the problems of dance notation or the like; and he
did not deal with the particular sort of movement or pan-
tomime one encounters in most dances. Instead, for Nietzsche,
dance is fundamentally a human activity symbolizing a specific
ethico-metaphysical stance. And what is unique about dance is
that it represents this stance better than any other human activity (though singing and laughing can play a similar role). This
"stance," as I have called it, concerns one's attitude toward such
things as the possibility of a transcendent god, the meaning of
life, one's cultural (especially moral) tradition, and even science, scholarship, and, more broadly yet, the "pursuit of
truth."[2]

A Rejoinder to Silenus

Lillian Lawler, in *The Dance in Ancient Greece,* reports the
words of an ancient Greek writer who expresses pity for the
inhabitants of an invaded city: "For them there is no
significance in life; they have no dancing, no Helicon, no
Muse."[3] These people are not to be pitied because they have
been defeated in battle but because they are not acquainted
with the arts and religious stories, the things which, above all
else, give meaning to human life. Nietzsche would have agreed
with the general proposition suggested here, and he would
have admitted that the meaning of life is a proper, or perhaps
simply unavoidable, issue of human concern.

One of the pervading themes in German philosophy, from
the late Kant to Nietzsche, is the question of the meaning or
purpose of human existence. Kant concerned himself especially with the question of human progress, particularly in light

of the barbarity and excesses of the French revolution during the Reign of Terror.[4] Hegel tried to discover a thread of reason and reasonableness in the apparently senseless course of human events called history.[5] And Schopenhauer, to mention just one more figure concerned with the meaning of life, decided early in his philosophic musings that human beings are subject to an insatiable, blind will that renders their existence less desirable than their nonexistence.[6] Though it is not always recognized, and almost never sufficiently emphasized, Nietzsche should be placed in this current of nineteenth-century German thought.

Nietzsche's first book, *The Birth of Tragedy,* was published in 1872. In the preface of that early work, the subtitle of which is "Hellenism and Pessimism," Nietzsche asserts that "art represents the highest task and the truly metaphysical activity of this life" (*BT,* 31–32). But what exactly is this task and this truly metaphysical activity? It is, I submit, the construction—or perhaps, formation—of something that will be seen as "justifying" human life. There is no doubt but that in *The Birth of Tragedy* Nietzsche attempts to account for the "birth" of Greek tragedy (which, of course, he locates in the duality, and in part antagonism, of the Apollonian and Dionysian "energies"), but there is also no doubt that Nietzsche ties up that historico-aesthetic question with a profound metaphysical question when he asserts that

> the same impulse which calls art into being, as the complement and consummation of existence, seducing one to a continuation of life, was also the cause of the Olympian world which the Hellenic "will" made use of as a transfiguring mirror. Thus do the gods justify the life of man: they themselves live it—the only satisfactory theodicy! Existence under the bright sunshine of such gods is regarded as desirable in itself (*BT,* 43).

It was through the (artistic) creation of the Olympian world that the ancient Greeks provided themselves with a meaningful existence.

"The Greek," Nietzsche claims, "knew and felt the terror and horror of existence" (*BT,* 42). This is confirmed, he said, by the story of folk wisdom in which King Midas interrogates Silenus (who, incidentally, had once been the companion of Dionysus). Upon being asked "What is the best and most desirable of all things for man?" Silenus at first refused to answer but finally cried out:

> Oh, wretched ephemeral race, children of chance and misery, why do you compel me to tell you what it would be most expedient for you not to hear? What is best of all is utterly beyond your reach: not to be born, not to *be*, to be *nothing*. But the second best for you is—to die soon (*BT*, 43).

Silenus's words reflect the Titanic reign of terror, Nietzsche suggests, but that reign was overcome and replaced by the Olympian order of joy that finally emerged. "It was in order to be able to live that the Greeks had to create these [Olympian] gods from a most profound need" (*BT*, 43). In creating Helicon, the Greeks formed gods who lived much as human beings—who fought each other, who envied and often stole each other's possessions, who harbored overpowering jealousies, who suffered great misery and pain, but who celebrated life, no matter what its quality. As a consequence, human existence is "justified," or perhaps "sanctified," for it is now seen as akin to divine existence. And so the "wisdom of Silenus" is reversed: "To die soon is worst of all for [men], the next worst—to die at all" (*BT*, 43). In a well-known episode of *The Odyssey*, Homer has Achilles say that he would prefer to live as a lowly day laborer rather than inhabit the realm of the dead.[7]

The Greeks, according to Nietzsche, had experienced the horror of human existence. How then, he asks, is their peculiar gaiety, exuberance, and joy of life to be explained? Only on the supposition that they saw their existence as a work of art, and indeed as a work of art that they themselves had created. Nietzsche writes:

> In the Greeks the will wished to contemplate itself in the transfiguration of genius and the world of art; in order to glorify themselves, its creatures had to feel themselves worthy of glory; they had to behold themselves again in a higher sphere, without this perfect world of contemplation acting as a command or a reproach. This is the sphere of beauty, in which they saw their mirror images, the Olympians (*BT*, 44).

But, Nietzsche says, there is one form of artistic creation in which human beings do not simply "see their mirror images" but become that which justifies themselves—and that is in dance. For in dance, man "feels himself a god," just like those gods he saw in his dreams: "He is no longer an artist, he has become a work of art" (*BT*, 37).[8] Although, as Nietzsche twice says, "It is only as an *aesthetic phenomenon* that existence and the world are eternally *justified*" (*BT*, 52, 141), there is something "self-justifying" about dance. For if man is justified by his artistic creations, and if, in dance, he becomes one with an artistic creation, then he is, as it were, "self-justified." This idea—that man is not really in need of anything outside himself for justification—is just hinted at in *The Birth of Tragedy*, but it becomes a major emphasis in Nietzsche's later works.

Inquiring into a possible "justification" of human existence, asking what, if anything, can "make life possible and worth living" (*BT*, 35), wondering how we human beings can endure the utter senselessness of human history and bear the meaningless sufferings of life, Nietzsche—not wholly unlike Schopenhauer and, a bit later, Oscar Wilde—saw at first no answer but to appeal to artistic creation. It was the same appeal, he speculated, that governed the ancient Greeks' creation of the Olympian order. Later Nietzsche replaced the gods, and perhaps even artistic creation, with the overman, who, Zarathustra announces, is "the meaning of the earth" (*Z*, 125); in other words, the overman takes over the role of justifying human life, and the task of human beings—that which gives their life meaning—is just that of preparing the way for the overman's appearance. In a sense, of course, the overman is a creation, but perhaps even more than the gods of old and the transcendent God of Judeo-Christianity, he seems to stand apart from human beings—indeed, too far apart to justify their life. So finally, I think, either the notion of the overman drops out of Nietzsche's thought, being replaced by the doctrine of *amor fati*, a thesis of active acceptance of what is and of what will possibly be again and again, or else the notion of the overman comes to stand not for something "beyond" man but for an attitude of *amor fati* expressible by man. And that attitude is symbolized by Zarathustra's dancing. For after all, and perhaps above all, "Zarathustra is a dancer" (*EC*, 306). Elements of this all too brief summary will be clarified as we continue. Here I simply want to stress that for Nietzsche dance signifies, throughout his career, the proper stance to adopt toward many things (including numerous human activities), but what he regards as proper varies somewhat from time to time.

Zarathustra's Devil

In part 1 of *Thus Spoke Zarathustra* there is a passage that many dancers and dance critics are familiar with.

> I would believe only in a god who could dance. And when I saw my devil I found him serious, thorough, profound, and solemn: it was the spirit of gravity—through him all things fall.
>
> Not by wrath does one kill but by laughter. Come, let us kill the spirit of gravity!
>
> I have learned to walk: ever since, I let myself run. I have learned to fly: ever since, I do not want to be pushed before moving along.
>
> Now I am light, now I fly, now I see myself beneath myself, now a god dances through me (Z, 153).[9]

In part 3 Zarathustra returns to the same theme, remarking that "above all, I am an enemy of the spirit of gravity" (Z, 304). But what exactly is meant by the "spirit of gravity"? What, in other words, is Zarathustra's "devil"?

One's devil is that which tempts one most sorely; it is one's greatest weakness, or that which one is most inclined toward—and, by suggestion, that which one must guard against most assiduously. In Nietzsche's case (he says through the figure of Zarathustra), the devil is the "spirit of gravity." This "spirit," I think, takes on many guises, of many different forms; but every form is to be combated by some form or other of dance.

Nietzsche's "spirit of gravity," according to George A. Morgan, symbolizes "all the burdens of life." And "completed love of fate means a victory over this spirit [of gravity], which [Nietzsche] symbolizes by dancing, flying, laughing, and singing—when the world has become *light,* that will be the divine culmination of existence for man."[10] On this view, Nietzsche portrays the ultimate victory over the spirit of gravity as the renunciation of anything otherworldly and the acceptance of this world as the only world. These attitudes are represented in Nietzsche's thought by an unwavering atheism, the thesis of *amor fati,* and finally the doctrine of eternal recurrence, all of which, it should be noted, are adopted by Zarathustra.

Morgan's interpretation is not incorrect, I think, but it is far from complete; it also can perhaps be stated somewhat more precisely. For when Nietzsche speaks of the "spirit of gravity," he has in mind much more than the "burdens of life": he is thinking of what may be called melancholia or nausea (see *Z,* 408–9), which is a much more general malaise than the phrase "the burdens of life" signifies. Indeed, Nietzsche would say that he who felt no such "burdens" might still very well feel a pervasive *Weltschmerz* or *mal de vie.* These terms remind us of twentieth-century existentialists (especially, I think, Unamuno and Camus), but Nietzsche would have been thinking of the doctrine of pessimism that is associated with the name of Schopenhauer. The idea of pessimism—roughly the thought that "all is vanity" and "life is not worth living"—is explicitly referred to—and soundly rejected—by Zarathustra (*Z,* 302, 316). It is worth noting that pessimism, according to Nietzsche, is likely to result, first, in self-pity and then in pity for others. For if one holds that life is fundamentally miserable, one will probably feel sorry for those who must endure life. Recall that Zarathustra's final temptation—one facet of his "devil"—is pity for others (*Z,* 439). To summarize, then: victory over the ever-threatening "disease" of melancholia is the acceptance of *amor fati* along with its most pronounced version, the doctrine of eternal recurrence; and this victory, as Morgan states, is symbolized by dancing, singing, and laughing.[11]

Melancholia may manifest itself in an area seemingly far removed from comprehensive world views like Schopenhauerian pessimism and ethical theories based on pity. It may lead one to seek solace and security in (a certain conception of) science—more specifically, in that sort of intellectual pursuit that posits absolute laws—whether of natural phenomena or of moral relationships—and stable entities and eternal verities. In short, melancholia may manifest itself in, for lack of a better term, scholarliness and the discipline of scholars, namely, "grave science."

Nietzsche begins *The Gay Science* with a section entitled "The Teachers of the Purpose of Existence." In opposition to the pessimists and to those (nihilists) who bewail the "human condition"—neither of which positions, of course, Nietzsche favors—

the teachers of, say, purposiveness cry out, "Life is worth living" (*GS*, 74). Life is to be taken seriously; certain things are to be valued without qualification; purpose and design are to be assigned to human life. So announce the teachers of the purpose of existence. But, Nietzsche maintains, it is solely because they perceive the "comedy of existence" that these teachers decree, "There is something at which it is absolutely forbidden henceforth to laugh" (*GS*, 75). They decree, in other words, that there is something solemn, serious, and, in a way, divine—hence, something standing beyond question or scrutiny. According to Nietzsche's analysis, even the pursuit of science, knowledge, and truth is motivated by the "human, all-too-human" desire for stability, solidity, and firmness. It is the "spirit of gravity" that moves us to hold to that which is firm; and it is the "spirit of laughter, song, and dance" that lifts us sufficiently above the firm so that we become capable of questioning it. "Gay science" is, among other things, a science that shrinks from no hypothesis, no matter how much tradition and convention may oppose it, and that leaves no conviction unexamined. Even "truth" itself can be made a subject of criticism (*GM*, 153).

The unquestionable, the immutable, the sanctified, the inestimable—this is also summed up by the word *God*. And, not unremarkably, it is in *The Gay Science* that Nietzsche first brings up the death of God—an event that "unchained this earth from its sun" (*GS*, 181) but that also explains "our cheerfulness" (*GS*, 279). For now, to speak metaphorically, we may sail "open seas" (*GS*, 228, 280, 283), and, to speak literally, we may put everything up to examination and experiment. With the death of God, something else goes by the board: one and only one world, or rather one and only one way of conceiving the world. "Grave science" would tell us that the old way of conceiving reality—with its perfectly straight lines, its exact triangles, its enduring substances, its causes and effects—is the only proper way, but "gay science" opens up the path for new ways of viewing reality, for "perspectivism." For reality, particularly human reality, is ambiguous, rich, and inexhaustible (*GS*, 334–36). This is not to say, however, that for Nietzsche there are no facts at all but only interpretations. What he does hold is that there are no "pure," theory-free—that is, nonperspectival—facts. He writes in the *Will to Power* "Against positivism, which halts at phenomena—"There are only facts"—I would say: No, facts is precisely what there is not, only interpretations. We cannot establish any fact 'in itself': perhaps it is folly to want to do such a thing" (*WP*, 267). Clearly, then, Nietzsche's espousal of perspectivism should be seen as a feature of his advocacy of "gay science," which in this case amounts to a rejection of the doctrine that there is one and only one way of perceiving reality.

What the "gay scientist," the genuine "scholar," needs to do is to stand back from his or her own tradition far enough to subject it to question. This scholar is not to carry "alien burdens"—the values and concepts handed down from earlier generations, which he or she has not personally "laughed at" or "danced over." These alien burdens are, primarily, one's culture's notion of "good" and "evil" (see *Z*, 305). Scholars, Nietzsche tells us, are prone, like asses, to "pull the people's cart" (*Z*, 216) rather than decide for themselves what is and what is not worthwhile. But how is one to, as it were, transcend one's time? Is it possible? Here Nietzsche is required to recommend a stance which, it seems, he has precluded from the realm of possibility—namely, the stance of "objectivity." He explicitly claims that every science—that is, every sort of inquiry—begins with certain presuppositions, which is to say, alternatively, that "science . . . rests on a faith; there simply is no science 'without presuppositions'" (*GS*, 281). This is one meaning of perspectivism, and it is one feature of Nietzsche's rejection of Schopenhauer's "pure knowledge" (see especially the section in *Z* called "Immaculate Perception," 233–36). The question is, then, "How is one to 'dance over' one's tradition?" In part, Nietzsche's answer is this:

> "Thoughts about moral prejudices," if they are not meant to be prejudices about prejudices, presuppose a position *outside* morality, some point beyond good and evil to which one has to rise, climb, or fly—and in the present case at least a point beyond *our* good and evil, a freedom from everything "European," by which I mean the sum of the imperious value judgments that have become part of our flesh and blood (*GS*, 342).

To carry out the project of "thinking about morality," one must be, Nietzsche says, "very light": "One must have liberated oneself from many things that oppress, inhibit, hold down, and make heavy precisely us Europeans today" (*GS*, 343). In fact, one must not only guard against being of one's own time; one must equally guard against aversion to one's own time and the suggested preference for another time—which is a form of romanticism.

Nietzsche suggests that only from a standpoint outside morality can one treat morality objectively. Other philosophers have said that one can speak of the justification of mathematics only from a nonmathematical standpoint—for example, from a linguistic standpoint—and that appears to be the sort of thing Nietzsche is saying in the passage just cited. But what would a nonmoral standpoint be? Perhaps aesthetic, or physiological? The answer to all of this depends on how one characterizes the various standpoints, particularly the moral point of view. But there is no time for that here, nor is there even time to argue that Nietzsche is probably conflating "morality" as a point of view with "morality" as a particular system of morals operative in a particular historical period for a particular society. Although Nietzsche says a good deal about—or around—these matters (e.g., in "A Thousand and One Goals," *Z,* 170–72, and throughout *Beyond Good and Evil* and *The Genealogy of Morals*), he does not directly pursue the issue of delineating a nonmoral standpoint from which one might view "morality."[12] In *The Genealogy of Morals,* however, there is a hint as to Nietzsche's version of "objectivity" when he remarks that "the *more* affects we allow to speak about one thing, the *more* eyes, different eyes, we can use to observe one thing, the more complete will our 'concept' of this thing, our 'objectivity,' be" (119). By way of summary, I think it fair to say that Nietzsche (1) rejects Schopenhauer's notion of "pure"—that is, will-less and nonperspectival—knowledge; that he would (2) reject one version of contemporary phenomenology, namely the idea that there are "pure givens" that human beings are in principle capable of describing in a presuppositionless, theory-free manner; but that he would (3) not oppose that version of phenomenology—and other theories—that instructs us to seek "objectivity" by approaching the objects of our inquiry from as many perspectives and with as few "biases" as possible.[13]

Elsewhere Nietzsche suggests a somewhat different sort of interpretative approach—at least with regard to, but not exclusively with regard to, "a scholarly book." He writes, for example:

> We do not belong to those who have ideas among books, when stimulated by books. It is our habit to think out-doors—walking, leaping, climbing, dancing, preferably on lonely mountains or near the sea where even the trails become thoughtful. Our first questions about the value of a book, of a human being, or a musical composition are: Can they walk? Even more, can they dance? (*GS*, 322)

Nietzsche goes on to say that he can tell when a book was written by someone bent over a desk, with "a pinched belly" and "cramped intestines." The nature of such a book, he suggests, will correspond to the setting in which it was composed: it will be stale, "cramped," and narrow—that is to say, it will re-hash old ideas, constrict the reader's mind, and erect barriers against novelty. Rather than expand the mind, such a book will shrink it. Nietzsche's thought here can be put more literally, I think. He is expressing his preference for books (and other things) that suggest new ideas to the reader, that question ac-cepted relationships and inferences, that arrange matters in unusual and, on first glance at least, bizarre ways, that leave no assumption untested and no "first principles" unexamined. He is expressing a preference for the sort of books he wrote.

Actually Nietzsche thinks much more highly of scholars, with their specialties, than he does of "men of letters," with their purported knowledge of everything (*GS*, 323). But there is an alternative: there is the philosopher. And again Nietzsche uses the analogy of dance, but here with regard to ingesting what might be called "morsels of knowledge." He writes:

> It is not fat but the greatest possible suppleness and strength that a good dancer desires from his nourish-ment—and I would not know what the spirit of a philosopher might wish more to be than a good dancer. For the dance is his ideal, also his art, and finally also his only piety, his "service to God" (*GS*, 346).

This, I think, is simply another way of saying that genuine philosophers are not tied down to their own cultural milieus or, like scholars, to particular specialties that will no doubt affect (if not determine) the way they view reality and human relation-ships. And the dance, Nietzsche suggests, represents the genu-ine philosopher's "triumph over gravity."[14]

Meaning And Immortality

The third essay of Nietzsche's late (1887) book, *On the Genealogy of Morals,* is entitled, "What Is the Meaning of Ascetic Ideals?" Therein Nietzsche is discussing, I think, the various forms of, say, "self-deprivation," which range from the "sacrifice" of intellectual self-discipline (a sort of harshness or even cruelty directed toward oneself), to mortification of the flesh, and, perhaps finally, self-murder. What do all of these manifestations of the ascetic ideal have in common? What do they all express? This is Nietzsche's question, and his answer is "the basic fact of the human will, its *horror vacui: it needs a goal*— and it will rather will *nothingness* than *not* will" (*GM,* 97). Why self-deprivation? In order to give some meaning, some reason, to suffering and misery which, in themselves, are recognized as lacking all meaning. As long as people believe in gods, they can hold that human misery is the will of the gods: "It's God's will that your six-year-old was raped and tortured to death." But when people no longer believe in gods, *they* must give sense to human misery—and it does not matter what source that sense is derived from. All that is needed is some absolute devotion to something, so that once scholars and philosophers gave up literal self-mortification, they devoted themselves unqualifiedly to the "truth," to which they now "sacrifice" themselves. But this "will to truth," Nietzsche reminds us, is just one more version of the ascetic ideal: it is one more attempt to give meaning to human existence, which otherwise lacked all meaning. Says Nietzsche,

> *This* is precisely what the ascetic ideal means: that something was *lacking,* that man was surrounded by a fearful *void*—he did not know how to justify, to account for, to affirm himself; he *suffered* from the problem of his meaning. He also suffered otherwise, he was in the main a sickly animal: but his problem was *not* suffering itself, but that there was no answer to the crying question, "*why* do I suffer?" (*GM,* 162).

Suffering is tolerable for man, but finding no reason for suffering is not. But "*the ascetic ideal offered man meaning!*" Unfortunately, Nietzsche judges, that meaning resulted in an aversion in general terms to human life, the body, happiness and beauty, appearance, change, death; it resulted, therefore, in a "will to nothingness"—that is, to "God," to the otherworldly, and the "beyond." Undeniably, then, "man would rather will *nothingness* than *not* will" (*GM,* 163).

Nietzsche does not say, but he strongly suggests, that the "will to meaning," as found in the ascetic ideal, is a "human, all-too-human" weakness, for it purports to find meaning for human existence in something beyond human existence, indeed, beyond all of this life. Nietzsche presumably holds, however, that the will to meaning is not always or necessarily indicative of human weakness, for, as Zarathustra claims, "the overman is the meaning of the earth" (*Z,* 125), and those who find meaning through preparing the way for the overman are apparently not weak. They indeed "remain faithful to the earth," and—again like Zarathustra—they rejoice in crying out, "What are the gods to me now?" (*Z,* 200). This means, no doubt, that nothing beyond the earth and human life, with all its instability, flux, and unpredictability, is to be invoked for the fulfillment of man's "will to meaning."

But is the overman not simply a surrogate god? Is he not "beyond?" And does not the reliance on the overman reveal a weakness in man? Is not the overman too distant from man to give man's life a meaning? The answer to these and related questions depends entirely on what the overman is meant to signify—and on that issue Nietzsche was far from clear. I suggest here, as I suggested earlier, that the overman becomes, not something beyond man—certainly not a new biological species—but an attitudinal stance that man is capable of adopting; and that stance is the yea-saying to all of human life that is exemplified by Zarathustra, especially in "The Drunken Song," the penultimate section of part 4 of *Thus Spake Zarathustra.* It amounts to taking joy in, or feeling joy upon the occasion of, certain experiences, and so the simultaneous welcoming of all woeful experiences. For in Nietzsche's judgment, everything is interlocked:

> Have you ever said Yes to a single joy? O my friends, then you said Yes too to *all* woe. All things are entangled, ensnared, enamored; if ever you wanted one thing twice, if ever you said, "You please me, happiness! Abide, moment!" then you wanted *all* back (*Z,* 435).[15]

Here there is no appeal to anything beyond man: there is simply Zarathustra's dancing acceptance (he says, "my soul dances") of all things, even such contradictory things as joy and woe.

In discussing Zarathustra in *Ecce Homo,* Nietzsche writes that in Zarathustra "all opposites are blended into a new unity." Above all, Zarathustra exhibits no rancor: "How gently he handles even his antagonists," and how cheerful and good-natured he remains. "Here man has been overcome at every moment; the concept of the 'overman' has here become the greatest reality" (305). Although Zarathustra says noto almost everything, he is the opposite of "a no-saying spirit," he is not a despiser of life, the body, the earth. He thus represents, Nietzsche claims, the concept of Dionysus, the dancing god, though this conception of Dionysus differs a bit from earlier ones; for here it stands for the affirmation of human existence despite insight into its eternal recurrence. What Nietzsche calls the "psychological problem" of Zarathustra is this:

> How the spirit who bears the heaviest fate, a fatality of a task, can nevertheless be the lightest and most transcendent—Zarathustra is a dancer—how he that has the hardest, most terrible insight into reality, that has thought the "most abysmal idea," nevertheless does not consider it an objection to existence, nor even to its eternal recurrence—but rather one reason more for being himself the eternal Yes to all things (*EC,* 306).

In a successive passage of *Ecce Homo,* Nietzsche reminds us that "Zarathustra has mastered the *great nausea* over man"—that is, the disgust with man or love and, what is worse, pity for man. Now Zarathustra views man as matter, an un-form, that needs a sculptor (309).

These passages might be taken to mean that Zarathustra's task is to help bring form and structure to human beings, to help raise them up above themselves; in short, to help them achieve the status of the overman. But this, I think, is a faulty interpretation of Nietzsche's thought. For the sculpting that Zarathustra is assigned is to be practiced on himself: his sole task is to perfect himself (cf. *EC,* 309). And if he achieves perfection, he will thereby have redeemed all of existence, "even all of the past" (308); for since, on Nietzsche's view, everything is tied in with everything else, anyone's achievement of perfection—anyone's becoming a sort of god—will have justified everything else, and he or she will have done so without the need for the old gods (cf. *EC*, 309; *Z*, 200). And how is this done? Above all, by joy in the face of personal and general suffering—the sort of suffering that only a god can bear, and welcome. Such a god, says Nietzsche, is Dionysus.

Gods are immortal. And joy wants immortality. Woe, Nietzsche says, wants heirs; it wants that it itself should go away but leave its "fruit" behind. But not joy: "Joy . . . does not want heirs, or children—joy wants itself, wants eternity, wants recurrence, wants everything eternally the same" (*Z*, 434). In a dialogue with life, Zarathustra whispers that all things recur and nothing disappears forever (*Z*, 339). And this knowlege, I submit, is the source of Zarathustra's (and perhaps Nietzsche's) suffering, and his joy. He is immortal.

It is a joy that he expresses, not surprisingly, by dancing. Indeed, the metaphysical significance of dance—in Nietzsche's thought and generally—is immortality. This significance takes various forms: belief in personal immortality, defiance of human mortality, frenzied postponement of death. It is almost as if staying off, and out of, the earth is the literal (and not so completely literal) significance of the dancer. And if the dancer does feel him- or herself to be a god, as Nietzsche often notes, this too is not surprising; for gods are immortal. Even those people who acknowledge their mortality use the dance to defy that fact; for as long as they dance, leap, fly, control their bodies, so long they achieve a spirituality that scorns death, perhaps even "until Charon himself is dead."[16]

Notes

1. See especially Plato, *Laws* 2.653–57, 672; 7. 814–7.

2. In the citation of Nietzsche's works the following abbreviations are used: *BT* (*The Birth of Tragedy*); *Z* (*Thus Spoke Zarathustra*, in *The Portable Nietzsche*, ed. Walter Kaufmann); *WP* (*The Will to Power*); *GS* (*The Gay Science*); *GM* (*On the Genealogy of Morals*); *EC* (*Ecce Homo*). All are translated by Walter Kaufmann (or, in the case of *WP* and *GM*, by Kaufmann and R. J. Hollingdale) and are published by Random House in the Vintage Books series (*BT*, 1967; *Portable Nietzsche*, 1977; *WP*, 1968; *GS*, 1977; *GM*, 1967; *EC*, 1967).

3. (Middletown, Conn.: Wesleyan University Press, 1964), 12.

4. See Kant, *On History*.

5. See Hegel, *Reason in History*, the introduction to Hegel's monumental *Philosophy of History*.

6. Schopenhauer, *The World as Will and Representation*, trans. E. F. J. Payne (New York: Dover, 1966), 324 et passim. Of course Schopenhauer thought salvation possible, through aesthetic contemplation and ethical compassion or pity.

7. *Odyssey* 11. 489ff.

8. Nietzsche reports and agrees with Lucretius's remark that gods first appeared to men's minds in dreams (*BT,* 33–35).

9. In *WP,* 535 (par. 1038), Nietzsche reminds us that Zarathustra is "merely an old atheist: he believes neither in old nor in new gods. Zarathustra says he *would:* but Zarathustra *will* not—Do not misunderstand him."

10. Morgan, *What Nietzsche Means* (1941; reprint, New York: Harper & Row, 1965), 312.

11. Perhaps the most graphic portrayal of victory over the "spirit of gravity" is Zarathustra's dream of the young shepherd who awakes to find that a snake—representing most specifically the "abysmal thought" of eternal recurrence—has crawled into his throat and bit itself fast there. Gasping and gagging, the shepherd finally bites the snake's head off. And "he bit a good bite. Far away he spewed the head of the snake—and he jumped up. No longer Shepherd, no longer human—one changed, radiant, *laughing!* Never yet on earth has a human being laughed as he laughed" (*Z,* 272).

12. In our own time sociobiology might be understood as a discipline largely concerned with "interpreting" moral phenomena, hence as something like a nonmoral standpoint on morality.

13. Edmund Husserl's notion of a "presuppositionless science" can be understood as a goal, not as an accomplishment—i.e., as an unrealizable ideal, not an achievable aim.

14. For yet another characterization of the genuine philosopher's activity, see part 6 of *Beyond Good and Evil,* entitled "We Scholars." The early essay, *"Schopenhauer as Educator,"* is also relevant of course.

15. It is Faust, in Goethe's poem, who ultimately wishes the moment of happiness to "abide." The general idea of everything being necessarily connected with everything else typifies German idealism from Leibniz on, with Fichte a particularly impressive example.

16. There is no better literary example of what I am suggesting than certain passages in Nikos Kazantzakis's novel *Zorba the Greek,* from which this final quotation is taken.

What Is Going on in a Dance?

Monroe C. Beardsley

I begin these rather tentative and exploratory reflections by calling upon some provocative remarks by George Beiswanger, from an essay written some years ago and later reprinted:

> Muscular capacity is the physical means by which dances are made. But the means becomes available to the choreographic imagination only through the operation of a metaphor, a metaphor by which a *moving* in the muscular sense takes on the character of a *doing* or *goings on*. . . . Strictly speaking, then, dances are not made out of but *upon* movement, movement being the poetic bearer, the persistent metaphor, by which muscular material is made available for the enhanced, meaningful, and designed *goings-on* that are dance.[1]

Though this passages summarizes a view that I shall try to defend and articulate, the attempt to apply the concept of metaphor troubles me: it seems a strained extension of an otherwise reasonably clear and useful term. So instead of Beiswanger's rather mysterious "operation of a metaphor," I shall suggest that we employ some concepts and principles borrowed from the philosophical theory of action. But I still like his favored expression for what we are all trying to understand better—those special "goings-on" that constitute dance.

This chapter was originally presented as a paper at the conference "Illuminating Dance: Philosophical Inquiry and Aesthetic Criticism," cosponsored by CORD and Temple University at Temple University, Philadelphia, 5 May 1979.

A partial, though basic, description of what is going on would be to say, using terms provided by Beiswanger (but I am also borrowing language from legal theorists such as John Austin and Oliver Wendell Holmes), that there are willed muscular contractions that cause changes of position in human bodies or parts of bodies. Such caused changes we may agree to call "bodily motions," or simply *motions,* assuming them to be—with surely few exceptions—voluntary. (For even if push comes to shove in a certain symbolic sense, I take it that no one is actually knocked off balance. But for a dancer to be lifted up or carried from one location to another is not a motion, in my sense, of that dancer, though it requires motions by other dancers.)

Bodily motions are actions; they are, in one sense, basic actions, the foundation of all other actions, at least as far as we are concerned today; for even if there are such things as purely *mental* actions, in which no muscle is disturbed, these cannot be the stuff or raw material of dance. But as Beiswanger says, bodily motions are not themselves the goings-on we label *Afternoon of a Faun* or *Jewels.* It is actions of another sort that we witness and wonder at; how, then, are these related to bodily motions?

An extremely fruitful discovery of philosophical action theory is that actions build upon, or grow out of, each other in certain definable ways. The wielding of a hammer, say, can become, in capable hands, the driving of a nail, and that in turn a step in the building of a house. One action, in a technical sense, is said to "generate" another action that is its fruition or even its aim. Thus we can analyze and come to understand certain actions by examining their *generating conditions*—that is, the conditions that are to be fulfilled in order for act A to generate act B. This is easy in some cases; clearly it is the presence of the nail and the wood, in proper relationship, that converts the swinging of a hammer into the driving of a nail and that enables the former action to generate the latter action: *in* or *by* swinging the hammer, the carpenter drove the nail. Now there is, of course, an endless variety of such sets of generating conditions; however, they fortunately fall into a limited number of classes, and these classes themselves belong to two fundamental categories. The first is *causal generation.* Since the swinging of the hammer *causes* the nail to penetrate the two-by-four studding, the swinging of the hammer *generates* the (act of) driving the nail into the wood. If the hammer misses or the nail is balked by a knot, this act-generation does not occur.

In this first category of act-generation, one action generates a second action that is numerically distinct from it: swinging the hammer is not the same action as driving the nail (or building the house). In the second category, no new action, yet a different kind of action, is generated. If a person mistakenly believes that his or her divorce is final and legal and so marries a second spouse, that person has (unintentionally) committed bigamy; given the generating conditions (the persisting legal bond), the act of marrying generates the act of committing bigamy. The person has not done two things, but two kinds of thing: the same action was both an act of marrying and an act of bigamy. This I call *sortal generation:* the act-generation that occurs when an action of one sort becomes also (under the requisite conditions) an action of another sort—without, of course, ceasing to be an action of the first sort as well.

These concepts, simple as they are, can help us clarify idioms sometimes used by dance theorists. Thus when George Beiswanger says that "dances are not made out of but *upon* movement" (and remember he is using the term *movement* the way I am using the term *motion*), we can interpret him, I think, as saying that a dance is not composed of, does not have as its parts or elements, bodily motions, but rather is in some way sortally generated by those motions: under certain conditions, the motion "takes on the character" (as he says) of a dance-movement. And if I may be permitted the license, I should like to take advantage of the dancer's cherished special use of the word *moving* and use it in a nominative form to refer to *actions that have the character of a dance:* I shall call them *movings*. Thus when Beiswanger adds, "Dance does consist of *goings-on* in the act of coming to be," I shall adopt a somewhat more cautious paraphrase: *in a dance, movings are sortally generated by bodily motions.* And this proposition must be supplemented at once to forestall an imminent objection: certainly there are rests in dance as well as doings, and these, however passive, are part and parcel of what is happening (it happens for a time that nothing happens). Muscular contractions may be needed to maintain a position as well as to change one—especially if it is to stand on tiptoe with arm and leg outstretched. So, besides motions we shall have to include *bodily pauses* or cessations of motion; and we can add that just as motions can generate movings, so pauses can generate *posings* (using this term for peculiarly dance states of affairs). Thus we may now propose the following: *dancing is sortally generating movings by bodily motions and posings by bodily pauses.*

Thus I find myself in disagreement—not wholly verbal, I think—with a recent valuable essay by Haig Khatchadourian.[2] It has been effectively criticized on several points by Julie Van Camp,[3] and I shall not review her objections here but only call attention to a few other matters. According to Khatchadourian, "Dancing consists of movements and not, or not also, of actions of some kind or other."[4] First, although this distinction—which I hope to clarify shortly—may seem oversubtle, I believe (with Beiswanger) that dancing consists not in what Khatchadourian calls movements—that is, motions—but in actions generated by them. And second, I think it is a mistake—and there seems no warrant for this in action theory—to divide bodily motions from actions: they *are* actions of a certain kind, though in themselves generally not as interesting as the actions they generate. However, Khatchadourian's distinction between (as I would say) bodily motions and *other* actions is important; but then the distinguishing features of these other actions need to be spelled out.

Taking off from the first of these two objections to Khatchadourian, I must now try to explain why I say that movings are more than motions: that there is indeed act-generation, a transformation of motions into movings. I have two main reasons.

My first reason rests on two propositions that will probably not be challenged. (1) It seems we do not dance all of the time—not every motion is dancing—so there must be some difference between the motions that generate dancing and those that don't, however difficult it may be to get a fix on. (2) It seems there is nothing in the nature of motions themselves that marks off those that can be dance from those that can't; practically any kind is available. Some insight into the puzzles here may be derived from Marcia Siegel's discusssion of Anna Sokolow's *Rooms*. She describes the various motions of the performers—for example,

Then, drooping across the chair seats, they lower their heads to the floor, lift their arms to the side and let them

drop, slapping against the floor with a dead sound. . . .
Slowly they lean forward and back in their seats, staring at
the audience.

　None of this can be called dance movement, but neither
is it merely the prosaic activity that it seems to be at first.
Sokolow gives these ordinary movements a dancelike
character by exaggerating the dynamics and the timing,
sometimes beyond "natural" limits. Instead of just raising
or lowering a hand, someone might take a very long time
to raise it, giving the gesture great importance, then drop it
suddenly and heavily, as if, having made all that effort to
prepare, there was nothing worth doing with the hand
after all. Besides the intensified way everything is carried
out, each move or repeated series of moves is a separate
gesture that finishes in some way before the next series is
undertaken.[5]

I am not sure I fully understand this passage, which is not as
clear as Siegel's writing usually is. When she says that "none of
this can be called dance movement," she is apparently not denying that what is going on is a dance; I think she means that
these motions are not the usual stuff of dance, not conventionally used in dancing. When she adds that "Sokolow gives these
ordinary movements a dancelike character," I take this to mean
that Sokolow shapes the motions so that they actually *are* dance,
not merely *like* dance. Of course this kind of performance is
difficult to talk about, but if I understand her, Siegel is marking
an important distinction. Of two motions, abstractly classified
as, say, "raising an arm," one may be a dance and the other not,
depending on some distinguishing feature contributed by the
choreographer—so that, more concretely described, they may
be somewhat different motions, though they belong to the
same shared type. One motion generates moving, in my sense
of the term, and the other doesn't. (Some would add that
merely transferring an "ordinary" movement to a stage, under
a bright spotlight, could give it a quality that makes it a dance.)

　My second reason for distinguishing the concept of *motion*
from that of *moving* is that this very distinction seems to be
deeply embedded in a large special or technical vocabulary that
is used for talking about dancing. Take the term *pirouette*, for
example. We can explain "how you do" a pirouette, and we can
say that in turning rapidly on her toe, the dancer pirouetted. A
turning of a certain sort generated a pirouetting, and they were

the same event; yet if we first describe the event as a rapid turning on the toe we are adding something to this description when we say that it was also a pirouette, for that is to say it was dancing. So with numerous other familiar terms: *jeté, glissade, demi-plié, sissone fermé, pas de bourrée.* (And, since we must not forget to include posings as well as movings, we should add *arabesque.*) My thesis is that all these terms refer to movings as such, not to the motions that generate them. When the technical terms are supplemented by other words, borrowed from ordinary speech—*leap, lope, skip, run*—these take on a second sense in the context of dance description, though I do not think this is a case of metaphor.

The question that looms next is evidently this: how does it come about that—or what are the generating conditions that make—motions and pauses become the movings and poses of dance? Without pretending to offer much of an argument, I will illustrate some features of action theory by reflecting briefly on a few possible answers to this rather large queston.

First, then, let us consider an answer that is not without plausibility and is in fact suggested by Marcia Siegel. You will recall her remark that a dancer in *Rooms* "might take a very long time to raise [his or her hand], giving the gesture great importance, then drop it suddenly and heavily, as if . . . there was nothing worth doing with the hand after all." She speaks of "the intensified way everything is carried out." If we are wary, I think we can make do with the word *expressive* to mark her meaning—and mine. When I use the word in this context, I refer to *regional qualities* of a motion or sequence of motions: it has an air of momentousness or mystery or majesty; it is abrupt, loose, heavy, decisive, or languid. To say that the motion is expressive is just to say that it has some such quality to a fairly intense degree. And this is *all* I mean by "expressive." We might then try formulating our first answer in this way: *When a motion or sequence of motions is expressive, it is dance.*

Selma Jeanne Cohen, in her well-known essay,[6] apparently holds that expressiveness is present in all true dance—though her defense of this view is, I think, marred by a tendency to confuse expressiveness with other things I shall shortly touch on, such as representation and signalling. Khatchadourian, in reply, says that expressiveness is not a necessary condition of dance but a criterion of *good* dance.[7] An objection to making it a *sufficient* condition is, for example, that an actress in a play might appropriately make exactly the same expressive motion as Sokolow's dancers yet would not be bursting into dance but dramatically revealing a mental state or trait of personality. Thus to make the first answer work we would need to introduce further restrictions on the range of regional qualities that are to be taken into account. If we look about in writings on dance, we find a diversity of terms but some convergence of meaning; take two examples from rather different quarters. As is well known, Susanne Langer speaks of "virtual powers" as the "primary illusion" of dance; and though I don't see the need for talking about illusions, I think "powers" conveys some general truth. Then there is a remark by Merce Cunningham, reported by Calvin Tomkins:

> He has remained firmly committed to dance as dance, although he acknowledges that the concept is difficult to define. "I think it has to do with amplification, with enlargement," he said recently. "Dancing provides something—an amplification of energy—that is not provided any other way, and that's what interests me."[8]

This remark is noteworthy in part because of what it tells about Cunningham's own taste and preferences, but I think "amplification of energy" conveys a general truth.

To put my suggestion briefly, and all too vaguely: in dance the forms and characters of voluntary motion (the generating base) are encouraged to allow the emergence of new regional qualities, which in turn are lifted to a plane of marked perceptibility; they are exhibited or featured. It is the featuring specifically of the qualities of *volition,* of willing to act, that makes movings of motions. This is most obviously true when we see power, energy, force, zest, and other positive qualities of volition; but it also applies to such qualities as droopy exhaustion and mechanical compulsion—weaknesses of the will, as well as strengths. Dances of course may be expressive in other ways, have other qualities besides these volitional qualities. But the first answer to our basic question might be reformulated this way: *When a motion or sequence of motions is expressive in virtue of its fairly intense volitional qualities, it is dance.*

Some will say that this sounds like sport, and the proposal does seem to extend beyond dance. Not that it is necessarily a mistake to find an affinity, but it seems we must continue our search. There are of course several familiar suggestions, which are dogged by equally familiar objections. Some of them are rather nicely brought together in this passage from St. Augustine:

> Suppose there is no actual work in hand and no intention to make anything, but the motions of the limbs are done for pleasure, that will be dancing. Ask what delights you in dancing and number will reply, "Lo, here am I." Examine the beauty of bodily form, and you will find that everything is in its place by number. Examine the beauty of bodily motion, and you will find everything in its due time by number.[9]

Some of these ideas are worth following up, when the opportunity presents itself. There is, for example, the suggestion that what transforms motions into dance is a certain *intention* that accompanies them: the intention to perform the motions for the sake of pleasure (I suppose, either of the performer or of the audience). This seems too narrow a restriction, even if it applies to most dancing; other intentions can be prominent. There is also the suggestion that the relevant pleasure is one derived from mathematically ordered motion (i.e., pulse and rhythm, which together form meter). This, too, has been regarded as central to dance (by both Khatchadourian and Cohen, for example), but we cannot take it as a necessary or sufficient condition, even if it may be a very useful criterion of dancehood. (St. Augustine, at some stages of his thought, was a bit obsessed with number.) There is also the suggestion that it is somehow the *absence* of practical intent ("no actual work in hand," he says) that distinguishes dance from other actions. This calls for another look, after we have gained a clearer notion of what "actual work" might encompass.

To get to this topic, we may take a short detour by way of another answer to our basic question, one that tries to capture an essence of dance through the concept of representation. Consider an *act-type* (that is, a kind of action, having numerous actual instances): say, snow shovelling. This involves, for effectiveness and efficiency, certain characteristic *motion-types*. If we select certain of these motion-types that distinguish snow shovelling from other activities and perform them for the benefit of someone else, we may enable the other person to recognize the action-type from which the motions have been derived. This, roughly put, is the representation (or depiction) of one action-type by an action of another type—for in representing snow shovelling, we are not actually doing it (the actor smoking a pipe onstage does not represent a man smoking a pipe, for he is one; but he may represent a detective smoking a pipe, which he is not).

Now representation by motions clearly comes in many degrees of abstraction, of which we can perhaps distinguish three degrees in a standard way. In *playacting* (as in drama) we have the most realistic degree: the actor may wield a shovel, and the director may even call for artificial snow for the actor to push about. In *miming*, we dispense with props and verbal utterance, and we allow room for witty exaggeration: the mime would be rushing about the stage, busily moving his arms in shovelling motions, stopping to blow on his fingers or to rub his aching back. In *suggesting*, we merely allude to the original action-type, borrowing a motion or two, sketching or outlining, and mingling these motions with others, such as whirling or leaping. This might be the *Snow-shovelling Dance*, to be performed, of course, after the actual job has been done, by way of celebrating the victory of humankind over one more assault of nature. Playacting, taken quite narrowly, must be comparatively rare in dance, miming much more common, though in short stretches, I should think. Suggesting, on the other hand, is pervasive; it appears in many of the most striking and cogent movings.[10]

Indeed, it is this pervasiveness that prompts another answer to our question: *When a motion, or sequence of motions, represents actions of other types in the mode of suggestion, it is dance.* This will undoubtedly cover a lot of ground, but it will not, of course, be satisfactory to all dancers today. For beyond the third degree of abstraction in representation there lies a fourth degree, where representation disappears; we have loping-back-and-forth and panting dancers, sitting and bending dancers, who don't represent anything. Or pirouetting dancers. Now one could argue that these fragments of moving only become dance when embedded in larger sequences that do represent by suggestion. But I should think many a pas de deux as well as many a contemporary dance episode is utterly nonrepresentational.

Snow shovelling is an example of a class of actions in which we effect a change in the physical world outside our skins; it is causally generated. Many of these actions have their own char-

acteristic, and therefore imitable, forms of motion: corn planting, baby rocking, knitting, hammering. I should like to call
such actions *workings,* because they perform work in the physi-
cist's sense—even though some of them would ordinarily be
called play: kicking a field goal or sinking a putt. It is plain that
dances include many representations of working actions, nearly
always at a fairly high degree of abstraction. And this contributes to their expressiveness: seen as baby rocking, the motions
may yield a more intense quality of gentleness.

Besides workings, we may take note of two other broad
classes of action that have some bearing upon the subject of this
inquiry. In one of these we are concerned, not with physical
states of the world, but (indirectly) with mental states of other
persons. The actions I refer to, when they are performed with
the help of, or by means of, verbal utterances, are called "il-
locutionary actions," and they are generally of familiar types:
asserting, greeting, inviting, thanking, refusing, insisting.
These types have subtypes: insisting on being paid time-and-a-
half for last week's overtime, for example, is a subtype that may
have numerous instances. Many of these same types of action
can also be performed without words; we can greet by gestures
as well, or sometimes better. Nodding, shrugging, winking,
bowing, kneeling might be called "para-illocutionary actions"
when they are done with this sort of significance; so biting the
thumb generates insulting, as in act 1, scene 2 of *Romeo and
Juliet.* With or without words, such actions can be called *signal-
lings* or *sayings,* in acknowledgment of the messages they carry.
I choose the latter term, and the way to put it is: in waving a
hand a certain way, the infant is saying good-bye. Sayings, like
workings, are representable: in waving his or her hand, the
dancer is representing someone saying good-bye. And, like
working-representations, saying-representations can contribute much to the expressiveness of motions in dance. The quality of that waving, as a moving, may be intensified by its
semantic aspect. The dancer summons up and draws into the
texture of his or her moving something of the sorrow or finality
of the action-type he or she is representing. Sayings involve a
form of sortal generation, what is (very broadly) called "conventional generation." It is the existence of a social convention
that enables arm waving to generate good-bying; the dancer
does not make use of that convention to say anything, but recalls it to intensify expressiveness.

This raises an important question that there is no time to do more than glance at now: do dances not only represent, but also constitute sayings? That is, can motions that generate movings also generate sayings? I have read an odd remark attributed to John Cage: "We are not, in these dances, saying something. We are simple-minded enough to think that if we were saying something we would use words."[11] This is indeed simple-minded, given the extraordinary richness of bodily motions as generators of para-illocutionary actions. It might even be argued that representations of para-illocutionary actions can hardly help but be para-illocutionary actions themselves, since by selecting the suggestive elements and giving them a different context we may seem to comment on the sayings we quote. But this claim goes beyond what I am prepared to argue for at the moment.

The third class of actions I shall call attention to consists of motions that are goal-directed, though not necessarily goal-attaining, and that have a point or purpose, even though they move neither other bodies nor other minds. Take, for example, running a race (with the aim of winning), or reaching out, or shrinking away. We might call these actions "strivings." They are generated by the presence of mental states, such as intentions (a form of "circumstantial generation"). Of course strivings, too, can be represented.

Workings, sayings, and strivings seem to belong together at some level of abstraction, as entering into social interactions that have a function, that end in achievement or are so aimed. If it is not too misleading, we may use the label "practical" for them all—and at least we will have tried to delimit the scope of this notorious weasel word somewhat more scrupulously than is usual. With its help, as so defined, we can state St. Augustine's proposal in what seems to be its most plausible form: *When a motion, or sequence of motions, does not generate practical actions, and is intended to give pleasure through perception of rhythmic order, it is dance.* But even at its best the proposal will not serve. Perhaps if we were to add a suitable insistence on expressiveness as another source of the pleasure, we would come close to an adequate characterization of dance as an art. But I assume that we do not wish to limit our concept of dance in this way. Suppose the pueblo corn dance, for example, is not only performed in order to aid the growth of corn but is actually effective; then it is a working, just as much as seed planting or hoeing. Dance shades off into and embraces some part of ritual, which is a kind of saying. If the dance is done at a festival in competition for first prize (although that may be opposed to the true spirit of dance), I suppose it is no less a dance for being at the same time a striving.

Thus we cannot define dance in this negative way as excluding motions that generate practical actions. Yet there is something to this opposition, something about dancing that is different, even if those other actions can be, in their various ways, expressive. Perhaps we can come nearer to it in one final line of thought. If *every* motion of the corn dance is prescribed in detail by magical formulas or religious rules to foster germination, growth, or a fruitful harvest, we might best regard it as pure ritual, however expressive it may be as a *consequence* of its mode of working. Like soldiers on parade or priests officiating at Mass, the participants would verge on dance but they would not really be dancing. But if some part of what goes on in the ritual helps it to achieve expressiveness (of volitional qualities) that is to some degree independent of any practical function, then whatever else it may be, it is also a moving. If, in other words, there is more zest, vigor, fluency, expansiveness, or stateliness than appears necessary for practical purposes, there is an overflow or superfluity of expressiveness to mark it as belonging to its own domain of dance.

Notes

1. "Chance and Design in Choreography," reprinted from the *Journal of Aesthetics and Art Criticism* 21 (1962):14–17, in *The Dance Experience: Readings in Dance Appreciation,* rev. ed., ed. Howard Nadel and Constance Nadel Miller (New York: Universe Books, 1978), 88.

2. "Movement and Action in the Performing Arts," *Journal of Aesthetics and Art Criticism* 37 (1978):25–36.

3. See Haig Khatchadourian, "Movement and Action in Film," *British Journal of Aesthetics* 20 (1980):349–55. In writing this essay I have benefitted much from studying Julie Van Camp's dissertation, "Philosophical Problems of Dance Criticism" (Ph.D., Temple University, 1981) and also from her helpful comments on an earlier draft of my essay.

4. Khatchadourian, "Movement and Action in the Performing Arts," 25.

5. Marcia B. Siegel, *The Shapes of Change: Images of Modern Dance* (Boston: Houghton Mifflin, 1979), 280.

6. "A Prolegomenon to an Aesthetics of Dance," *Journal of Aesthetics and Art Criticism* 21 (1962):19–26, reprinted in several places, including Nadel and Miller, *Dance Experi-*

ence, and *Aesthetic Inquiry: Essays on Art Criticism and the Philosophy of Art,* ed. M. C. Beardsley and H. M. Schueller (Belmont, Calif.: Dickenson, 1967).

7. p. 36, n. 13.

8. Calvin Tomkins, "An Appetite for Motion," reprinted from the *New Yorker* (1968) in Nadel and Miller, *Dance Experience,* 273.

9. *De Libero Arbitrio,* 2.16.42; trans. H. S. Burleigh, in *The Library of Christian Classics,* vol. 6 (Philadelphia: Westminster Press, 1955).

10. Where playacting or miming is prominent, we are tempted to say what Anna Kisselgoff wrote of a Jerome Robbins work: "The line between dance and nondance has been obliterated in *Watermill*" (*New York Times,* 27 May 1979).

11. Quoted by Erica Abeel in "The New Dance," reprinted from *Dance Scope* 2 (1965):21–26, in Nadel and Miller, *Dance Experience,* 117.

Dance, Whitehead, and Faustian II Themes

Maxine Sheets-Johnstone
David B. Richardson

"How does the human body dance the world?"[1] What we want to examine in this paper is the possibility of understanding dance as an incarnation of a civilization's world view. The approach in this preliminary inquiry takes for its horizon the Faustian II *Weltanschauung* of Western civilization, the common world view that contributes so significantly to our picture of reality. The world view of a civilization—for example, the Chinese, Hindu, Graeco-Roman or Faustian—is a shared way of seeing things; members of the culture assimilate it during their growth into adulthood. It is integrated with their own individual outlooks and with various other points of view associated with family, vocation, religion, and other facets of culture. A civilizational world view is made up of an unconscious group of ideas, images, feelings, and attitudes that have considerable unity and self-consistency, so that the significant deeds and works of the civilization have a strong family resemblance. The moment we recognize Faustian I and II tonal music, or Greek tragedy with its classical unities of time, place, and action, for example, we apprehend a particular *Weltanschauung*. A world view fulfills an unconscious need to bring a specific order, shared with members of one's own culture and not shared with alien civilizations, into one's life.

Our methodology in this enterprise will be to utilize present-day critical writings on dance, particularly those of the *New Yorker* dance critic Arlene Croce. By employing this quasi-hermeneutical procedure, we hope to show not only how dance fulfills a Faustian II image of the world but further, how in fulfilling this image dance exemplifies as well significant aspects of the process philosophy of Alfred North Whitehead (1861–1947). Since from a world view perspective Croce and Whitehead share a Faustian II *Weltanschauung,* a convergence of thematic motifs in their viewpoints on dance and on the world, respectively, should not be surprising.

The tremendous revitalization of the arts that began in the early nineteenth century and which has continued into the twentieth indicates that a rejuvenation has been occurring in all significant activities of Western civilization during the past 180 years. We shall consider Western dance from this Faustian II point of view, although we will also be referring to present-day Western world culture as a continuation of an original Faustian civilization. We follow current usage and designate Western civilization—Europe since 950 A.D., and later, Europe and America—as the "Faustian" civilization, so termed by Goethe, Spengler, and others. It is known as a Faustian world outlook because its dramatic character, represented by Dr. Faustus of Marlowe (sixteenth century), Goethe (nineteenth century), and Mann (twentieth century), has become the personality type characteristic of the civilization. Although Spengler's pessimistic thesis in *The Decline of the West* (1922) held that the Faustian style had run its course by 1800—he believed Western civilization was decadent and that the decline and fall would begin in about the year 2000—we have, on the contrary, like many scientists, philosophers, and artists, taken an optimistic view, in light of the tremendous cultural revitalization over the past 180 years. The arts especially have taken on new life during this period, and dance has been at various times in the forefront.

Faustian II Themes

It is the thesis of this essay that the following Faustian II themes are regnant in Western culture: (1) a psychology in which feeling and emotion are supreme human values; (2) a physical world engaged in never-ending movement and change; (3) a curvilinear and ever-flowing space; a space–time plenum with local regions of force fields; (4) a durational or "seasonal" form of time (in contrast to a clock time); (5) an organic interrelation and correlation of events; (6) cherished complexities of a new concrete reason; (7) rhythmic kinetic energies permeating the universe, creative sources of never-ceasing emergent novelty. It is not the purpose of this paper, of course, to analyze each of these themes in depth in relation to dance. Such a project would warrant book-length treatment. The purpose is rather to suggest the richness of connections between contemporary dance and the Faustian II world view, a richness that promises much in the way of future endeavors. At the same time, we want to suggest a dovetailing of dance and process philosophy through their mutual participation in the Faustian II *Weltanschauung*. This mode of joining dance and philosophy is especially intriguing, since Whitehead's philosophy is oriented in unique ways toward the kinetic world of the dancer and choreographer, in particular, and toward the world of art in general. Let us begin by identifying in a general way some of the above Faustian II ideas in both dance and process philosophy.

Whitehead's metaphysics reflects the Faustian II world view so vividly that his thinking appears to have been thoroughly permeated by Faustian II images, values, and ideas. Emotional expression, for example, which has become a high value in the Faustian II civilization, is equally prized by Whitehead: the very stuff of reality for Whitehead is feeling, of which emotion is the highest form. Emotional expression was not part of the Faustian I world outlook, but by the time of the Romantic era it had entered into the core of the Faustian II world view. In contrast, the love of reason is common to both Faustian dispensations; the Faustian II reason, however, is disposed to encompass intricacies and complexities to which the old Faustians were unaccustomed. Theirs was a more abstract, ours is a more concrete reason. We shall see that Whitehead carried the Faustian II idea of reason to an extreme in his notion of active interrelationships throughout the universe and that some of the greatest contemporary choreographers embody a similar structural density of relationships in their dance.

Both the Faustian I and Faustian II world views have envisaged things as engaged in ceaseless process and change. This process point of view is of course emphatically and elaborately expressed by Whitehead. The phenomenon of dance, in turn, can so naturally epitomize process and change that its enormous popularity today may in part be seen as a natural result of its embodiment of this Faustian II value.

What is perhaps most conspicuous in the *Weltanschauung* of any civilization is its concept of space because, after all, its members experience and envisage things and actions in the context of space. Here there is a striking difference in Faustian I and Faustian II world views. In the former, spatial theories centered around the image of an infinite empty space into which bodies moved in a straight line. As early as 1277, Bishop Tempier of Paris prohibited the heresy of denying the possibility of *linear* motion to heavenly bodies. The new envisagements of space—after 1800—were thoroughly different. All Faustian II spaces relate to an Einsteinian, curvilinear space–time, a spatiotemporal autogenesis in which radiant energies, particles, and bodies generate a space that expands through time as a curved geodesic surface. It is a space, at times, like that of an expanding flower, moving out from a local center in all directions, or of a *grande pirouette*, the spin generating a swelling volume. And yet it is a space in which relativities and mutual relationships are so important that an oceanlike plenum, with multiple centers of high density, is generated. The plenum is fluidlike in its eddies and currents and in its constant reciprocal relationships with the space-making or space-changing energies and forces moving through it. Laban, whose "Labanotation" is the most widely used system of dance notation throughout the world, analyzed movement in part in terms of an icosohedron, a twenty-faced geometrical form having both cubical and spherical attributes. The spatial reality represented by this multidimensional form accords thoroughly with an Einsteinian or Faustian II concept of space. It is texturally exemplified in Arlene Croce's description in *Afterimages,* of George Balanchine's *The Four Temperaments:* "Space itself is liquified," she writes, "and planes on which we observe the dance rise, tilt, descend. Sometimes we are launched and roving in this liquid space."[2] The description is reminiscent of Kraus's characterization of Mary Wigman's envisagement of space as a waterlike medium through which the dancer must swim.[3]

The use of chance—not improvisation, but the deliberate use of fortuitous elements—has been a means for some choreographers to enhance creativity in their work and to discover kinetic novelty. In Whitehead's process philosophy, as in the Faustian II world view, novelty has also a central place. Whitehead held that creativity is an ultimate category of all things insofar as the ultimate constituents of reality, the actual entities that constitute all things—whether micro-particles or macro-bodies—are each a "potentiality for process,"[4] that is, they offer the possibility of novelty through the rhythmic interplay of becoming and change.

The idea of organic unity has found expression in modern dance from the time of Isadora Duncan, who expressly choreographed her dances from natural movements emanating from the organic unity of her own body. A manifestly organic intention is equally apparent in the technique demanded by Balanchine's choreography and, of course, in the dancers who dance it. As Croce writes of a vividly striking moment of movement in *Liebeslieder Walzer,* "The girls didn't have to understand the sentiment of the music in order to express it; they had a technique which did it for them. In fact, the technique *was* the sentiment" (*A,* 420). In one of his masterworks, *Science and the Modern World,* Whitehead, for his part, fully endorsed the English Romantic poets' rhapsodic assertions which celebrated the organic influences that unify human and nonhuman nature.[5] Closely associated with this Whiteheadian idea of organicism is the Faustian II preoccupation with relativities and correlations. In Whitehead's philosophy, and in contemporary process philosophy in general, the Faustian II preoccupation is of seminal importance. It is expressed in the idea that any one thing is related to all other things. No matter how large or small, each thing is actually or potentially related to everything else. Like creativity, this idea is a central category of reality, "the one general metaphysical character attaching to all entities."[6]

With the above general sketch of Faustian II ideas, we can turn our attention now to a finer study. We will focus in turn upon three of the regnant ideas: (1) a psychology in which feeling and emotion are supreme human values; (2) cherished complexities of a new, concrete reason; and (3) rhythmic kinetic energies permeating the universe, creative sources of never-ceasing emergent novelty. A fourth regnant idea—that of a durational or "seasonal" form of time—will be woven into the analysis of rhythmic kinetic energies permeating the universe.

Choreographic and Whiteheadian Expressions of Faustian II Ideas

A preoccupation with qualities of feeling is one of the Faustian II traits that has been present in dance since the Romantic era. As noted before, feeling experience was not part of the preceding Faustian I world picture, even though of all the ultimately metaphysical preoccupations of Westerners since the tenth century the most significant has been emotional expression. The explanation is that intense feeling has always been the supreme psychological function in Christianity. Christian emotion, after a habilitation of eight hundred years (1000–1800), entered into the civilizational world view of Europe. The Faustian II world style is thus different from the more austere, relatively phlegmatic Faustian I outlook. While early Renaissance and late Gothic cultures were of one mind in their high evaluation of strong emotion, this assessment stemmed from religion; today it is the emotional quality of the world view itself that influences modern times. Sometimes that quality is depicted in extraordinarily vivid psychological dramas. The ideas in Balanchine's *La Sonnambula,* for example, clearly derive from the emotional tradition of Romantic ballet (A, 415), but the emotion is keyed up to an extreme characteristic of all Faustian II expressionistic art. "It would be hard to exaggerate the bitterness of *La Sonnambula* or the hysteria of *La Valse,*" says Croce (A, 411). Even "party scenes"—"festive atmosphere[s] like great parties where everyone behaves charmingly and has a wonderful time" (A, 409)—are, perhaps oddly enough, keyed up in a similar way: "Party scenes that Balanchine has staged for his story ballets are likely to be less effervescent, stranger, and more troubling by far in their sensations than . . . ballets of pure dancing. They are full of disturbing, violent, and even grisly happenings." (A, 409).

According to Croce, Stephane Mallarmé, the renowned French poet of the nineteenth century, distinguished between ballet and dancing: ballet was poetic theater and not, in Croce's terms, "a mere business of noodling around on point" (A, 76). In this sense Mallarmé could be said to have looked for the same purity of form in dance that he strove to attain in the new, unaffected, clean images of his own poetry. His personal poetic search anticipated the next century's beginning quest in dance and the other visual arts for ambivalently meaningful but visually clear forms that would not be confined within the mundane human sphere. They would be forms of movement that would contain gestalten or "physiognomies" of perhaps cosmic breadth. Consider, for example, Croce's description of Annabelle Gamson's re-creation of Isadora Duncan's *Prelude:* "There was only one gesture—a slow walk in four directions with an arm lifting now to this, now to that corner of the stage. . . . It was a question not of repetition but of a single idea stated with complete conviction" (A, 256). But Mallarmé's ideal of dance may also be seen to anticipate an abstract, expressionistic form of dance, one similarly capable of both human and cosmic reference, as the dances of Martha Graham and Mary Wigman attest. As Croce notes, "For Mallarmé, whose ideal in dance was the purity of expression we have since come to recognize in great abstract choreography, the signature of the classical ballerina was her ability to summon up elemental visions" (A, 76). Such visions were precisely those to be summoned forth by the greatest of modern dance pioneers, as well as by nineteenth-century classical ballerinas. Although Mallarmé was uninterested in the expression of passion, the abstractness he prized in dance was destined to be joined with symbolic expression.

Martha Graham's choreography is typically and intensely symbolic of emotion: nondecorous, shocking, expressing not only joy and grief, but guilt, anguish, remorse, and a range of other feelings. Croce writes of Graham's *Dark Meadow*, for example, that it is "an extravaganza of preconscious emotion, all rumbling subterranean fantasy. There is no way to grasp its meaning unless one allows its intense subjectivity to meet one's own unrestrained conscience" (A, 193). Of course there is the much earlier Graham classic, *Lamentation* (1930). Croce describes in the most congealed but telling way the stunning and mesmerizing impact of this work: "The form of the dance says it all—solid geometry as live emotion" (A, 163). She goes on to say that "the same organic principle is seen in the space-slashing design of *Diversion of Angels*" (A, 163). But perhaps it should be noted, too, that the integral expressivity of a Graham dance can be grossly distorted—by overly enthusiastic performances, for example. Of one rendition of *Diversion of Angels*, Croce writes, "[It] has no plot but does have a gooey layer of desperately acted-out and dearly cherished emotion poured over the dances by the company. (It's good choreography; why can't it just be danced instead of hugged to death?)" (A, 55). In this respect the very emotional power of Graham's work would seem to be at the same time its most vulnerable element. At times "We get very little idea of how the [Graham] technique worked itself into expression through its use of the body's weight as an obstacle" (A, 195).

When the non-Romantic inspiration entered into dance in

the twentieth century, as it entered into the other arts, the symbolically expressive element was destined to remain one of the most durable of choreographic values. The range or play of emotion among contemporary dance artists is extreme, with the intense symbolic passion and sense of organic unity of Martha Graham at one end of the spectrum; the virtuosity in experiment, mood, and technique of Merce Cunningham in the middle; and the capacity for a compulsive or formal-but-unpredictable logic—as in the works of Yvonne Rainer or Twyla Tharp (A, 340, 342–43)—at the other end of the spectrum. Whereas Martha Graham's *Deaths and Entrances*, for example, "gives us so fearful a glimpse of domestic insanity . . . [in which] the household is alive . . . , [where] we sense, rather than observe, whispered conversations, footfalls in the dark corridor . . . [and where] upstairs a shutter bangs in the rain, a lamp burns all night," (A, 300), Merce Cunningham's dances deliver no such emotional punch and drama. "the sense of human emotion that a dance can give is governed by familiarity with the language," says Cunningham in his lower-case style; "joy, love, fear, anger, humor, all can be 'made clear' by images familiar to our eyes. and all are grand or meager depending on the eye of the beholder."[7] Emotion here is not symbolically expressed but discovered; it is not put in, so to speak, but neither is it taken out. It is a question of the priority of movement over form. "In Cunningham's own best work, as in all works of art, a negotiable idea becomes transparent expression; nothing is left out of it but the talent that produced it in the first place" (*GD*, 69). At the latter end of the spectrum, emotion enters casually by chance or by audience choice, as it were: "The consistent compulsive logic of a Rainer group concert can be as perversely fascinating as the look of her beat-up performers" (A, 339). After describing something of the nature of Rainer's work and its choreographic affinities with Cunningham and Tharp, Croce warns, "Yet to know about Rainer is not the same as to know her; she has to be seen. In the first place, no description can impart the duration, calculated shock, or graded monotony of her effects" (A, 340). Clearly dance at this end of the spectrum can be entrancing to the point of being captivating—or boring; it depends on one's expectations and point of view. "What you see," as Croce writes of another choreographer at this end of the spectrum, "is what [you] have to be willing to see" (*GD*, 47). All the same, the renegade character of the newer generation of choreographers can give their dance an air of qualitative unpredictability not unlike the inconstant flux of emotion in everyday life, which also has to be "seen"—that is, lived—in order to be known.

Feeling is so central to Whitehead's metaphysics that for him all actual entities are constituted by an assemblage, a concrescence, of feelings or prehensions. In various ways Whitehead actually arrives at a universal category of experience in the sense that the ultimate components of all things and of all events are experiencing the world, and this in spite of the fact that consciousness is absent in most of the universe. For Whitehead the primitive experience of all entities, even the simplest elements—that is to say, the "stuff" of which they are made—is emotional feeling. No matter how elemental or removed from animate life, everything in the universe is experiencing in ways which are analogous to the human experience of feeling. Whitehead thus deliberately uses terms previously limited to descriptions of humans—*emotion, valuation, satisfaction, subjective aim,* and so on—to describe all levels of reality. Causal efficacy, for example, whether in the transference of radiant energy or of mechanical force, involves "the primitive experience, . . . emotional feeling, felt in its relevance to a world beyond."[8] From the perspective of Whitehead's philosophy, not only does the expressivity of the dancer's body considered in itself have implicit affirmation, but the emotional suggestiveness of choreography, quite apart from outright symbolic expression, is ultimately acknowledged as well.

When we turn to the theme of concrete reason, it is first and foremost descriptions of Balanchine's dances that strike the attention. In her review of a revival of *The Four Temperaments*, Croce has occasion to recall Balanchine's dances of the 1940s, and she recalls that period of time as choreographically "a monumental decade." In these dances, she writes, there is "an intertwining of echoes and cross-references. . . . The dancing grows from simple to complex structures, and every stage of growth is consequentially related to every other. It is partly because of their structural logic that his ballets make such great sense—or such vivid nonsense" (*A,* 186). If any art concretizes reason, none would seem to be able to do so with greater vividness or diversity than dance, and no artist's concretizations would seem to surpass in intricacy those of Balanchine.

The density of a composition is a stylistic aspect of concrete reason readily apparent in the Faustian II arts in general. It is precisely a compositional density that is at the bottom of Croce's appraisal of Balanchine's work in general: "No Balanchine ballet," she writes, "no matter how enjoyable, is assimilable at first sight—there's too much going on" (*GD*, 58). Density is readily seen in the other arts as well, in Stravinsky's and Webern's music, for example, and in Faulkner's and Pynchon's novels. Avoiding redundancy, the Faustian II artist puts into play an intricate value: compacted, complex images fashioned with calculated precision. The choreography of Twyla Tharp is equally outstanding in this respect. Not only is her highly complex style "singularly unemotional . . . [and] objective" (*A*, 394), but hers is an art "that can absorb jazz," for example, "without getting carried away by it, that can release and even galvanize the senses without ever slipping into self-indulgence or going out of control" (*A*, 394). Tharp's capacity to fuse different styles of dance and movement in the same work, and, within a given work, to fuse styles in the same body at a single kinetic stroke, is testimony to a further aspect of structural complexity in her work—"high-concentration" dance.

Performers too can contribute, and contribute incisively, to the density of a dance. Of Baryshnikov, for example, Croce writes that

> in his debut performances this season [1974] with the American Ballet Theatre, he danced "on top of" the solos in *Giselle* and *La Bayadère*, giving us two and three times as much to look at as anyone had ever given us in the same unit of musical time. High-concentrate dancing is what the most progressive twentieth-century choreography is all about, but the idea has never been expressed before by a performer on so high a level of virtuosity (*A*, 75).

What might be called the mining of a dance by a performer is one of a number of tendencies in dance in this century to have converged toward the exploration of the new concrete reason, a reason that is not a matter simply of controlling an artistic process but a matter of finding outlets in the complexities and possibilities of the artist's craft. Croce's statement that "Baryshnikov's promise lies not in novel steps but in his power to push classical steps to a new extreme in logic, a new density of interest" (*A*, 75) is a precise identification of this push toward complexity from the point of view of the performer. On the choreographic side, of course, there are innumerable examples, as the previous discussion suggests. But it should be explicitly pointed out, too, that a primary focus of the new Faustian reason has been the exploration of movement exclusive of any message or story, and further that that exploration at times has included the exploitation of chance as a prime determinant of movement. This use of chance does not result in a casual, anything-goes medley of movement; it too is a matter of calculated precision and as such is clearly the work of a consummate artist. To paraphrase Pasteur, "Chance in dance favors the prepared body."

Whitehead has persuasively expressed the new Faustian bent for a highly concrete reason in his notion of the great complexity of all experiences, of which rational human thought is only a miniscule part, and in which meaningful, potentially intelligible structures are literally everywhere to be found. An aspect of this complexity is spelled out in his theory of the interrelatedness of all things. From this perspective, phrases in Croce's description of Balanchine's dances of the 1940s could, with minor changes, stand as a commentary on a Whiteheadian text: where "every stage of growth is consequentially related to every other," where there is "an intertwining of echoes and cross-references," a pattern of meaning is built up from the very flesh and character of each thing in relation to all others and to the whole. Indeed, Whitehead's account of reality might begin with the statement: "The Theme is full of elementary particles, jostling, caroming, crisscrossing space in strokes" (*A*, 187). Everything is in process. But, to carry the analogy further, using another passage from the same dance review, it should be clear that if we are able to see "a foot becoming a point"—a foot curling, then flexing and arching—"the detail looms [only] for an instant, then quickly takes its place in the grand scheme of the ballet" (*A*, 187). Process is ordered interrelationships, not anarchy; it is marked by concrescences, not insularities.

If the Faustian II ideal of concrete reason is transparent in contemporary dance, the Faustian II notion of rhythmic energies permeating the universe is no less so. The rhythms of dance have either flowed from the physical rhythms of the body (including the rhythms of movement itself) or, with a varying strictness, been transposed from music to the pulsations of the performers' bodies. In either case, there is a greater mildness, that is, a less obdurate force, in the Faustian II than in the Faustian I rhythmic energies. Moreover the extraordinary emphasis on directional energies and mechanical forces in the sciences and the arts of the Faustian I eighteenth century is no longer apparent. The extreme sense of directional forces moving into space was symbolized by an unvarying rhythmic beat, as if a single metronomic rhythm were itself a pulsation of force propelling bodies on a straight line into space. This old Faustian musical beat, so far as it occurred in the baroque or in the rococo periods was symbolic of the idea of dynamic mechanical forces organizing cosmic nature. In twentieth-century dance, by contrast, there occurs a new flexibility of rhythmic articulations, as opposed to a single metronomic beat, and an exploration of rhythmic diversity. There is, for example, an interest in plumbing and following rhythmically the experiences of the organic body in whatever way those experiences might unfold, thus permitting an exploration of biological cycles or historicities. A rarified example of this focus is Deborah Hay's *Circle Dances,* which are "the result of thirty years of moving and studying dance."[9] Of these dances she writes that "the body is one quiet, breathing, sensitive generation of energy and movement. The movement is repeated slowly and comes from each individual's own feeling and breath."[10] In a commentary on one of her own performances of these dances, she elaborates on her central theme that "breath is movement" and "movement is breath": "It was almost as if I became another person in whom breathing and movement were unified. I like to call this person 'dancing-breath.'"[11] A less extreme example of body-centered rhythms is found in Trisha Brown's *Accumulation,* initially accompanied by the Grateful Dead's "Uncle John's Band" but subsequently performed in silence. It was not simply the durational aspect of rhythm that changed in the silent version of the dance, the piece being in the first instance four minutes long and in the second fifty-five minutes; the tempo of movement "fluctuated in relation to biological changes in temperature, fatigue and second winds."[12] Body-centered rhythms, in the sense of cyclical energies, can not only be a source of inspiration for dance; they can also at times, and in a quite determined way, exercise a choreographic control over the dance itself.

Where music and dance do come together, the new Faustian choreography is not usually dominated by a single rhythm;

again, it is a matter of complexity—or diversity. Of Twyla Tharp's group pieces in general, for example, Croce writes that "[they] employ an all-over pattern, with the dancers moving to simultaneous but disparate counts" (*A,* 342). Erick Hawkins elliptically pinpoints the rhythmic complexity and diversity of Faustian II dance when he writes of "dance that loves time as a *sensed* duration, and all the subtle asymmetrical divisions of time, and yet *always* the pulse of time."[13] Even in Laura Dean's dances, which Croce describes as "planned primitivism"—"only primary colors are used, and they're meant to burn us with their purity" (*A,* 137)—there is an intense and complicated rhythmic patterning. *Drumming,* for example, uses a score by Steve Reich which Croce describes as follows:

> [It] consists of a single rhythmic pattern enunciated in turn by bongo drums, marimbas, and glockenspiels; to each of these bands are added male and female vocalisers, whistling, a piccolo; in the fourth and final section all voices are heard together. Since the instruments frequently play out of phase with each other and introduce further variations in pitch and timbre, the effect is sumptuous—a multilayered sonic veil of which the dance is only able to pick up two or three threads (*A,* 136).

Although Croce finds the choreography thin in comparison with the music, she notes that "when, to the marimba section of *Drumming,* the Dean dancers go into their bobbin-like spins, their faraway trance corresponds to the remote whirr of the music, and their different bodily rhythms correspond to its multiplicity" (*A,* 136).

Whether primarily body-centered, movement-centered, or music-centered, rhythm in contemporary dance presupposes a time that is "seasonal" rather than momentary. This notion of seasonal time, in fact, enters into the whole matrix of cultural deeds and works of contemporary Western civilization. It is a notion that is congenial to the idea of the historical, for example, an idea that is at the core of the Faustian II *Weltanschauung.* As contemporary Westerners, we intuit sometimes the slow and languid, sometimes the agitated and rapid; we intuit dynamic themes embracing fellow humans, animals, seasons, growing vegetation, and a pulsating cosmos—themes that are vibrations of the ceaseless, expanding energy of the world. In such intuitions, time tends to be organically divided into qualitative durations of variable extent. It is no longer merely clock or watch time, artificially divided into moments, ticks, and seconds. Part of the ultimate meaning of Faustian II life stems from the affirmation that patterns in time can be intuited, as well as the more usual patterns in space. Faustian II dance literally embodies these qualitative temporal intuitions.

Whitehead's epochal idea of time is a particular expression, too, of the Faustian II idea of seasonal durations. His temporal concerns stretch to the smallest constituent processes of physical reality: "actual occasions." Quite in harmony with the Faustian II notion of the historicity of macro-events, Whitehead depicted micro-events—actual occasions—as time quanta that could not be broken down into instants. Carried to the level of human experience, this of course means that there is no immediate present as such, and indeed, for Whitehead, the present "is the vivid fringe of memory tinged with anticipation."[14] In short, at both the macro- and micro-level, nothing is static but everything is in process; everything is becoming. But within that span are overlapping volumes of time, so to speak. In his earlier philosophy, Whitehead spoke of events *extending* over other events. Thus dancing a dance "extends" over dancing any phrase of the dance, just as dancing any phrase of the dance extends over dancing any movement within the phrase. From this perspective, there are stratified durations or processes that are as polyrhythmic as Reich's "multi-layered sonic veil."

There are two further aspects of Faustian II rhythm, each of which is as much at the core of dance and of Whitehead's process philosophy as seasonal spans; in fact each is already suggested in the above account of historical durations. The twin values of dynamic energy and dynamic process came into their own around the year 1800, after having been overlaid for eight hundred years by the Greek notion of static substance— although within the eight hundred-year Faustian I dispensation, the idea of an ultimate materiality gradually lost credibility. But the regnant value truly metamorphosed when it was no longer a question of the mechanism of force or the energy of the inertial impetus of substances, but instead, the energy of force-fields or regions, emanating not wholly determined energies but energies capable of creating novelty. To a large extent, modern dance is a consummation of "energy ideas" which spread throughout Western civilization, especially after 1800.

Dynamic energy and fluency are aspects of Whitehead's

world picture, according to which feeling, prehension, or emotional valuation occurs everywhere, even in the least conscious and simplest of entities. Whitehead's concept of a quantitative "emotional" intensity is translatable by the term *energy,* and his concept of "specific form of feeling" is translatable by the phrase *form of energy,* or *dynamic process.* The transference of physical energies throughout the universe is literally a transference of throbs of emotional energy. Hence the universe is seen to be as dynamic and changing as Einsteinian physics and quantum mechanics presuppose it to be: a thoroughly vibrant, pulsing world to its tiniest and most primitive parts.

If we were to take a critical dance review at face value, these two Faustian/Whiteheadian themes—dynamic process and dynamic energy—appear each to have been separately incarnated in Balanchine's ballet *Metastaseis and Pithoprakta.* The ballet—really two separate works—was described as follows:

> In *Metastaseis* (a coined word meaning dialectic transformation), an enormous disk at the center of a bare stage reveals itself to be 28 male and female dancers in chalk-white garments that look like winter underwear. Slowly they writhe, rise, and begin to surge about the stage, combining and recombining, touching and turning, with arms and legs outstretched like diagrams of molecular linkage or a microscopic view of the proliferation of cells—an impression heightened by bright white crosslighting. *Pithoprakta* (meaning actions by probabilities) has twelve dancers skittering, scuttering, rolling across the stage like nodes and waves of electrical energy.[15]

The critic's preoccupation with metaphors of molecular and submolecular energies remarkably verifies the idea of a dynamic process and of a dynamic energy becoming visibly incarnate. Indeed, the dancers of *Pithoprakta,* by symbolizing nodes of electrical energy, could be centers around which moving cosmic forces revolve as electrons revolve around the nucleus of the atom. Through the very kinetic energy that defines it, the art of twentieth-century dance fulfills, in the most unique way among the arts, the powerful and metaphysical penchant of Faustian II civilization to draw close to and symbolize the kinetic energy of the micro- and macro-cosmos—its "dialectic transformations" and its "probabilistic events."

Earlier than Whitehead, at the very beginning of the Faustian II era, Hegel had described the rhythmic dialectic of things and events, in cosmic nature and in the human world, as the basic logic in the formation of Western civilization. His theory of a universe in the dialectical process of becoming is made plausible by the visible rhythms and organic maturations and decay of growing things. The dialectic is evident in the temporal successions of opposite states: of seedlings becoming trees, or of living leaves becoming lifeless, falling to the forest floor and turning to humus. In a not unrelated way, Whitehead depicts actually existing entities neither as substances nor as beings, but as *becomings*. He sees every entity as a growing concrescence of its constituent parts, and thereby sees the macrocosm as engaged in constant process.

Movement, too, is a process. It is not a property of an object or merely a change of position; it is a concrescence of kinetic powers. The meaning for dance of the notion of becoming is perhaps most aptly summed up in Merce Cunningham's comment that "any movement can become part of a dance." Because movement itself is first of all a transformation—a becoming par excellence—it is extraordinarily plastic. It is open to change—to new interweavings, new contexts; one movement can grow into, out of, and with, a limitless number of other movements. Here again, Twyla Tharp's talent for compounding a variety of dance styles provides a ready and particularly vivid example. Perhaps the richest illustration is had, however, in Croce's general description of the aftermath of "mercist" (Croce's preferred term for "post-modern" dance) lecture-demonstrations:

> Audiences will sometimes ask how much they should know of the creative methods used in a dance in order to appreciate it. The question, not at all a dismissible one, means that they've detected the presence of a process that doesn't disappear into a result. It may also mean that the process looks as if it would be more interesting to watch or to know about than the actual dance it has produced. Process is often deliberately on view in mercist pieces (*GD*, 68).

The process/product dichotomy is a well-recognized and acknowledged one in dance, and it has been further refined in different ways—for example, in the distinction between symbolic and existential meanings.[16] What is new here is the idea of the visibility of process; in Whiteheadian terms, the visibility of concrescences, of things growing together before one's very eyes. It is one thing for a choreographer to focus upon process and to embody the concept of process in a dance; it is quite another for process to show itself forth, for it to achieve a palpable, visible reality and significance: for it neither to "disappear into a result" nor to be of only passing or parenthetical interest.

But the notion of dynamic process—of becoming—is only half the story. There is also the Faustian II notion of dynamic energy itself, an energy whose paths are either unpredictable or foreseen only as probabilities. Whitehead avoids the word *chance,* and the concept has in fact little place in his philosophy. Yet novelty and its generative source, creativity, are of ultimate value in Whitehead's philosophy. Creativity is indeed the "Category of the Ultimate"; it plays a role in Whitehead's metaphysics similar to the role that matter plays in Aristotle's. Novelty generated by creativity is not utterly novel, since the world is in process; that is, feelings or prehensions—the basic processual stuff of actual occasions—provide the basis upon which novelty emerges. According to Whitehead, these processual forms are attracted toward the novel; they are "lured" by novelty, and the lure is an expression of rhythm. Through rhythm, then, there is not only historical duration or seasonal time, but the creative emergence of novelty in the world. Rhythm fuses sameness and novelty; it offers at the same time regularity and contrast, stability and change. In the unfolding or flow of worldly things and events, rhythm accounts for the copresence of continuing sameness and creative innovation; it is a quality of all living and nonliving things.

Were one asked to encapsulate unpredictability or innovation par excellence in dance, the name of Merce Cunningham would undoubtedly be invoked. As Croce has pointed out, "Cunningham has initiated more new ideas for theatrical performance than any other choreographer" (*GD,* 69). So much are newness and chance associated with his work, it is not surprising that the whole of it is undergirded by a philosophy of flux:

> The impression of fleeting phenomena, of mutability, that we get from so much of Cunningham's work is the controlling metaphor of his theatre. . . . His idea of nature-in-the-theatre rests on the flux that is common to both nature and

the theatrical performance; as he says of one of his ballets, "the continuity is change" (*GD*, 11).

But Cunningham's philosophy of flux is not an endorsement or an embodiment of change willy-nilly. Cunningham makes dances by listening to the actuality of movement, so to speak. Croce notes earlier in her description of Cunningham and his work that he is a classicist: " 'That a dance be,' as he once wrote, 'unprompted by references other than to its own life' is the first requirement of classicism. Cunningham has eminently satisfied it" (*GD*, 10). For Cunningham, the new or the unpredictable are anchored in the very real process of movement itself. That is, they emerge out of the very unfolding of movement, and it is only insofar as one is witness to that unfolding—attentive to the kinetic passage itself, whether as choreographer, dancer, or audience—that one is able to create, discover, or appreciate unpredictabilities or new possibilities. Cunningham's logic is unforeseen but it is a thoroughly discriminating logic.

A radically different kind of novelty but a parallel structure is epitomized in the world of ballet by Balanchine. Actually, a counterexample—Croce's appraisal of a "failed" work—makes the point most lucidly. Croce begins a review with the question,

> Is there a greater theatrical adventure than a new Balan-
> chine ballet seen for the first time? . . . At first, swept along
> at intergalactic speeds, we feel nothing but the novelty and
> peculiarity of it all—the sensation of being bombarded by
> clean particles of image and sound. And we are likely to
> think, as the strokes and details build up to a total impres-
> sion, Why, how strange—he's never done anything like this
> before (*GD*, 58).

She goes on to note that when seen for the second time a ballet may lose some of its singular novelty and "become an inte-grated core expression of the company that produced it" (*GD*, 58). Yet her answer to the seemingly rhetorical question at the beginning of the review is, "Yes: a new Balanchine ballet seen for the second time" (*GD*, 58). As fresh and as mesmerizing as a first performance might be, the second may be even more so. But the focus of Croce's temporizing remarks here is *Kammer-musik No. 2*, a ballet which she has now seen four times and which seems to fall into the category of "estimable" but "avoidable" ballets (*GD*, 59). "The ballet boils with precisely directed energies," she writes, "it's the mirror of an impersonal yet human process. . . . I find the process poetically incomprehensible and I believe it isn't going to become less so, yet the way it's worked out and timed down to the last microsecond is something for other choreographers to study and for all of us to admire" (*GD*, 61).

From a Whiteheadian perspective, what makes the ballet "avoidable" is a rhythmic imbalance: the clarity and precision of the choreography are impeccable, but the choreography remains at the same time "poetically incomprehensible." The ballet "has a powerfully thick and busy surface" but "lacks depth" (*GD,* 59); "without ever getting mechanical and therefore predictable in his moves, [Balanchine] yet finds a visual rhyme for everything he hears" (*GD*, 60). Estimable moments aside, on the whole, the dance is clearly tedious: "Though the atmosphere of the piece never deepens, it never dies either" (*GD*, 60). A dynamic process is there, but the dynamic spark itself—a full-bodied radiant energy—is lacking. There is a consummately perfected but empty unfolding of movement. Thus, Croce writes, *Kammermusik No. 2* is "a member of the family, but a fairly unappealing member—the kind that sets out to gain by hard work and good credit what it lacks in bloodlines" (*GD*, 59).

Where dynamic process and dynamic energy fail to come together in a dance, novelty in a Whiteheadian sense is jammed, and choreography can come literally to a dead halt. A comparison of Croce's general remarks on "ballets without choreography" and on Twyla Tharp's choreography throws into relief the hazards of a preoccupation with movement gone dry, with a dynamic energy unanimated by dynamic process. "Good choreography," Croce writes, is an "intellectual delight" (*A*, 322). Where

> no interest is being generated at an intelligent level, which is to say at the level of choreography . . . movements the dancers do merely state the situation without developing it, and you realize as the piece wears on that there is no reason why they should be moving at all. And the more sterile the means of expression, the more compulsive the effort becomes to create excitement through kinetic emphasis. These ballets are full of overenergized kinetics, of the *will* to choreography. Like sex in the head, the movements are overreasoned at the expense of reason itself" (*A*, 322).

In contrast, Croce speaks of Tharp's dancers as

> giving us so much more to see than most companies ever
> think of giving, and they let us see them giving it. . . . At
> peaks of furious activity, they may get breathless and a
> little giggly, but they stay calm . . . because they're being so
> carefully objective. It's this objectivity that fascinates and
> carries us from one moment to the next. We get interested
> in the task they have set themselves; we try to follow the
> intricate logic of it. But we can also enjoy the dancing
> another way as a burst of nonsensical excitement. We can
> leave the dancers to their purpose and wrap ourselves in
> the illusion that it's all happening spontaneously. . . . As the
> dance flickers between its two aspects I become convinced
> that I'm watching the most exciting performing in the
> theatre (*A*, 390–91).

Where there is intellectual delight in the form of good
choreography, there is the possibility of attending either to the
process of movement or to the spontaneity of kinetic energy
itself. When juxtaposed in this way, Croce's assessments thus
point toward a double vision at the heights of aesthetic appreciation, a vision that mirrors the Faustian/Whiteheadian notion
of becoming and change as the double cornerstones of novelty.
Taken together, the critical vision and philosophical notion
point toward a bona fide aesthetic standard for the criticism of
dance. Novelty cannot be generated by itself; it cannot be
"willed." On the one hand, sheer energy alone, "overenergized
kinetics," does not make a dance. But neither does sheer process alone. One could refer here not only to *Kammermusik No. 2*
but to Croce's estimation of "baby-step concerts" as well, concerts where, as Croce sees it, baby's first steps "are repeated
over and over in wonderment, as if choreographers hoped to
discover for themselves the secret of why on earth man dances"
(*A*, 138). In short, the suggestion is unmistakable that good
choreography is doubly inspired and may be doubly appreciated. A closer accord with the Faustian/Whiteheadian notion of a creative emergence into novelty could not be asked.
Perhaps a richer and more promising basis for assaying critical
judgements of dance as well as dance itself could not be asked
either.

A final and concluding comment might be made in light of
the above comparison. When Croce speaks in one instance of

movements being "overreasoned at the expense of reason itself" and in another instance of an audience's following "the intricate logic of the task the dancers set for themselves," there appears to be a choreographic contrast not only in respect to the embodiment or nonembodiment of a double-valued Faustian/Whiteheadian dynamic but in respect to the Faustian II notion of a concrete reason as well. The point is that where one regnant idea goes, so also go the others; if one has gone amok, the others are not likely to be far behind. Regnant ideas are not ingredients that a choreographer puts into a dance; they are intertwined aspects of a global world view. Not only this, but they are only apparent in retrospect, after the creation of a dance, not in advance of it. No more than classical aesthetic principles of composition are Faustian (or Whiteheadian) ideas the stuff from which a choreographer weaves a dance. As Erick Hawkins has said, "I think it is almost impossible to speak of aspects of the movement, such as its style, before it is found, before it comes out of my body as I choreograph, as a spider spins its web."[17] If dance embodies Faustian II ideas and if it is a reflection of Whiteheadian process philosophy, it embodies and it reflects not out of a self-conscious appropriation but because the body is as much the living source of these ideas and the ground of their everyday living reality as it is the source and ground of the living reality of dance.

Notes

1. From "Phenomenology as a Way of Illuminating Dance," this volume.
2. *Afterimages* (New York: Vintage Books, 1979), 189. *Afterimages* is hereafter cited as *A,* and Croce's *Going to the Dance* (New York: Alfred Knopf, 1982) is hereafter cited as *GD.*
3. Richard Kraus, *History of the Dance* (Englewood Cliffs, New Jersey: Prentice-Hall, 1969), 162.
4. Alfred N. Whitehead, *Process and Reality: An Essay in Cosmology* (New York: Harper Torchbooks, 1960), 33.
5. *Science and the Modern World* (New York: Macmillan, 1967), 84–86.
6. Whitehead, *Process and Reality*, 33.
7. Merce Cunningham, *Changes: Notes on Choreography*, ed. Frances Starr (New York: Something Else Press, 1968), unpaginated.
8. Whitehead, *Process and Reality*, 247.
9. *Contemporary Dance*, ed. Anne Livet (New York: Abbeville Press, 1978), 128.
10. Ibid.
11. Ibid., 130.
12. Ibid., 45.

13. From booklet sold to audiences of Erick Hawkin's concert performance at Utah State University, Logan, Utah, in August 1965, p. 13.

14. Whitehead, *The Concept of Nature* (Cambridge, England: Cambridge University Press, 1955), 73.

15. Time Magazine 26 January 1968, 45.

16. Maxine Sheets-Johnstone, "The Passage Rites of the Body: A Phenomenological Account of Change in Dance." A rigorously abridged version of this paper appeared in *Leonardo* 11 (1978): 197–201, under the title "An Account of Recent Changes in Dance in the U.S.A."

17. "Pure Poetry," in *The Modern Dance,* ed. Selma Jeanne Cohen (Middletown, Conn.: Wesleyan University Press, 1965), 50.

The Autographic Nature of the Dance

Joseph Margolis

The salient, indisputable fact about philosophical studies of the dance is their conceptual poverty. I think it is accurate to say that the dance is the single principal art that is either very nearly unmentioned in comprehensive overviews of aesthetics or else treated (almost as a second thought) by way of adjusting arguments strongly and directly grounded in the other arts—principally, drama and music—or by way of notions of representation and expression, linked even with the analysis of the literary arts.

There are also some natural difficulties in theorizing about the dance. For one thing, there can be no question that notational efforts at scoring a dance are radically less interesting intrinsically than musical scores or the texts of dramas. The reason undoubtedly lies in the central importance of the tempered keyboard in Western music and the use of an articulated language in drama. For the sequences of actual notes in a musical score cannot fail to exhibit formal properties (often quite complex) that may be detected even in the absence of acoustic assistance, and the internal properties of the elements of language are, as the history of criticism and appreciation attests, very nearly inexhaustible. Dance scores, however, are primarily heuristic devices for recovering a minimal sense of the principal positions and movements of a given dance, and aside from

This chapter was originally presented as a paper at the conference "Illuminating Dance: Philosophical Inquiry and Aesthetic Criticism," cosponsored by CORD and Temple University at Temple University, Philadelphia, 5 May 1979.

the classical ballet, which has a finite vocabulary of distinct bodily positions and movements and of the history of its own evolving style, the notational convenience of Labanotation, for instance, has rather little to do with the formal conditions of actually learning to dance or to perform a particular dance.[1] Dance notation, on the whole, tends to capture the movement of a dance by drawing the path or sequence of trajectories that statically approximates it—very nearly in the sense in which Henri Bergson despaired of any conceptual capture of human movement. Although there are efforts to correlate movements and distinct expression notationally, such efforts appear to be noticeably awkward and unconvincing.[2] Furthermore there is no sense in which the perception of related positions and movements, ordered perhaps in an interesting way and legible from the notation itself, could possibly be grounded in an understanding of the deeper structures of the dance by means of a closer attention to the notation itself: no such structures are there presupposed by the notation that are in any sense comparable to the structures of music and language. The reason seems to lie with the emphasis in dance notation on visual recognition *tout court* and the requirements for generating dance movements in terms of the dynamics of motor activity controlled proprioceptively.

This cannot be taken as a weakness in the dance, only as a weakness in attempts to treat the dance primarily as an art that can be satisfactorily construed as allographic—in Nelson Goodman's sense[3]—or as a performing art suitably subsumed under generalizations readily drawn from music and literary theater. It is abundantly clear that even musical notation fails to achieve its ideal allographic function, since it is both impossible to exclude notationally variations of tempo and tone that are musically pertinent, produced in apparent accord with notation, and quite irrelevant to insist on the allographic for the reidentification of particular compositions or the serving of musical interests.[4] There are, of course, other complaints about putative allographic restrictions on identity—in particular, those bearing on the familiar practice of omitting portions of a drama or musical composition or dance, or of replacing dance steps or instruments or the like, in order to accommodate local contingencies—without the least damage to fixing the identity of a piece. *Hamlet* is often cut in performance; the *Brandenberg Concerti* are often played with modern instruments; the thirty-two *fouettés* that appear in *Swan Lake* are often reduced to six-teen, the remaining measures replaced by other steps. In fact, Georges Balanchine has quite regularly replaced steps in the choreography of well-established dances of his that in rehearsal seemed, because of the overriding movement and spirit of the dances, to be required.

These reflections point to a second feature of the dance that tends to set it somewhat apart from the principal performing arts. The divergence among performances of what purports to be one and the same dance tends, if anything, to be less easily discounted than the counterpart phenomena in the other arts. I should not deny that divergent performances or interpreta-tions obtain in music and drama as well, but the abstract con-straint of a common keyboard and a common language encourages the fiction that such divergencies in music and drama are either practical concessions to the imperfect condi-tions of performance (for instance, acoustical differences among concert halls and the convenient slackness of require-ments for tempo and pitch) or else degrees of interpretive free-dom permitted once conformity to certain strict but minimal requirements is achieved. The illusion that this holds for dance as well may be seen in the following remarks by Mary Sirridge and Adina Armelagos in which they reject what they term "the modified expression theory": "excluding the case of explicit mime, which is remarkable precisely because it is not continu-ous with the traditional vocabulary of ballet, the ballet dancer may be said to be concentrating on two things: doing the right thing and staying in line."[5] With an important qualification, Sirridge and Armelagos follow Goodman's theory of style,[6] holding that "a general dance style, such as ballet, solves the problem [of expression] by providing the dancer with an inven-tory of movements or sequences of movements, which we will call a 'spatial vocabulary.'" Against the "classical expression theory," they hold that "the dancer [need not] actually be feel-ing what he projects," and against the "modified expression theory" they assert that the dancer need not be concentrating on expression at all. In fact, they say, "It is quite important that the dancer not concentrate on expressing something or 'play-ing to the audience.'" They go so far as to hold that "the ex-pression or projection of personal feeling or emotion has nothing to do with the dancer's expectations of him- or her-self or with the focus of the dancer's artistic concentration." The dancer restricts him- or her-self somehow "almost entirely" to "the kinesthetic sensations associated with executing steps properly" and to the comparable "sense of being *en rapport* with the other dancers or with the music."[7]

There is no reason to hold to the classical expression theory. In fact, it is rather difficult to find advocates nowadays. The modified expression theory is similarly occupied with a contingency that is either marginal or associated with the work of a special sort of dance, possibly not unlike the mime Sirridge and Armelagos have in mind. But their emphasis is designed— deliberately or not—to conform with the allographic model of the dance, for, by the ordered regularities of a putative style, they suppose that the aesthetically relevant expressive qualities of a performance may be grasped by a sensitive *audience* without affecting the sense in which performing *dancers* conform only with the notational requirements of a given piece. The movements and positions of the body, then, notably in the classical ballet but by no means confined to that, serve as the extensional counterpart in dance of sequences of notes in music and of sentences in drama.

But this is a decidedly defective view—a view, in fact, that Sirridge and Armelagos themselves in effect undermine in an apparently contemporaneous paper. (We shall turn to it shortly.) There simply is no reliable correspondence between a dancer's performing a set of movements in accordance with a mere notation and an audience's seizing the expressive qualities somehow conveyed by those movements, and there are no kinesthetic sensations that could guide a dancer with regard to much more than congruence with a rhythmic beat and with the beat of other dancers. Also, a dance coach or director normally does not correct a dancer with respect only to the notational minima of a dance; and to say that the director corrects the dancer with respect to the requirements of "style" is: (1) to say, at least, that the dancer *is* expected to attend to the expressive features of a dance; and is (2) not to say that the style invoked is systematically or algorithmically coordinated with the performance of movements demonstrably correct on notational grounds.

The body is not an instrument for a dancer in the same way in which a violin is for a musician or a brush for a painter. We cannot help but see the peculiarly intimate and sui generis sense in which the dancer and the mime use *themselves* in performance. The same sense is at work in the singer, the actor, and the instrumentalist—and even, if the point needs to be pressed, among visual and literary artists, for all artists compose and perform with the organized materials of their experienced life. To watch Rampal perform on the flute, for instance, is to appreciate his command of the idiosyncratic energies and habits of his own body that he must tap in order to bring his notes into accord with the notational requirements of the score and his own conception of the appropriate style of a given composition. The authority of a performing artist characteristically extends to the invention of an expressive style—not merely to the confirmation of a canon—which, in any case, is too subtly linked to the niceties of particular performances to be captured generically. Similarly, the dancer does not work simply with positions and movements but with the naturally expressive use of positions and movements generated (not altogether consciously) by that *person's* use of his or her own body through the accumulated grooming of a continuous life; *and* imposed on and altering this natural and acquired expressiveness, individuated through an exclusively privileged experience with a single body, the *dancer* learns the expressive possibilities of different styles and the way in which his or her own performing body, stylistically informed, is viewed by knowledgeable observers.

Such considerations obviously affected the appraisal of Tanaquil Leclerc's efforts to play the principal role in *Swan Lake*. Leclerc's tall and extremely slim body, naturally trained in a sort of humorous and informal manner, had much more to overcome than the more classically proportioned body and more formal manner of Maria Tallchief. In this sense, quite contrary to Sirridge and Armelagos, since the body is naturally expressive (essentially in the way that Wittgenstein emphasized), dancers are obliged to be concerned with the expressiveness of their movements—even if both the classical and modified expression theories are false, and in addition to whatever convention about *denoting* emotions and the like may obtain. Leclerc managed to produce a rather deviant version of the Swan Queen, whose expressive features may very possibly have required an adjustment in taste and perception precluded by her sudden malady. The adjustment, however, was no different in principle from the general diachronic shifting of balletic style through the historical influence of strongly authoritative dancers. Still, it is certainly clear that she produced the requisite movements that notation of the ballet would have required, exhibited the generic features of the Romantic style favored in the transatlantic version of the Russian ballet, and remained kinesthetically *en rapport* with other dancers. What Sirridge and Armelagos fail to account for is, precisely, that the Leclerc performance had to be orchestrated around the novel bodily expressiveness of Leclerc's manner of dancing; and this both required attention on Leclerc's part to expressive considerations and now exposes the sense in which style and expression in dance cannot be satisfactorily captured as the correlates of correct movements. Here it is extremely important to notice—it is often misunderstood—that the expressiveness of performance is *intentional,* but when we say this we are not referring only to that which is psychologically deliberate or consciously intended. This kind of intentionality cannot be satisfactorily represented by any extensional notation. It has to do rather with the individuality and idiosyncrasy of human expressiveness as the intersection of biologically and culturally contingent processes, raised at least to an essential place in the medium of the dance. Conceptually, this signifies that the history of production, including particularly the personal resources and expressive motivation of individual artists, tends to dominate the characterization of whatever may be called the style of performance.

There is, of course, a logical distinction between denotation and expression: neither entails the other. But in a highly conventionalized art like the classical ballet, what is reflexively representational at the level of mental states tends to be expressive because it is denotative. This is, in one sense, a matter of style, but it is neither necessary nor even characteristic of more recent ballet, which has accommodated the freer forms of so-called modern dance. It is rather more a matter of certain genres of representation. The expressiveness of the natural movement of the body belongs, first, to the human animal and, second, to the groomed member of a particular culture. It is conceivable that in very highly stylized societies conventions obtain that are at once both denotative and expressive of emotion—perhaps in the public behavior of the geisha or of the temple dancers of Southeast Asia, for example—and that the natural expressiveness of one's own body is suppressed or ignored. Logically, however, that natural expressiveness of the body is implicitly recognized wherever, with regard to actual mental states, the expressive and the denotative are not viewed as coextensive. But when the division obtains in the dance— conceivably, even in the classical ballet, if the point about Leclerc and Tallchief is well taken—"personal style" cannot be treated as "a dancer's characteristic articulation of a more general spatial vocabulary" or of some generic style that fixes the particular denotative vocabulary of a distinctive form of dancing.[8] For that thesis involves a confusion. There may be a conventional representational system of beliefs and emotions, in which what is expressed is no more than what is denoted; style in this sense will be correlated with correctly executed movements, as Sirridge and Armelagos claim. But where the expressiveness of bodily movement intrudes, either in the sense of natural expression or in the sense of culturally favored modifications of such expression (not incorporated in the denotative conventions of a dance), what we designate as "style" cannot, for conceptual reasons, be merely correlated with the proper execution of notationally specified movements. There is, therefore, a deep equivocation about the notion of style: it may refer to a conventionally developed system of denotative (*and therefore,* expressive) correlates of notationally specified sequences—which of course relieves the dancer of any need to attend to expression; or it may refer to a mode of performance that combines the natural and culturally groomed expressiveness of the body with some approximate denotative convention—which of course imposes on the dancer a need to attend to the proprieties of expression. In the latter sense, but not the former, expressive qualities need not be construed in terms of denotative symbols at all, though they will clearly depend on the conventions of a particular culture. They are, when present, literally present—as extensions of the naturally expressive—in whatever sense cultural phenomena are actual phenomena irreducible to purely physical systems, with respect to which they might well have been treated as metaphorical.

Interestingly enough, Sirridge and Armelagos qualify their acceptance of Goodman's well-known thesis about expressive qualities, namely, that a work expresses those properties that it metaphorically exemplifies.[9] For, conceding the natural expressiveness of the body, they are prepared to admit that "human movement may be literally sad." They go on to say that a good performance of *Swan Lake* may have properties that "are surely metaphorically exemplified, hence expressed. With others [that is, other properties], the answer is not at all clear-cut. Since both kinds of properties are aesthetically important ones to which the work is symbolically related, it makes little difference."[10] Here, however, we see how the complexity of the dance refuses to yield to their formula and how, at the same time, it betrays a characteristic weakness in Goodman's theory of expression. For, if a certain movement may be literally sad, then it must "possess" the property without needing to refer to it; in that sense it possesses it without exemplifying it, without being in any way symbolically linked to it. But that, precisely is what is denied by Goodman (whom Sirridge and Armelagos profess to follow).[11] The point is not a mere quibble. For, if the performance of a dance exhibits such properties, dancers cannot restrict themselves to what may be notationally represented. Given that dance notation has a rather restricted use, refining our sense of the nature and role of expression points directly to the sui generis nature of the art of dance.

The mystery of this aspect of the dance, the intrusive expressiveness of the body, of which the dancer may not initially be entirely cognizant, is probably most nearly captured in Merleau-Ponty's well-known essay, "Eye and Mind"—except that Merleau-Ponty never mentions the dance and apparently believes (for rather curious reasons) that the art of painting best exemplifies the primordial sources of artistic expression.[12] Nevertheless, his insight concerns the interior, the lived, effort of the body to orient itself at once perceptually and in movement, with regard to external objects and other incarnate systems, originally and also in a way that cannot completely overcome the essentially tacit dimension of our bodily orientation and expression.[13] Put this way, the theory of the dance and of bodily performance cannot be completely formulated without attention to the deeply intentional, ultimately *autographic* features of the expression and significance of bodily movement itself. In effect, notably in our own time, the dance cannot be appreciated without some sense of how movements are actually generated, and this perception, however disadvantageously managed in third-person situations, relies very heavily on our sense of the manner of movement of distinct and particular bodies. This is why, perhaps, one feels that Martha Graham could hardly have been replaced in certain of her dances. In a second paper, Armelagos and Sirridge admit as much about

Graham's *Frontier,* though they persist in thinking that a dancer's personal style (style$_2$) is somehow "both an articulation and
a further development of style$_1$" (that is, an inventory of acceptable positions and position sequences, including, one supposes,
denotative import).[14] On their own admission, and according to
the preceding argument, moreover, this is quite impossible:
either dances of Graham's kind cannot be notationally fixed—
for if they could someone else could dance them; or else what
may be noted must be confined to questions of style$_1$, which
then fails to specify for us what is often crucial both to the
appreciation of a particular dance *and* to a group of its distinctive properties. While Armelagos and Sirridge hold that "some
surrogate explicitly designated by [Graham]"[15] might replace
her, because, precisely, the intended sense is that the lucky
replacement could not be judged suitable on the basis of notationally specified details. It is also not particularly telling that
they hold, reasonably enough, that José Limon's *The Moor's
Pavanne* could be performed by dancers other than Limon and
his company; although, allegedly because it failed to preserve
the intended style, the classical balletic performance of *Pavanne*
by Nureyev and Fonteyn either radically transformed the work
or in a sense destroyed it.[16] The reason is simply that it is not
essential that token instances of the same (type) composition
agree in all aesthetically relevant features or even (again, *contra*
Goodman) that different performances exhibit some common
set of necessary and sufficient features in order to be construed
as "compliants" (instances) of the same work.[17] In fact, there is
every reason to believe that the performing style of nineteenth-
century ballets, to the extent that they may be thought to have
been preserved, has evolved under the pressure of the personal
style of leading dancers. And, although on an argument already given, the dance may be less accommodating notationally
than music and drama (because it is more autographic, in spite
of being a performing art), there is no antecedent reason to
preclude a classical rendition of *The Moor's Pavanne.* If Nureyev's version failed, it did so because it was a failed performance—even an inappropriate one—not because it was in
principle impossible to perform the dance in such a different
style. Or, alternatively, if the classical balletic style was indeed
inappropriate, other styles might have proved unexpectedly
congenial, and other dances might show a greater hospitality
toward divergent styles of performance. It is hard to see that a

Shakespearean performance of *Julius Caesar* and a contemporary one—even Orson Welles's modern-dress version—could not fairly be construed as alternative, stylistically quite different performances of one and the same drama. In any case, resistance to the propriety of the Nureyev version can hardly be restricted to notational constraints and points in the direction of the autographic.

The upshot is that once we give up relying on notational constraint on the reidentification of a dance from performance to performance, there is no logical necessity or advantage in holding that personal style (in effect, expressiveness) is nothing more than, or is primarily, "an articulation and a further development of style$_1$," or that considerations of style$_1$ set fixed notational constraints on the identity of a dance. Treat the dance in a frankly autographic way, and one accommodates at a stroke the history of the dance (and of every other performing art) and the peculiar importance of personal style in the dance (even in the classical ballet, where perhaps the strongest resistance might have been possible).

This, then, is a third distinctive feature of the dance. Adjusting Goodman's category considerably, we can say that dance is a largely autographic art (with some notational facilities), rather than an allographic one. I say that Goodman's category must be adjusted, but then it must be adjusted on independent grounds. For Goodman introduces two quite different notions of the autographic/allographic contrast: in one, art is autographic "if and only if . . . the most exact duplication of [a work] does not thereby count as genuine"; and in the other, a work ceases to be autographic, becomes allographic, "only when . . . [it] is fully determined independently of history of production, in terms of a notational system."[18] Insofar as there are no works of art that are "fully determined independently of history of production," there are no allographic arts, though there are arts with partially allographic features. *All artworks are such in virtue of some history of production,* and that history may even include the intention that they be susceptible to notational constraint. But apart from this, it is certainly clear that contrast with forgery is not essential to considerations bearing on the history of production. If one stressed the notational features of the dance, then it would still be possible to insist that an unauthorized dance performance of Graham's *Frontier* might well be a forgery—much in the sense in which a printing of a Dürer etching, pulled from the true plate but unauthorized, might be called a forgery. And if one stressed the productive history of *Frontier,* then one could still insist that there was no useful sense in which an unauthorized performance must be a forgery. Useful as the notion of forgery is in obliging us to admit the non-perceptual features of all the arts, it is not really central to the effort to characterize particular arts as autographic or allographic. The truth is that ascriptions of forgery—even more benign characterizations such as "in the style of," "of the school of," "influenced by"—are contingently affected by prevailing practices, productive control, market value, and the like, in a way that cuts across the distinction. Forgery, for instance, is a perfectly reasonable charge against the reproduction of unauthorized copies of couturiere designs—which (*contra* Goodman) are particularly apt to be regarded allographically.

Armelagos and Sirridge appear to concede the point of the difficulty of construing the dance as allographic in the sense that Goodman favors—that is, that a dance score is more or less the equivalent of a music score. They stress the unlikelihood of incorporating notationally reference to such "integral 'incidentals'" as the bearing of the accompanying music, lighting, and costumes, *and*—in the same breath—the personal style of individual performers. But their intention, ultimately, is to correct Goodman's thesis, not to abandon it, for they go on to argue that "choreography, correctly understood, *is* one of the main criteria for identifying a performance as a member of the class of allographic compliants which counts as a performance of the work" [italics added].[19] If one thinks of the work of Fokine and Nijinsky, however, it is difficult to see how the *choreography* of a particular artist can fail to anchor the very features of a work in the history of its production, in features of personal style that cannot satisfactorily be incorporated into some generic *notation*—even if the choreography yields a partially instructive notation. Armelagos and Sirridge admit as much in at least some cases, but they are committed to the idea of the gradual development of the dance as a fully allographic art. The principal counter-considerations, are reasonably clear, however. Even the notion of a style, style$_1$, loses all sense of an allographic nature if it is produced by a dominant choreographer, is associated with a particular dance ensemble, tends not to become a canon for the profession as a whole, is closely linked with the personal expressiveness of this or that dancer, is principally taught by example, is noticeably easily lost in performances guided solely by the notation of correct positions and movements, is essentially linked with a relatively transient spirit or style of some distinct society or group, or maximizes improvisational forms and the recognition of stylistic congruence within actual performance. Armelagos and Sirridge speak of style (style$_1$) as a choice of "spatial vocabulary and characteristic kinesthetic motivation," but in effect they admit that at the present time it appears quite impossible to free reference to "kinesthetic motivation" from biographical reference to a particular choreographer, that is, from the personal expressiveness of the style (style$_2$) of a particular choreographer. "Style as we construe it," they concede, "is difficult, if not impossible to record in a notational scheme"; but if so, they go on, "then identity criteria based solely on notational scores are inadequate." Nevertheless, they look forward to "the increasing homogenization of dancer training already underway," which, they feel, "will gradually free dance works from the idiosyncratic control of their creators and increase the number of persons who can adequately interpret inadequate scores."[20] But this may well be a betrayal of the inherent difficulties they themselves take notice of, as well as of the essential sense in which dancers use their personally and culturally idiosyncratic selves as the very medium of their art—*not* steps, movements, positions, or styles primarily focused on denotative and symbolic import.

What reason is there for thinking that the evolving styles of the ballet or the plural styles of modern dance can be fixed canonically and freed from the expressive styles of an enveloping society? The two-storey picture of style$_1$ and style$_2$ is intended to accommodate the allographic conception, but it fails utterly to come to terms with the obvious fact that the dance is not insulated against the world and that dancers are recruited from the living culture that sustains it. One need think only of the eclectic, mixed, and pop-culture features of the work of Jerome Robbins, Anna Sokolow, and Twyla Tharp to see the implausibility of the expectation.[21] New dance forms are bound to exploit the expressive styles of life that themselves emerge contingently and change without end. Georges Balanchine, who wrote the preface for the original edition of Hutchinson's *Labanotation,* had already tactfully observed there the inability of the extraordinarily detailed extensional analysis of dance

movement to capture "the style of the finished product and . . .
the general overall visual picture and staging." He admired the
precision of the notation, particularly its fidelity with respect to
"time values," but he also saw the advantage of a film record—
which is to say, he saw the impossibility of a notation for the
intentional, autographic features of the dance.[22]

The point is easily misunderstood. It is quite possible, of
course, that a kind of dance notation may well facilitate a grasp
of the intentional and expressive complexities of a particular
dance. What is at stake is not notation but allographic notation,
notation confined to purely extensional features of the dance
(such as position and path of motion) that may be supposed to
be theoretically adequate to identifying particular pieces or
identifying them in an aesthetically relevant way. It is instructive, for example, that the enlargement of Rudolph Laban's
extensional dance notation into so-called Effort/Shape analysis
and choreutics presupposes relatively fixed correspondences
between psychological attitudes and dispositions, and movement complexes.[23] But the adequacy of such a system is certainly doubtful beyond the most elementary forms of natural
expressiveness. For aesthetic purposes, it is not particularly important to confine notation allographically; in fact, in musical
notation, we normally supplement putatively extensional notation with such notational instructions as *andante, allegro,* and the
like, which are intended to capture a quality that belongs to a
certain historical practice or spirit (or dance style) that normally
cannot be fixed allographically.

In any case, it is impossible to advance the allographic ideal
without attention to the theory of how dance is produced and
related to the expressiveness of human life itself. To consider
these matters—in all the arts as well as the dance—is to grasp, I
should insist, the sense in which dance is essentially autographic, with some notational conveniences. The allographic
model is not mistaken because it is too inflexible or because the
dance has not yet emerged at a stable enough level to be
properly thus characterized. It is mistaken because it tends to
separate questions of identity from questions of aesthetic interest and because it ignores the profoundly intentional nature of
all art—not primarily in the sense of the psychologically deliberate but in a sense grounded at once in the biologically and
culturally shaped forms of historical human expression. The

very fact that some of the arts are recognizably autographic in nature demonstrates conclusively that the reidentification of particular works—to say nothing of their appreciation—does not require compliance with any allographic system. Reject the extraneous complication of the theory of forgery, and no barrier exists against admitting the autographic nature of the performing arts as well. To understand that characterization properly is to recognize how the production, recognition, and appreciation of art depend upon the emergent and personally shifting powers of the individual human members of historically contingent cultures.

Notes

1. See Ann Hutchinson, *Labanotation,* rev. ed. (New York: Theatre Arts Books, 1970). Cf. Merce Cunningham, *Changes: Notes on Choreography* (New York: Something Else Press, 1968).

2. Cf., for instance, the observation by Mary Sirridge and Adina Armelagos, "The In's and Out's of Dance: Expression as an Aspect of Style," *Journal of Aesthetics and Art Criticism* 36 (1977): 23–24, n. 7.

3. Nelson Goodman, *Languages of Art* (Indianapolis: Bobbs-Merrill, 1968), 121–22.

4. See William B. Webster, "Music Is Not a 'Notational System'," *Journal of Aesthetics and Art Criticism* 29 (1971):489–97; and Joseph Margolis, *Art and Philosophy* (Atlantic Highlands, N.J.: Humanities Press and Harvester Press, 1979), chap. 4.

5. "In's and Out's of Dance," 16.

6. Nelson Goodman, "The Status of Style," *Critical Inquiry* 1 (1975):799–811.

7. "In's and Out's of Dance," 18, 15, 17, 16.

8. Ibid., 19.

9. Goodman, *Languages of Art,* 85.

10. "In's and Out's of Dance," 18.

11. Goodman, *Languages of Art,* 85–86. Cf. Margolis, *Art and Philosophy,* chap. 5.

12. Maurice Merleau-Ponty, "Eye and Mind," in *The Primacy of Perception and Other Essays,* ed. James M. Edie (Evanston, Ill.: Northwestern University Press, 1964).

13. An attempt to apply this general phenomenological account specifically to the dance may be found in Maxine Sheets-Johnstone, *The Phenomenology of Dance* 2d ed. (London: Dance Books, 1979). Cf. also Susanne Langer, *Feeling and Form* (New York: Scribner's, 1953).

14. Adina Armelagos and Mary Sirridge, "The Identity Crisis in Dance," *Journal of Aesthetics and Art Criticism* 37 (1978):130–31.

15. Ibid., 130.

16. Ibid., 131.

17. On the type/token distinction, the ontology of art, and the untenability of Goodman's notational criteria of identity, see Margolis, *Art and Philosophy.*

18. Goodman, *Languages of Art,* 113, 198.

19. Armelagos and Sirridge, "Identity Crisis in Dance," 133.

20. Ibid., 138.

21. See Marcia B. Siegel, *The Shapes of Change: Images of American Dance* (Boston: Houghton Mifflin, 1979).

22. Hutchinson, *Labanotation* xi–xii.

23. See Rudolph Laban, *The Mastery of Movement,* 3d ed. rev., ed. Lisa Ullman (Boston: Plays, 1971), and *The Language of Movement: A Guidebook to Choreutics,* ed. Lisa Ullman (Boston: Plays, 1974).

Personal Style and Performance Prerogatives

Adina Armelagos
Mary Sirridge

To understand dance is to grasp its particular symbolic nature. It is no accident that dance is the most problematic of all the arts. The difference in understanding the symbolic nature of dance lies in the direct use of the human body as material. In dance, the individual body as medium or instrument appears to have a greater effect on the consistency and identity of the work than in the other performing arts. It is because of the seemingly overriding effect of the body in dance that any theory of dance must include a description of how the body is used in the production of the dance performance. There is the inevitable temptation to rely on an unanalyzed notion of "natural expressiveness." A more fruitful approach to the problem is through the analysis of style. This approach is the main feature of our model. The use of the body, we claim, is largely dependent on factors that are related to style.

Joseph Margolis, in "The Autographic Nature of the Dance" (this volume), attempts to explain the often overwhelming effect of the dancer's movement as a culturally conditioned "natural expressiveness" that he equates with personal style. This equation, rather than illuminating style and the dance process, threatens to obscure the relationship of the performer to the work and therefore to covertly minimize that relationship. A celebration of the body as "naturally expressive" mystifies it. When dancers speak of the body's presence as overwhelming or powerful, it is a statement about the effect of the dance, not a description of what they do.

Style is the most important concept we can use to understand dance, while "natural expressiveness" is not a part of style and contains no explanatory power. We take style to be not only a static concept by which performances are grouped as performances of a given work but also the dynamic force that in effect is responsible for producing performances. In our view, style is a twofold concept. Style$_1$, or general style, consists of a spatial vocabulary, a set of movements or allowable movement sequences held together by a system of kinesthetic motivation.[1] Style$_2$, or personal style, is the dancer's particular contribution within style$_1$.

Both levels of style are involved in the two major symbolic modes, representation and expression. Following Nelson Goodman, we consider a work to represent what it denotes and to express what it metaphorically exemplifies.[2] The difference between several different general styles (style$_1$'s) is at once a kinesthetic phenomenon and a characteristic difference in representation. Both are related to the work and not to the individual dancer, even though the dancer is responsible for producing the properties that are seen as expressed or represented. The distinction between the qualities of the dancer and the qualities of the work—a distinction that might lead us to a theory of interpretation—is one that Margolis consistently fails to make. It is essential to view the performer as someone who embodies, fulfills, and generates the work and to understand the sense in which the dancer is and is not the dance.

Margolis's criticisms of our thesis seem to have two foci. First, he claims that although we deny that dance is an allographic art in Goodman's sense,[3] we veer towards him covertly in construing a given style (style$_1$) as a general spatial vocabulary through which a personal style (style$_2$) emerges. This seems, at least, to be the force of Margolis's remark:

> [Sirridge and Armelagos's] emphasis is designed—deliberately or not—to conform with the allographic model of the dance, for, by the ordered regularities of a putative style, they suppose that the aesthetically relevant expressive qualities of a performance may be grasped by a sensitive *audience* without affecting the sense in which performing *dancers* conform only with the notational requirements of a given piece (this volume, p. 73).

Margolis assumes that we equate style and notatability, and by doing so draw the dancer's attention away from style-relevant features, thereby separating the expressive qualities of the performance from the dancer's efforts. Margolis's second criticism is that we thereby downplay the role of "natural expressiveness" and of the "deeply intentional, ultimately *autographic* features of the expression and significance of bodily movement itself" (p. 77).

The specifications that Goodman imposes on what he calls "compliance"—that is, a performance counting as an instance of a work—does not take into account style in any sense. But style, as we construe it, is an essential factor by which works are grouped as compliants. Seeing performances as belonging to a class of works is not just a convenient device but a critical concern of dancers, a concern that involves the expressive qualities of the work. Our stated position is as follows:

> Dance will become autographic only when either notation succeeds in capturing style, or general practice decides that style is incidental. Either might occur, but neither has to date. It is unlikely that style will ever be considered incidental, given the tight connection between stylistic compliance and authenticity (*IC*, 138).

This is a position of which Goodman could not—indeed, does not—approve.[4] Thus Margolis attempts obliquely to attack Goodman through criticisms of our model, even though we diverge from Goodman in some of the ways that Margolis suggests. Nowhere are we claiming that style is equivalent to "the proper execution of notationally specified movements." (Margolis, p. 76). Our view is diametrically opposed to this claim. We maintain that one cannot ignore the importance of the still extant autographic links of specific dance works with their creators and primary performers. We take seriously the claims of some choreographers that their works are theirs to control, alter, and pass on when they see fit. In fact, we argue that

> style as we construe it is difficult, if not impossible, to record in a notational scheme. This does not mean that traditional notation systems cannot serve as mnemonic or analytic devices, or that choreography is not an important element in determining what work a performance is a performance of. Indeed it is precisely the importance of the

choreography as a link to the specific choreographer which causes difficulties for "common-denominator" notation schemes which aim at bypassing this link (*IC*, 138).

There is a sense in which we agree with Goodman. We believe that dance is heading towards the allographic, but not that it is *intrinsically* autographic.[5] Rather, *given the state of the art,* there is an element of performance essential to determining what work a performance is a performance of, which is not notatable, and that element is style. Though we do not think that style will ever become irrelevant, we do believe that the necessity of reper-formance will diminish its importance in ever more different circumstances. Even if we were to view dance as a totally auto-graphic art, we would not take Margolis's position, which equates the autographic with personal expression. This equa-tion is flatly wrong.

We emphasize the importance of explaining general style (style$_1$) in terms of spatial vocabularies not out of any desire to edge closer to Goodman but in view of plain fact. As we see it, dancers are trained to select certain movement patterns and to think in terms of style-relevant kinesthetic motivation. *It is the factor of kinesthetic motivation that is recalcitrant to notation.* Mar-golis's claim that "there are no kinesthetic sensations that could guide a dancer with regard to much more than congruence with a rhythmic beat and with the beat of the other dancers" (p. 73) is wrong as well as narrow. It makes a difference in the movement generated whether a dancer is trained to think of him- or her-self as strung by the top of the head to the ceiling, strung by the breast bone to the ceiling, or working with or against the force of gravity. These are all legitimate everyday examples of kinesthetic motivation that provide for the dancer his or her felt success at attaining the style of the work. Why these differences in kinesthetic motivation matter is an interest-ing question in itself but one that we will not pursue here.[6] That the differences exist and have their effect on the production of style is what is important.

Margolis's reference to the corrections of the dance coach (p. 73) reveal a failure to understand what style-relevant con-siderations are. The lack of exactness or completeness of dance scores is a reflection of the inadequacy of physical demonstra-tion itself in communicating to the dancer what is relevant in learning a style. On a nonelementary level, the dancer must formulate an external model of the dance movement as a cohesive style, irrespective of what is being demonstrated by the teacher. To be told that a teacher's movement is "fundamentally Cunningham" is to be told something that makes it possible to execute the movement that is demonstrated. The fundamental characteristics of that vocabulary (style$_1$) are known to most dancers. For example, to stare at one's arm in Cunningham style *is* to stare at one's arm; likewise a turn at the waist involves the whole upper body moving in a single plane. There is no point in trying for a personal implementation of the movement—for a personal style—until one understands the general movement idiom involved (style$_1$).

It is the way in which general style$_1$ demands are understood by the dancer that allows personal style to emerge. This emergence, as markedly distinct from the general style, is highly prized in most Western dance styles. In dance forms where personal style does not seem to matter or where personal and general style seem to be coextensive—for example, in Noh theater or Balinese temple dance or other non-Western dance idioms—it may appear that the dancer is submerging his or her personality or suppressing his or her personal style. Often the dance training in these cultures ensures the style$_1$ demands by the teacher's direct physical positioning and manipulation of the body. While visible aspects of style$_2$ seem to be submerged, it would be more accurate to say that to the outsider personal style seems to be contained within the execution of the style$_1$. In Western dance it is more customary to stress idiosyncratic development of personal style within a general style. But it is extremely misleading to view any dance tradition as "confining" the personality. Given the very special ideologies associated with non-Western dance, its performers are supposed to—and do, if they are to be believed—see what we regard as confinement as a kind of limitless freedom. There is no evidence that personal style does not develop. Some performers are more accomplished than others, and this is a matter of personal style. But for the uninitiated, the close association between personal and general style may be imperceptible.

For the dancer, the link between self and style is individual temperament. We have, we think, made it sufficiently clear elsewhere that due to individual temperament the dancer may have to decline to operate within a given set of general constraints.[7] Thus, notation aside, we *do* insist, for the ordinary dancer, on the primacy of general style$_1$ constraints as a pre-condition for the development of a personal style$_2$. The issue of whether or not the style$_1$ has a long developmental history, has been influenced by the characteristic movements of its inceptor or star performer, or is what has been thrown together in a rehearsal when someone decided that everyone would "move normally" is irrelevant. But for the dancer, the kinesthetic "feel" of a given style is *not* irrelevant. Without the developed kinesthetic feel of the particular style, the style simply cannot be produced.

Spatial vocabularies free rather than confine the dancer's movement. It is for this reason that "natural expressiveness," on the other hand, is likely to limit the dancer to the movements he or she already knows or leave the dancer to fit the movements he or she knows arbitrarily into a style$_1$. The issue of natural expressiveness as an inherent feature of the dancer's body is one that we have never broached. When we use the term *expression,* we always use it in Goodman's sense, as the relationship *of a work* to a property that it metaphorically exemplifies. We have always spoken, then, of properties of movements or of works, and in terms of expressive acts. Our position is that the notion of natural expressiveness is one that is at best inapplicable to dance and at worst devoid of content. As Goodman notes, in *Ways of Worldmaking,*

> Worlds differ in the relevant kinds they comprise. I say "relevant" rather than "natural" for two reasons: first, "natural" is an inapt term to cover not only biological species but such artificial kinds as musical works, psychological experiments, and types of machinery; and second, "natural" suggests some absolute categorical or psychological priority, while the kinds in question are rather habitual or traditional or devised for a new purpose.[8]

Margolis concedes that natural expressiveness is a rather complex phenomenon that contains a strong culturally determined component,[9] but his argument for its existence is based on the case in which the dancer's temperament (Tanaquil Le-Clerq in *Swan Lake*) appears to override the work. Actually, Margolis's example of a mismatch between the dancer and the work is not the most serious case of apparent dominance of a dancer's "natural expressiveness." Choreographer Paul Taylor provides a stronger case; he claims to predicate his works on the "natural" abilities of his dancers.[10]

But neither the Tanaquil LeClerq or the Paul Taylor case demonstrates a direct connection between the temperament of the dancer and the work. Rather, they are examples of a disparity or connection between the effects a dancer can produce and the known qualities of the work. A more serious case can be made by referring to the "autonomous choreographer,"[11] where specific, deeply felt qualities of the dancer seem to emerge through and to be identified with the work itself. Both the autonomous choreographer and the audience may feel that this is the result of unconscious, happy accident. This apparently unconscious coincidence between the dancer's idiosyncratic movement and its effect has been brought to the conscious level by experimental choreographers like Yvonne Rainer and David Gordon. Experimental choreographers who use ordinary movement claim that it can be equated with "natural expression" because it seems to be outside the artificial imposition of known dance styles.

For reasons of clarity we would like first to deal with the case of the autonomous choreographer, secondly with cases of the LeClerq-Taylor type, and lastly with the challenge presented by the advocates of ordinary movement.

As the primary performers in their own works, autonomous choreographers exercise exclusive control over the work. It stands to reason that they should best exemplify the qualities of the particular roles that they conceive. These qualities, once established, fix the specific content of the work so that, in effect, only they can freely alter it. Is it then the direct "expression" of emotions, qualities, and so forth that is being communicated to the audience by means of "natural expressiveness?"

Martha Graham has created a long list of anguished heroines. There seems to be nothing intrinsically tragic about her body, qua physical body. Rather, she has developed her body as a tragic medium. Graham has made use of angular movement and of contraction and release in developing her movement vocabulary. These movements often stand for the anxiety and conflict of her heroines. Graham has had to teach the world that her movements symbolize anxiety and conflict— some of the time (for in some of her dances they do not). It was in developing her general style that Graham taught herself how to use movement meaningfully.

Graham's release of these roles to others when her own abilities failed suggests her having made a rather complex decision. It is a decision that all autonomous choreographers must eventually make if their roles are not to die with them (one that some autonomous choreographers, such as Isadora Duncan and Ruth St. Denis, never made). The decision is difficult, not because it involves a surrender of native expressiveness but because it introduces a nonexclusive flexibility of interpretation. For the autonomous choreographer, the privilege of changing the choreography or developing particular nuances keeps the works alive for him or her as an individual, while at the same time securing idiosyncratic control over the work and the general style. A general style develops through new works and altered interpretations of older ones.

In one sense the autonomous choreographer is correct. He or she has simultaneously originated a general and personal style and believes that because of that fact he or she has a unique understanding of the depth possible in the general style. Autonomous choreographers know that movement cannot be exactly duplicated by imitation alone, so that it is unlikely that their personal style could be copied exactly. But they also know that there are interpretations of old works, and new directions introduced by new works, that would not violate their general $style_1$ constraints. Autonomous choreographers thus consciously exclude developments that they wish to place beyond the bounds of their own $style_1$. This reinforces the connection among the autonomous choreographer's particular interpretations, despite the nature of changes made, while excluding other valid interpretations. In general, such choreographers overestimate the current dependence of their $style_1$ on their own personal decisions. There are limitations to $style_1$ expansion, and any interpretation is ultimately tested against audience acceptance of the general $style_1$ parameters. Graham, like most autonomous choreographers, has lost the battle of exclusion, as performances come to be judged with reference to their own $style_1$ ideals. The case of the autonomous choreographer is not one in which the temperament of the dancer is converted directly into the movement one sees.

A variation of the autonomous choreographer is the case in which dances seem to be "made on" particular dancers. Some choreographers claim that they are using the natural proclivities and abilities of their dancers to shape the work. We have elsewhere quoted Paul Taylor as saying:

> More often than not, the kind of dance we work on to-gether turns out to be dependent on these different danc-ers as individuals. Sometimes their limitations are as interesting as their strong points.
>
> These eight dancers are not exactly like tubes of paint with which to cover the canvas of space. Not exactly. They have character and personality which they assert. They have individual traits, and just when you think you know how to handle them, they change.[12]

Taylor takes his inspiration where he finds it, and he prefers to find it in a wide diversity of physical types. Taylor has an ex-tremely expansive spatial vocabulary. One need only compare *Aureole, Book of the Beasts,* and *Big Bertha* to see this. However, Taylor is not allowing the dancers' whims or personalities the directive hand. Taylor has a strong, recognizable general style. A Paul Taylor dance looks like a Paul Taylor dance, no matter what qualities he chooses to emphasize. Further, he claims that every member of his company is replaceable: if he were depen-dent on specific personalities that would not be the case. The Taylor case is not an exception. The long story of dance de-velopment of the classics is often the story of the abilities and inabilities of lead dancers.[13]

Even Margolis's own example of Tanaquil LeClerq's "comic" approach to *Swan Lake* demonstrates that the dancer is affected more by general style in which he or she performs than by his or her "natural expressiveness." It is peculiar that Balanchine tried to stage *Swan Lake* at all.

> There was a good deal of speculation as to *why* Balanchine mounted yet another Swan Lake. The program was almost apologetic about the enterprise. . . . The whole notion of reviving the classics seemed the very antithesis of the ideals of both Balanchine and Kirstein, particularly in the case of this ballet, which was already in the repertory of practically every ballet company worthy of a name.[14]

Swan Lake was not Balanchine's type of ballet. It is an old ro-mantic ballet which depends on its sweet, sad narrative and the

power and plaintiveness of the Swan Queen's acting. These
have never been Balanchine's characteristic aesthetic objectives.
But he tried to stage it effectively. He left certain features in-
tact, such as the meeting of the Swan Queen and the Prince, the
famous adagio, the Swan Queen's variation and coda, the *pas de
quartre,* and the first entrance of the swans. But he created new
choreography and completely refocused the ballet, drawing attention away from the soloists to the corps.[15] Balanchine was left
with a Swan Queen who did not fit into his ideas about how
soloists and corps complement each other. Maria Tallchief, the
first dancer to perform the Balanchine version, exemplified the
Romantic style in which she was trained, and not Balanchine's.
She explains the difficulties she had:

> It was one of the most difficult things I ever did. I remem-
> ber when George choreographed it. I could see what he
> wanted, but then I couldn't do it. . . . Technically it wasn't
> difficult at all as compared with my other roles, but it was
> the interpretation. . . . [Balanchine] left my role more or
> less in the traditional version.[16]

Tanaquil LeClerq was bred as a Balanchine dancer. She
fitted into Balanchine's new interpretation of *Swan Lake.* That
was precisely the problem. As her coach Barbara Walczak recalls,

> "None of them quite caught it right. [Balanchine's] major
> comment was always, "larger, wilder, more creature-like,"
> especially in the case of the very long-legged ballerinas.[17]

It was no bent for comic expression that may have ruined
LeClerq's version of *Swan Lake.* She had done serious roles for
the New York City Ballet in dances such as *La Valse* and
Afternoon of a Faun. It was her training—her education in a
specific style—that made her predictably ill-suited for the role.

In our view there are limitations to the development of a
given style$_1$ that have to do with propensities within the style
itself. When changes do occur, they are often resisted within
the dance world. This is not surprising, for unbridled change
would produce chaos in older works. But styles seem to have
evolved in spite of the resistance of dancers and original performers. The José Limon style as it is taught today has acquired
a lyric component. This has been accomplished by increasing

the number and decreasing the depth of torso-initiated im-
pulses. It has been suggested that this change is due to feminine
influence since the technique has passed mainly through female teachers.[18] Whether or not one wants to consider the
change a feminine influence, a genuine "free area" in the style
existed to be explored. Styles evolve as "free areas," and become designated within the original style. These "free areas"
direct the emergence of personal style and contribute to the
direction of the style's expansion. It is at this point that the
dancer's body is viewed as inhibiting or enhancing the general
style in which he or she performs. To confuse the personality
or the body type of the dancer with personal style is to ignore
the cohesiveness of a general style and the genuine contribution that the individual dancer makes. The originator of a style
has certain privileges, but in dance exclusive control over the
style, once it is well formulated, is not one of them. Certain
"free areas" of the style may not be apparent to its originator—
or the originator may not be interested in exploring them.

Thus the practice of choreographers and dancers is best described in terms of spatial vocabularies and kinesthetic motivation, not in terms of personality or "natural expressiveness."
The combination of spatial vocabulary and kinesthetic motivation that determines the effects of style$_1$ also preselects the
dancer who can fulfill those requirements. The link between
the temperament of the dancer and the expression of the work
is an *indirect one* mediated by style$_1$. Some postmodern choreographers, such as Yvonne Rainer and David Gordon, attempt to
eliminate preselection of dancers on the basis of training in a
particular style, hoping thus to establish between the dancer
and the work a direct link normally not present in known dance
styles. These choreographers choose "natural" or seemingly
unstylized movement that almost anyone can perform. Simple
movements such as sitting, walking, hopping, spinning, and
standing take place in an unstylized time-space and seem totally
natural to the audience. The dance is to appear just what it is
and no more. The audience is supposed to attend to the personal differences between the performers, and these differences are claimed to be "expressive" ones. In fact, the kind of
dance *where movement is just what it appears to be* effectively elimi-
nates the "virtual realities" for the audience.[19] The audience
literally sees what is there.

But a curious inversion occurs. The dancer pays the price of extreme concentration for this seemingly natural display. If we understand Margolis's characterization of the generation of expressive properties, this is the sort of attention dancers are usually required to give to the work. It is clear, however, that without the limits of a determinate spatial vocabulary the dancer must force concentration on those acts that are habitual and do not usually demand attention. For the dancer this is an extremely taxing undertaking. Movement that is recognized for what it is is not expressive for the audience. At least the audience can reflect on how difficult it must be to appear unwatched. This is a reflection not on the movement but on the project. There is, however, tremendous satisfaction for the dancer in these works. The significant virtual qualities now exist entirely on the dancer's side: studied unstudiedness, laboriously controlled naturalness.

In such dances, choreographers and dancers are attempting to establish a connection between kinesthetic motivation and the audience's perception. In more traditional styles, where determinate vocabularies exist, the connection is a matter of faith put into the training in a particular style$_1$. The usual process of learning a style relies heavily on physical demonstration as an example of kinesthetic motivation. *The dancer must learn to associate particular sensations with a particular motivation.* Dancers who experiment with ordinary movement hope to remove the artificially established link between kinesthetic motivation and audience perception of the form. Overall the experiment with ordinary movement has not been an unqualified success. Inevitably it has been discovered that to move "naturally" requires at least a concern for technique as in traditional dance, although the outcome of the technique is not apparent to the audience. What the dancer has succeeded in doing, at least temporarily, is placing the virtual qualities on the inside—and it is in this sense that the dance is expressive—at least for the dancer.

The inversion has placed the contemporary critic in the dilemma of having to resort to merely an accurate description of the movement. The audience can impute what meaning it will to the dance. Or the performer can be asked directly what the movement "felt" like—hence, what it meant. Far from bridging the gap between art and life, dance that is based on ordinary movement recreates it in a different form, a form that tends to exclude the audience. For the dancer it points to the impossibility of merging the two. As ordinary movement becomes material for dance, it becomes art and ceases to be ordinary. There can be no merger, only a kind of passing at the crossroads.

The strange effect of this tendency in dance is that the impact of the strong individual personal style, the kind that emerges in traditional Western dance, is nullified. The more ordinary the movement, the less room there is for individuality. Thus dances that emphasize ordinary movement are not an extreme example of personal expression but quite the reverse. They are similar to the aesthetic goals of some non-Western dance styles in which personal style and general style seem to be coextensive, with one qualification: only the dancer's side of the work has virtual qualities.

Personal style can be understood in terms of the way dancers themselves describe the process. Moving from a primary description, we are then in a position to describe with greater accuracy the creation of the artistic qualities that are crucial to dance. In dance, we have to take into account the statements of dancers about the relation of feeling to the effects produced for the audience. For example, Suzanne Farrell has said:

> I don't believe in "intrinsic reaction" to the music. I may find myself producing an effect sometimes that I didn't plan. But I'm never unaware of it. Afterwards, I'll analyze it and decide if it's worth keeping. Then I'll work on how to amplify or diminish it so it can become part of the palette I have at my disposal. . . . Any number of people may have the same "instinctive reaction" to that moment—but it doesn't matter what you feel. You've got to produce something visually and physically to indicate what you feel.[20]

She warns:

> when you reach the point where you absolutely *must* look a certain way, then you are no longer useful to Balanchine.[21]

To consider style as a twofold phenomenon, as we have, is to open the way for considering aesthetically relevant issues such as interpretation, intention, or the evolution of style. Any theory must account for the facts and have some predictive advantage. Our model has the advantage of explaining how, for instance, a formulated style$_1$ can add or limit modes of presentation. It explains why a humorous *Swan Lake* is likely to be seen as satire, rather than as an acceptable comic version of *Swan Lake*. It also explains how a dancer's personal style is directly dependent on his or her ability to produce and elaborate a general style.

It is, as we have stated elsewhere, the history of production that interests us, a history of production that can account for the complexity of dance. A model of personal style based on "natural expressiveness" places emphasis wrongly on the personal history of the dancer and not on the particular dance's history of production. What is being asked is how the dancer generates the properties that are the dance. Our model describes how the dancer's body is linked through individual temperament to the style in which he or she performs. The fact that this link is not "natural" but contrived within various styles gives us an understanding of how the dancer uses his or her body in the dance. As we see it, an appeal to "natural expressiveness" is a step backwards. Even those cases where "natural" movement is involved are not cases of "natural expressiveness." Understanding dance as it is *built* from the inside, whether the movement appears natural or contrived, is a significant part of understanding dance's effects.

Notes

1. *Spatial vocabulary,* as we use the term, is basically similar in meaning to the dancer's term *movement vocabulary.* There is, however, an important qualification. *Movement vocabulary* is often used in a more restricted sense to refer only to the discrete positions characteristic of a particular style such as ballet. In our view, a spatial vocabulary must involve "learning the characteristic inventory of movement and movement sequences as they relate to more general ideals of movement. . . . Spatial vocabularies and movement ideals are not ends in themselves—though they are the proximate terminus of the dancer's performing efforts" (Mary Sirridge and Adina Armelagos, "The In's and Out's of Dance: Expression as an Aspect of Style," *Journal of Aesthetics and Art Criticism* 26 (1977), 19. Hereafter cited as *IO*. From this we conclude that "a spatial vocabulary limits the exercise of spatial imagination and frees the dancer to move" (18). Spatial vocabularies derive their meaning through systems of kinesthetic motivation: "kinesthetic motivation is best described from the dancer's side as a sense of the pattern of the movement flow, the originating impulse, the stresses and transitions. From the audience's point of view, kinesthetic motivation is the quality and direction of movement thus produced" (Adina Armelagos and Mary Sirridge, "The Identity Crisis in Dance," *Journal of Aesthetics and Art Criticism* 37 (1978): 131. Hereafter cited as *IC*.

2. See Nelson Goodman, *Languages of Art* (Indianapolis: Bobbs-Merrill, 1968). Hereafter cited as *LA*.

3. According to Goodman, a work is "autographic if and only if the distinction between the original and a forgery of it is significant, or better, if and only if even the most exact duplication of it does not thereby count as genuine. If a work of art is

autographic, we may call that art autographic. Thus painting is autographic, music non-autographic, or allographic" (*LA*, 113). See also 198: "In sum, an established art becomes allographic only when classification of objects or events into works is legitimately projected from an antecedent classification and is fully determined independently of history of production, in terms of a notational system."

4. In private correspondence, Goodman has simply said that he thinks we are wrong about this.

5. Cf. Margolis, "Autographic Nature," 000: "[Expressive qualities] are, when present, literally present—as extensions of the naturally expressive—in whatever sense cultural phenomena are actual phenomena irreducible to purely physical systems, with respect to which they might well have been treated as metaphorical." See also p. 000: "Treat the dance in a frankly autographic way, and one accommodates at a stroke the history of dance (and of every other performing art) and the peculiar importance of personal style in the dance (even in classical ballet, where perhaps the strongest resistance might be possible)."

6. This is an issue we take up in a forthcoming paper.

7. "Dancers have temperamental limits which determine how they want to feel when moving, regardless of what is being produced for the perceiver. Any dancer who likes the feel of sinuous and sensuous movement is going to find ballet temperamentally unsatisfying. Dancers who claim that they are looking for a dance style whose movements allow them to express their feelings misspeak themselves. But they are saying something important. They come in fact looking for a dance style which will allow them to adopt movement whose kinesthetic expressive potential matches their own temperamental proclivities as concretized in their own style$_2$" (*IO*, 22).

8. Nelson Goodman, *Ways of Worldmaking* (Indianapolis: Hackett, 1978), 10.

9. "It has to do rather with the individuality and idiosyncrasy of human expressiveness as the intersection of biologically and culturally contingent processes, raised to an essential place in the medium of dance" 000.

10. "The more ordinary situation is that described by Paul Taylor. . . . For the choreographer, the natural proclivities of his dancers are much in evidence. They constitute and shape his work as it meets the beholder, and they influence his choice and implementation of spatial vocabulary. Even choreographers in such stable dance forms as ballet have consistently allowed their dancers to shape their vocabularies" (*IC*, 133).

11. The autonomous choreographer is one who choreographs and is the main performer in his or her own works.

12. Paul Taylor, "Down with Choreography," in *The Modern Dance: Seven Statements of Belief*, ed. S. J. Cohen (Middletown, Conn.: Wesleyan University Press, 1965), 91–92.

13. Cf. Frank W. D. Ries, "In Search of Giselle: Travels with a Chameleon Romantic," *Dance Magazine* 53 (1979): 58–74.

14. Nancy Reynolds, *Repertory in Review* (New York: Dial Press, 1977), 129.

15. Ibid.

16. Ibid., 130.

17. Ibid.

18. Ann Vachon of Temple University, former Limon Company member, provided us with this perception of Limon.

19. Susanne K. Langer, *Problems of Art: Ten Philosophical Lectures* (New York: Scribner's, 1957), 5–6: "Everything a dancer actually does serves to create what we really see; but what we really see is a virtual entity. The physical realities are given: place, gravity, body, muscular strength, muscular control, and secondary assets such as light, sound,

or things (usable objects, so-called "properties"). All these are actual. But in the dance, they disappear: the more perfect the dance, the less we see its actualities. What we see, hear, and feel are the virtual realities, the moving forces of the dance, the apparent centers of power and their emanations, their conflicts and resolutions, lift and decline, their rhythmic life. These are the elements of the created apparition, and are themselves not physically given, but artistically created."

20. David Daniel, "A Conversation with Suzanne Farrell," *Ballet Review* 7 (1977): 8.
21. Ibid., 12.

Movement Notation Systems as Conceptual Frameworks: The Laban System

Suzanne Youngerman

Movement notation is of more relevance to the arts, humanities, and sciences than is generally recognized.[1] Notation systems are more than tools for documentation; they are systems of analysis that can be used to illuminate many aspects of the phenomenon of movement. Notation scores embody perceptions of movement. Furthermore, they can provide data, in an unusually revealing form, for research on a variety of topics, including the exploration of the concept of style, of the ways in which movement can be conceptualized, and of the bases for aesthetic evaluations.

The writings of Nelson Goodman, Joseph Margolis, and Adina Armelagos and Mary Sirridge are significant in treating the issue of notationality as having value beyond the practicalities of recording dances.[2] They have discussed notation in the context of the problem of establishing and preserving the identity of a choreographic work. The goal of this paper is not to enter directly into their dialogue, but rather to supplement it with information and ideas that will rectify some of the misconceptions about notation that they express; the aim is also to widen understanding and appreciation of the *theoretical* aspects of notation. The focus will be on issues, especially the problem of notating movement intent, rather than on the presentation of detailed explanations of the mechanisms of notation.

There are many dance notation systems based on graphic signs in the European/American tradition.[3] Other dance cul-

tures have also developed notations.[4] Although some of these
are of historical relevance only, new systems are continually
being invented; for instance, there is now experimentation with
computers. There are, nevertheless, three major systems:
(1) the Laban system, consisting of (a) Labanotation (as it is
known in the United States) or Kinetography Laban (as it is
referred to in Europe), and (b) Effort/Shape. The two systems
together are now often called Laban Movement Analysis or
Labananalysis in the United States; (2) Benesh Movement Notation, also known as Choreology; and (3) Eshkol-Wachmann
Notation, which has been used primarily in Israel.[5] Each of
these systems can deal with many kinds of movement—not just
dance.

There is some controversy as to which is the "best" system.[6]
Since each analyzes movement from a different perspective, it
is likely that the "best" system may depend on the problem at
hand. For instance, the Benesh and Eshkol-Wachmann systems
place more emphasis on showing the end positions of movements; the Laban approach generally notates the process of
movement. This distinction is just one of the ways in which
movement can be conceptualized differently and in which notation can vary in capturing this conceptualization.[7]

The closest kin to dance notation is music notation. Although
the latter has had a longer history than its dance counterpart, it
still struggles to capture many aspects of its subject, especially in
the area of qualitative features. In addition, new kinds of
music, methods of composition, and performance criteria have
challenged the limitations of existing notation systems. However, the place of notation in the two arts varies in a crucial way.
In music, it is the composer who notates the work; the score is
the result of the creative process. In dance, it is very rare that
the choreographer produces the score. This situation is responsible for much of the skepticism that choreographers have had
about the reliability of notation. Although the usual procedure
is for the notator to work while the choreographer is either
composing, teaching, or rehearsing the piece, this practice does
not solve all the problems. The notator writes what the
choreographer asks for in terms of movement, even if no dancer present is actually performing according to the choreographer's intent. On the other hand, the choreographer's wishes
may not be absolutely clear; for example, instructions are often
nonverbal or metaphoric. The extent to which the choreog-

rapher, dancer, and notator share the same conceptual understanding of the movements in a dance is one of the central
issues of notation. Matching the symbology of the notation system to the movement intent is a major challenge.

Although the existing dance notation systems may not com-
ply wholly with Goodman's definition of a notation system and
may never fulfill his criteria for establishing dance as an allographic art, they have extensive capabilities of a practical and
theoretical nature. According to Goodman, "An established art
becomes allographic only when the classification of objects or
events into works is legitimately projected from an antecedent
classification and is fully defined, independently of history of
production, in terms of a notational system."[8] Goodman, Margolis, and Armelagos and Sirridge have discussed many of the
problems involved in reaching this goal. However, in considering the possible allographic nature of dance, they have
underestimated the capabilities of the existing notation systems
as well as the future potential of these and perhaps other not-
yet-developed systems. It is not the objective of this paper to
argue the extent to which present-day dance notation can provide accurate and complete records suitable to serve as the basis
for establishing choreographic identification. The systems
probably have not been tested adequately enough to draw any
definitive conclusions in that regard. On the other hand, I do
hope to show that the existing systems are much more techni-
cally advanced and conceptually interesting than has been acknowledged by Margolis or other writers. Thus serious issue is
to be taken with Margolis's comments that "notational efforts at
scoring a dance are radically less interesting intrinsically than
musical scores or the texts of dramas"; "dance scores are
primarily heuristic devices for recovering a minimal sense of
the principal positions and movements of a given dance"; and
"there is no sense in which the perception of related positions
and movements . . . could possibly be grounded in an understanding of the deeper structures of the dance, by means of a
closer attention to the notation itself."[9]

Armelagos and Sirridge also have misconceptions about the
value of notation in regard to capturing style. They define style
as a combination of

   a "spatial vocabulary" and a distinctive pattern of kinesthetic motivation. A spatial vocabulary is an inventory of

acceptable positions and position sequences; and kinesthetic motivation is best described from the dancer's side as
a sense of the pattern of the movement flow, the originating impulse, the stresses and transitions. From the audience's point of view, kinesthetic motivation is the quality
and direction of movement thus produced.[10]

They distinguish two types of style, as follows: "A cohesive
vocabulary and motivation choice produce what we call style$_1$
constraints. Contrasted with these are the style$_2$ characteristics
produced by the dancer's individual manner of execution at the
performance level."[11] Although one could challenge their
definition of style as well as differentiate more than two levels
(e.g., style of genre, style of movement technique, style of the
choreographer, style of the work, style of the dancer), the important point here is their insistence that there is a problem in
distinguishing what is "in the steps" from what is contrbuted by
the dancer. This difficulty is partially a function of the need to
discriminate the more elusive qualitative features of movement.
They argue that it may be possible for notation to handle most
spatial vocabularies, but that the crucial dimension of kinesthetic motivation is resistant to notation. "Labanotation," they
write, "is precise, but becomes descriptive, and even pictographic when it attempts to notate movement ideals and motivation." They concede that one system, Effort/Shape notation,
"does try to account for some such factors. But . . . it sacrifices
precision for completeness."[12] If precision is equated with quantitative measurement, then theirs is a valid criticism. Effort/
Shape, while covering the phenomenon of movement
holistically, does deal with qualitative and not (at this point)
measurable units. However, if precision is seen as the ability to
pinpoint the source of motivation, then their evaluation needs
to be reexamined. Notation, even of spatial vocabulary alone,
can reveal much more of movement intent and style than is
generally recognized. An example given later in this paper will
illustrate this potential. Furthermore, existing notations can
capture aspects of personal style, and they have both prescriptive and descriptive capabilities.[13]

Determining the range of interpretation permissible, and
thus the point at which a performance of a work ceases to be
part of that classification of performances that is identified as
the choreographic work, is a choreographic or aesthetic prob-

lem. Notational constraints are not in themselves the main handicap. The existing notation systems are in fact in a constant state of revision and refinement. As new problems arise, new solutions have been found.[14]

The Laban System: A Conceptual Framework for Dance

The Laban system originated as a corollary of a much wider search for an understanding of the principles of movement, of the sources of movement expression, and of the value of dance to humanity. Given its theoretical breadth, this system is of particular significance to the philosophy of dance. However, my use of the Laban system to illustrate the theoretical nature of dance notation is not meant to be a polemic for its superiority; rather it is intended to provide a concrete point of reference for the discussion of some underlying aspects of movement notation and of some specific capabilities that may or may not be possessed by other systems.

The name of Rudolf Laban (1879–1958) is of course associated with the development of Labanotation. What is little recognized is that this system of notation was not an end point of his career, but rather one part of a much more encompassing involvement with movement: choreographing; championing movement for the layman as well as for the professional dancer; innovating in the field of dance education; researching the movement of factory workers; and, above all, searching for a conceptual framework for the analysis and interpretation of movement. This latter aspect of his work is generally unknown in the United States; much of his writing has never been translated into English.[15] The body of literature he has left is but one example that refutes the common allegation that there have been virtually no studies of dance of philosophical import.

There are important distinctions to be made, however, between what Laban wrote and did in his lifetime and what has been developed from his ideas. The areas of movement analysis considered as part of the Laban system today have evolved over the decades and have been shaped by the contributions of many individuals. In the United States, his legacy has tended to be divided into two main areas, called *Labanotation* and *Effort/ Shape*. The latter has roots in an earlier system called *Eukinetics*.

The concept of *Effort,* and the notation for it, were not formalized until Laban became involved in analyzing the movement of factory workers during and after World War II. The *Shape* aspect of the system was not formally developed until later in this period by his student, Warren Lamb. Irmgard Bartenieff, who was instrumental in the growth and spread of Effort/Shape in the United States, developed an aspect of Laban's work based on the analysis of the kinesiological level of movement, a system called *Bartenieff Fundamentals,* which has been incorporated into the Effort/Shape system as it is taught in the United States. The study of spatial relationships, which Laban called *Choreutics,* is also included in Laban studies. The various subsystems of Laban's work have had different histories of development since his original formulations. His colleagues and students have been responsible for the transformation of Labanotation into a highly technical tool and of Effort/Shape into a system of movement analysis with diverse applications.[16] Currently there is interest in reunifying his work according to the principles that underlie all the systems. Thus, rather than separating Labanotation from Effort/Shape, the whole system is often referred to in the United States as *Laban Movement Analysis, Laban Movement Studies,* or *Labananalysis.* A brief description of the main areas of Laban Movement Analysis follows.

Labanotation. This is a system of notation for the description of the structure of movement. It deals with the "what," "where," and "when" of movement. The shape of the basic sign indicates the direction of movement, the shading of the sign refers to the level of movement (high, middle, low), and the relative length of the sign shows the time duration. The placement of the sign on a three-line vertical staff indicates the body part moving. Reading the staff vertically reveals succession in time; reading horizontally reveals interrelationships of body parts at one point in time. Thus, direction, level, and timing of an action are captured in one symbol. Sequencing of movement, the distribution of body weight, the configuration of movement in the body, the relationship between movers, and the orientation of the whole within the performing space can be readily grasped. Moreover, there is flexibility within the system as to the amount of detail provided. For instance, a walk can be broken down into minute detail or shown in a generalized form. Motif writing, developed by Valerie Preston-Dunlop as a derivative of Labanotation, can be used to abstract the general patterns of a movement sequence.[17]

Effort/Shape. This notation system describes the quality of movement, the "how" or adverbial dimension of moving. *Effort* studies deal with changes in the use of bodily energy: how one activates one's weight, attends to space, orients to time, and controls the flow of muscular tension. Each effort factor is conceptualized as on a continuum. Thus, weight or force runs from "light"—an overcoming of gravity—to "strong," a powerful engaging of one's weight. The space factor deals with attention to the environment: is there a "direct" focus or an "indirect" or "flexible" multifocus? Time can range from "sustained"—an indulging in or drawing out of time—to "sudden" or "quick"—an urgent crystallization of time. Effort flow ranges from "free"—an ongoingness of movement—to "bound," a controlled, stoppable attitude toward the flow of energy. A movement is rarely animated by just one effort quality; most actions combine two or more of the factors in the various permutations that are possible. For example, one could perform a plié by sinking with a sustained, bound quality and rising with a light, free, indirect quality. The signs for the effort elements are concise and can be easily linked together in combinations; they can also be written in sequences to reveal phrasing.

By describing the movement in terms of what the body does with energy and what it creates spatially, the ambiguity of descriptive adjectives is diminished, and the action can be performed and seen according to its movement intent. To describe a movement in adjectives such as "graceful" or in metaphoric terms such as "snakelike" can be evocative but says little about specific movement content. There may be a shared basis for everyone's interpretation of "graceful"—perhaps "lightness" is a common feature. Yet the term may encompass other references as well—for example, a light, sustained quality, or light, indirect, free-flowing movement, or light curvilinearity. Using the Effort/Shape terminology is a way of describing movement in movement terms. Although ordinary adjectives are used to describe these qualities, the use of the signs rather than the words helps to limit or fix their use according to their technical definitions.

Shape refers to the ways in which the body changes its form— how it adapts to or creates space. There are three different kinds of shape possibilities; each can be succinctly specified in the form of a question. Does the movement relate only to changes in the body shape, that is, to alterations in the relationship of body parts to each other—folding and unfolding, for example, or growing and shrinking—and not to interactions with the environment? Such body shape changes are called *shape flow*. Alternatively, does the movement relate to the surrounding space in a goal-directed manner, a shaping quality known as *spokelike* or *arclike* directional shaping, as when one reaches out for something? Finally, does the body actively sculpt space or adapt to the environment in two or three dimensions, as in shaping or carving movements? The concept of shape does not refer to the form or the design that is produced, but rather to the *manner* of creating a spatial form or bodily configuration.

Choreutics, or *Space Harmony.* This is the study of the relationship between the body and its spatial environment. Spatial harmonics are the proportionate relationships between paths of movement. This subsystem of Laban's work deals with such concepts as spatial designs, the relationship between the limbs and torso in moving, and movement scales built on linear dimensions, planes, or three-dimensional forms. Laban wrote: "Every trace-form [pathways creating shapes in space] has hidden dynamic connections which are followed intuitively by the moving person. To unveil these hidden relations is one of the aims of the study of choreutics and the art of movement."[18] Studying the relationship between spatial pathways and what later came to be called effort, and the manner in which they combine to form an expressive statement, was at the core of Laban's work. It is interesting to note that after Laban fled Germany and settled in England, the book that he began to write to introduce his ideas to the English-speaking world was on Choreutics. The manuscript, begun in 1939, was not published until after his death.[19]

Bartenieff Fundamentals. Laban included anatomical and kinesiological principles in formulating his ideas about movement and notation.[20] His student, Irmgard Bartenieff, applied concepts derived from the eukinetic and choreutic material to her work as a physical therapist. She then incorporated insights from her experience into the Laban system in the form of what is now known as *Bartenieff Fundamentals.* Some of the themes that are explored in this facet of Laban-derived work include the study of the principles of weight shift, initiation of movement, breath support, sequencing of movement, and interaction of body parts, especially between the upper and lower units of the body. The goal of Fundamentals is to promote integrated and efficient movement patterning and to reveal the interrelationship between body, effort, shape, and spatial relationships. The question of how the body supports movement in space and facilitates the expression of dynamics is the primary analytic question that ties this body-level work directly to the Laban system. Since Labanotating involves the analysis of what the moving body does, the Fundamentals perspective relates to Labanotation as well.[21]

It is important to note that most of the applications of Effort/ Shape and Choreutics in the United States frequently do not use the actual notation signs but rather develop the movement principles on which the notation is based.[22] The notation signs are an adjunct to the system. The relationship is analogous to that between music theory and music notation. Dance critic Marcia Siegel, for instance, has emphasized the use of Effort/ Shape as a movement vocabulary. She has written: "The widespread adoption of Effort-Shape analysis by critics could provide the objective verbal context which dance has always lacked."[23] It is significant, however, that the system does have a written symbology, for, as in music and mathematics, graphic signs facilitate the articulation, growth, and communication of ideas.

The Laban System: Its History and Underlying Principles

Laban considered all aspects of his work to be interdependent. To think of Laban Movement Analysis as simply a recording device is to miss the richness of Laban's contributions. This system provides a way of perceiving, describing, and analyzing movement, as well as a way of notating it.[24] The same could be said of all movement notation systems,[25] though to a lesser extent, because the developments of the other systems were not guided by theoretical goals beyond those engendered in the pragmatic desire to devise a means of recording movement in a clear and concise way.

Laban's original idea, in fact, was not only the practical one of inventing a system for the documentation of dances for posterity or for establishing the identity of a choreographic work. He was searching for a way of symbolizing what he felt to be the nature of movement. He wished to capture in graphic signs the totality of movement—its structural and expressive content. He proclaimed that "the ultimate goal of kinetography is not the Dance Script [*Tanzschrift*], but the Script Dance [*Schrifttanz*]."[26] Laban felt that "the form of the notation signs must grow from the knowledge about the innermost nature of the things to which we refer in order to denote for the instructed reader what is intended."[27] This dream was to give way to the practical exigencies of recording dances. Two separate notation systems developed. Labanotation (then called *Schrifttanz*) was first presented in a form similar to its current state in 1928; Effort/ Shape did not find notational expression until the 1940s and 1950s.

Historically, Laban's search for the principles underlying movement and for a sign system to express them developed together and concurrently with his creative work as a choreographer. The kernel of most of his theoretical work was formulated during the period from about 1910 until World War II, an era coinciding with the growth of central European modern dance. Mary Wigman and Kurt Jooss, two of the foremost choreographers of the time, were originally his pupils.[28] Many of the concepts of movement that Laban was exploring took form in their choreography. Jooss's *The Green Table* is the best known of these works.[29] Laban's theoretical as well as his artistic work evolved in the context of expressionism. The subsequent development of his ideas has freed them from this historical context so that his principles of movement and notation system can be applied universally.

Laban's ideas and their applications did not develop linearly. He approached the same problems from different angles and attempted to synthesize concepts from diverse fields. The results of his searchings reinforced each other. Some of his ideas are now dated, unverifiable, or disproved. His writings are often convoluted; sometimes the ideas are presented in a very abstract fashion, sometimes they sound almost mystical. Yet the core of his work remains as a rich conceptual framework for further exploration. Since all of his ideas did interrelate so closely, it is very difficult to explain sections of his work taken out of context. The following discussion illustrates some of the interconnections that exist or have existed between his notation

and the wider conceptual problems with which he was concerned. As noted earlier, notation was only a small part of his
work, and the description here does not pretend to cover all
aspects relevant even to this subject.

Laban believed that "motion and emotion, form and content,
body and mind, are inseparably united."[30] He felt that "every
emotional state coincides with a very definite body tension."[31]
He sought to discover what this relationship is and how it is
produced. He explained what he meant by body tension as
follows:

> The elements of each gesture are bodily tensions combined
> with intellectual and feeling excitations. The body tension
> we determined according to directions in space towards
> which they are executed; furthermore according to the
> application of force with which they are led into definite
> widths of space and with larger or smaller time-duration
> within which they follow each other.[32]

The "direction in space" to which he refers took on a greater
significance to him when it was seen as part of a larger system of
spatial orientation. Starting with the three dimensions of the
upright human body—the up/down vertical axis, the side/side
horizontal axis, and the forward/backward sagittal axis—Laban
outlined some of the basic possibilities of moving in space. One
can move linearly along these axes, or in cycles within two-
dimensional planes, or in three dimensions, with constant
change within the three spatial tendencies, as in spiralling and
twisting. Another basic spatial relationship is the diagonal cross,
the four diagonal lines that run through the center of the body.

Using these spatial axes as frameworks, one can visualize
polyhedral or crystalline structures or scaffoldings surrounding the body, creating various action spaces. The most basic of
these forms are the cube (formed by connecting the end points
of the diagonal cross); the octahedron (formed by connecting
the end points of the three axes); and the icosahedron (formed
by connecting the corners of the planes, outlining a form that
approximates a sphere). These spatial structures are seen as
"kinespheres," or personal "bubbles" surrounding the body,
defining not only the range of movement but also the underlying structural possibilities of movement sequences.[33]

It was the goal of Laban's work, especially in Choreutics, to discover the interrelationship of spatial pathways and dynamic stresses or emotional moods and to create a sign system to reveal this unity. He explained:

> One of the basic experiences of the dynamics of movement is that its different spatial nuances always show clearly distinguishable mental and emotional attitudes. It is possible to relate the moving person's feeling for dynamics to the spatial harmonics within trace-forms and to the zones through which the paths of the trace-forms lead.[34]

Laban found "certain correlations of dynamic nuances with spatial directions."[35] In addition, he proclaimed: "It is one of the most striking discoveries in the domain of choreutics that an oddness and an affinity exist between action-moods [expressive actions], and that this relationship can be expressed by space symbols."[36] These quotations demonstrate the close interconnection that Laban felt existed between dynamics and space and their expression in his sign system. In most of his writings Laban outlines clear correlations (known as "affinities") between movements in specific directions and specific effort qualities. The central European style of modern dance, which he helped to foster, seemed to support and to develop these relationships. Other styles of dance, different movement activities, and cultural variations, however, have challenged these correlations. Since one cannot assume a dynamic quality from a notation for a spatial direction, the degree to which the idea of inherent correlations is valid and can be applied to notation remains a point of controversy and a subject of research within the Laban system. Yet in an effort to understand the complexities of the form/content or movement/expression relationship, we can look beyond one-to-one correlations. For instance, we can conceive of these choreutic forms as spatial structures that limit certain movement possibilities and promote others, producing different expressive qualities. For example, moving along the vertical axis makes a statement about the body's relationship to gravity, that range of expressive potential that involves the possibility of being pulled toward the ground or rising toward the sky. Leaving the stability of the vertical axis by tilting or spiralling promotes lability, each in a different way. Tracing a path from a high point to a low point expresses a different quality from moving in the opposite direction. In addition, his theories alert us to the ways in which the body, effort, and spatial directions interact. Laban observed, for instance, that

> when a movement is accompanied by a secondary one in another part of the body in an opposite spatial direction, it can easily be understood that the secondary movement might inhibit or disturb the main movement; it might diminish its speed, decrease its dynamic power and deviate its direction. Sometimes in this way dynamic nuances can be explained by the spatial influence of secondary movements and tensions.[37]

One of the more general characteristics of movement that Laban wished to elucidate is the distinction between stable and labile movement. "The two contrasting fundamentals on which all choreutic harmony is based," he wrote, "are the dimensional and the diagonal tension."[38] He explained the significance of this discovery as follows:

> dimensional directions [along one of the three axes] are the carriers of stability while the diagonals *guarantee* the labile flow. The degree of diagonal tendency therefore will determine its flight intensity; influenced by dimensional secondary tendencies, the natural urgency to change is missing."[39]

Thus a sign for diagonal direction in Labanotation carries with it the connotation of lability. The movements that precede, accompany, and follow the diagonal movement and the effort quality of those movements may increase or decrease its dynamic impact. One can read spatial relationships from Labanotation symbols; for instance, one can detect whether labile, diagonal "cubic" choreutic forms or more stable, dimensional "octahedral" forms predominate in a dance, or how these spatial tensions interact with each other within a dance.

In addition to encompassing what could be seen—that is, both structural and dynamic qualities—and expressing their interrelationship in one sign, the ideal notation system that Laban wished to develop would symbolize also the structure, source, or motivation that produced the movement. In the following analogy he clarified what he wished his notation to symbolize:

The representation of the wheel by a circle gives its outer form as it is seen from the outside, so to speak. The representation of the wheel by the spokes shows us the inner tension forces which keep the wheel spokes apart. The wheel is seen from within here.[40]

Laban wanted his notation to show the "spokes" of movement; not the external form, but what one did with one's body to create that form. In Labanotation as it exists today, to take a step, for instance, is symbolized as a shifting of the center of weight in a certain direction, over a certain time duration, at a certain level. One is not given a picture of the final pose; instead one has to move or conceptualize the moving in order to discover the final outcome; one has to participate actively.

Knowledge of Laban's research into the complexities of movement—into body tension, spatial directions, dynamics, emotional mood, stable and labile movement, and so on, all in conjunction with a notational system—is important for two reasons. Goodman remarks that "the development of Laban's language offers us an elaborate and intriguing example of the process that has come to be called 'concept formation.' "[41] Some of the conceptual stages that the notational ideas went through can be traced in several of Laban's books, starting with his 1926 *Choreographie.* The second reason for valuing the research is that fundamental ideas resurface and are retained in the system, making the notation of interest from a theoretical point of view. Specifically,

1. Both Labanotation and Effort/Shape notation record the *process* of moving, not the resulting positions. This perspective focuses attention on *action* and *conceptualization,* rather than on architectonics. One experiences empathy with the mover rather than only observing shapes and patterns from the outside.
2. Each of these systems in itself provides a *choice of ways of describing and recording movement* that makes it possible to capture subtle distinctions; in this way, *the notation can be consistent with the particular conceptualization of the movement.* Together, the quantitative perspective of Labanotation and the qualitative perspective of Effort/Shape enrich our understanding of the movement.
3. Finally, the systems deal with notating *movement quality*

and *kinesthetic motivation,* especially through the use of Effort/Shape notation.

The following section illustrates these points by presenting examples of the kinds of distinctions that are made in scoring a choreographic work.

Using the Laban System

To exemplify the three characteristics of the Laban system mentioned above, let us analyze the simple action of raising the leg with bent knee from a standing position. Notice first that by describing the movement as "raising," rather than "with a raised leg," the focus is on human action and not on the result of an implied action. In this particular instance, what is the intent of the movement? Is the aim of the movement of the leg to create a distinct shape, or to travel a definite path, or merely to flex at the hip, the resulting shape and path being incidental? Is the movement traveling away from something or toward something? Is the intent to create a specific angle at the hip, at the knee, at both, or are the angles of no significance? Is the movement initiated by leading with the knee, or pushing with the thigh? Is the goal to create a specific relationship between the two legs, or is the aim to maintain balance or to experiment with the dynamics of movement? These are the kinds of distinctions that can be made using Labanotation.

Labanotation, however, cannot reveal all the qualitative nuances with which the movement was performed. This is where Effort and Shape notation are uniquely valuable: the attitude of the mover to his or her own weight, space, time, and flow qualities can be indicated. The manner in which the mover shapes his or her body in the environment also can be notated. For instance, was the raising of the leg a folding, body-oriented shape flow action?; or was it a directional, spatially aware movement from the hip, describing a clear arc in space? Was there careful attention to the path in which the knee traveled—that is, was there bound flow and direct space effort? Or was there, for instance, a quick, strong impulse into the floor followed by a light, indulging in time as the leg rises? These few questions do not begin to exhaust the possibilities for describing the very simple action of "raising the leg with bent knee from a standing position." It should be noted also how ambiguous the description of this movement is in English words; for instance, is the knee bent before it is raised, or does it bend while the leg is rising? Through the use of Labanotation and Effort/Shape notation, this kind of confusion can be avoided.

When the context or the motivation for a movement varies, there will be differences in how the movement looks. Although often subtle nuances, they are discernible and, in many respects, notable characteristics. Often it is these kinds of distinctions that may make all the difference in discriminating among styles or establishing choreographic identity. The Laban notator has a range of options in choosing a form of writing that can best capture the intent of the movement. Other movement notation systems can also deal with many of these distinctions, some with more accuracy and flexibility than others.

Because Labanotation and Effort/Shape evolved somewhat independently of each other, there are difficulties in reuniting the two systems for use in a score. This is one of the areas in which there is ongoing experimentation. The decision as to how much of the dynamic content of a choreographic work is to be left to interpretation should not rest with the notator. The crucial issue seems to be how to differentiate between those aspects that can or should be left to individual interpretation and so should not be scored and those that are basic to the characterization or style of the dance.

For instance, in *Swan Lake,* Odette and Odile are differentiated from each other not just by costume color, steps, and quantifiable traits like speed, but by a constellation of dynamic qualities. Many of these aspects of the choreography cannot be captured by a notation of "spatial vocabulary" alone. Although we cannot know today the original intent of the deceased choreographers, it is possible to score the results of tradition in the form of individual interpretations. If there were common denominators in the dancing of a role, they would emerge from the notations. Hypothetically, we might find that Odile tends to initiate phrases with quickness (not fast in terms of tempo, but rather as a crystallization of time), or that she rises with strength, whereas Odette may rise with lightness. This type of subtle manifestation of kinesthetic motivation can make a crucial difference in preserving the identity of a choreographic work. This is the level where Effort/Shape notation can prove itself.

By taking José Limon's *The Moor's Pavane,* an example given by Armelagos and Sirridge,[42] we can easily see how notational authority could prevent the interpolation of ballet steps into a modern dance work. It is less obvious how notation could prevent a dancer from performing the movement in a balletic manner. For instance, ballet emphasizes line, the architecture of movement and positions; Limon technique, among other traits, emphasizes breath as a motivating force. While a snapshot that captures a pose may possibly look the same in both techniques, the intent of the moving is different. Thus, a leg extension to the side, for instance, might be done in ballet with the goal of reaching as high a point as possible, whereas for the Limon dancer the intent would be for the leg to travel only as far as the forceful impulse of the breath would send it. Without knowledge of this stylistic characteristic, someone who read a notation indicating a pose or specifying a point in space for the leg gesture to reach would be misled as to the proper motivation for the movement. Labanotation and Effort/Shape in complementary use can make these kinds of fine distinctions.

It remains for the human being who is writing the movement to be able to ask the right questions, to see the myriad possibilities, and to select the best way to notate the particular instance. Most of the biases in the systems are in the humans using them, and are not inherent in the symbologies themselves. If the context is known, then one can take certain things for granted as clues to the motivation. For instance, the example given above of raising the leg with a bent knee might be written differently if it occurred in a Balkan folk dance, in a military march, in ballet, in Limon technique, in climbing a stair, or in rebounding from stepping on hot coals. When the style and genre of the choreography is known, then the completeness and proper choices in notating rely on the notator's skill and sensitivity and are not, for the most part, a function of inherent limitations in the notation. When the style is not known, say in notating a foreign dance form, knowledge of cultural conceptualizations would be needed as well.

Conclusion

Dance notation is more than an heuristic device or a pragmatic tool. The current state of notation and its potentials have

been underestimated; the various applications of notation beyond documentation have gone unrecognized; and the intrinsic
interest of notation systems as conceptual frameworks has remained unappreciated.

The preceding discussion has shown that the analysis of a
notation score can generate questions and provide answers for
many kinds of studies. In the field of aesthetics, these center on
the concept of style and the relationship between notation and
performance. Notating is not a mechanical process; it requires
knowledge about style and an understanding of the different
ways in which a movement can be conceptualized. The notator,
reconstructor of notation,[43] and the performer, on the one
hand, and the aesthetician, critic, and historian, on the other
hand, should be intimately aware of each other's work. *Notation
scores can be resources for aesthetic inquiry; philosophical writings
about dance can provide insight for the notation of scores.* Both processes can benefit from a closer interrelationship. Notation
scores are dances presented in another medium, a medium that
makes it possible to go back and in some way reexperience or at
least reanalyze the dance form and style. The notator often has
had "privileged" information through his or her close contact
with the choreographic or teaching process connected with the
piece being notated. Patterns or characteristics that might not
be apparent otherwise emerge from the notation, even some
that may not have been chosen consciously by the choreographer or notator. On the other hand, insights into the source
and essence of expression, style, and aesthetic criteria provided
by philosophical inquiry can be incoporated into the choice of
graphic representation of the movement.

Notations are embodiments of perceptions of movement. A
notation that is guided by an awareness of the ways in which
movement can be conceptualized can be a source of enlighten-
ment to anyone interested in the phenomenon of movement.
The perceptual and cognitive processes involved in notating
and in translating notation back into movement are unusual
manifestations of the human ability to symbolize. The clues to
style, aesthetic criteria, and movement intent that can be discovered in a dance notation score or through the use of notation systems as frameworks for movement analysis make the
understanding of the principles behind notation a valuable re-
source for the artist, humanist, and scientist.[44] Notation can be
an adjunct to the experience and understanding of dance and

has wide implications of both a practical and theoretical nature. It is a work in progress.

Notes

1. This paper originated as a response to Joseph Margolis's paper, "The Autographic Nature of the Dance" (now a chapter in this book), as it was presented at the conference "Illuminating Dance: Philosophical Inquiry and Aesthetic Criticism," co-sponsored by CORD and Temple University and held at Temple University, Philadelphia, 5 May 1979. My presentation of the Laban system derives from the understanding of it that I gained from my training under Irmgard Bartenieff and others in Laban Movement Analysis (Effort/Shape), from my reading of Laban's writings and those of his colleagues and students, and from my research and teaching experiences with Effort/Shape. Although I have studied Labanotation, I am not a Laban notator.

2. Nelson Goodman, *Languages of Art,* 2d ed. (Indianapolis: Hackett, 1976); Joseph Margolis, "The Autographic Nature of the Dance," this volume; Adina Armelagos and Mary Sirridge, "The Identity Crisis in Dance" *Journal of Aesthetics and Art Criticism* 37 (1978):128–39.

3. For a history of dance notation, see Ann Hutchinson Guest, "A Brief History of Dance Notation," in *Tracking, Tracing, Marking, Pacing* (art exhibit catalogue) (New York: Pratt Institute, 1982), and *Encyclopedia Britannica,* 15th ed., *s.v.* "Choreography and Dance Notation."

4. See, for instance, Frank Hoff, "Dance Notation Preserved at Mōtsuji," *Dance Research Journal* 9 (1977):1–4; Gloria B. Strauss, Camella Wing, and Leung Yuen-wah, "Translated Excerpts of Chinese Dance Notation," *Dance Research Journal* 9 (1977)5–12.

5. Principal sources on Labanotation are: Ann Hutchinson, *Labanotation,* rev. ed. (New York: Theatre Arts Books, 1970); Albrecht Knust, *Dictionary of Kinetography Laban,* 2 vols. (London: Macdonald & Evans, 1979); Valerie Preston-Dunlop, *Practical Kinetography Laban* (London: Macdonald & Evans, 1969); Rudolf Laban, *Laban's Principles of Dance and Movement Notation,* 2d ed., ed. Roderyk Lange (Boston: Plays, 1975); Nadia Chilkovsky Nahumck, *Introduction to Dance Literacy* (Transvaal, South Africa: International Library of African Music, 1978). For information on Effort, Shape, and Space theory, see Cecily Dell, *A Primer for Movement Description: Using Effort/Shape and Supplementary Concepts* (New York: Dance Notation Bureau, 1970); Irmgard Bartenieff and Dori Lewis, *Body Movement—Coping with the Environment* (New York: Gordon & Breach, 1980); Rudolf Laban, *The Mastery of Movement,* 3d ed., Lisa Ullmann (Boston: Plays, 1971), *The Language of Movement: A Guidebook to Choreutics,* ed. Lisa Ullmann (Boston: Plays, 1974), and *Modern Educational Dance,* 3d ed., ed. Lisa Ullmann (London: Macdonald & Evans, 1975); Rudolf Laban and F. C. Lawrence, *Effort: Economy in Body Movement,* 2d ed. (Boston: Plays, 1974); Valerie Preston-Dunlop, *A Handbook for Modern Educational Dance* (London: Macdonald & Evans, 1963); Marion North, *Personality Assessment through Movement* (London: Macdonald & Evans, 1970); Irmgard Bartenieff, Martha Davis, and Forrestine Paulay, *Four Adaptations of Effort Theory in Research and Teaching* (New York: Dance Notation Bureau, 1970).

For Benesh, see Rudolf Benesh and Joan Benesh, *An Introduction to Benesh Movement Notation: Dance,* rev. ed. (New York: Dance Horizons, 1969), and *Reading Dance: The Birth of Choreology* (London: Souvenir Press, 1977).

For Eshkol-Wachmann, the main source is Noa Eshkol and Abraham Wachmann, *Movement Notation* (London: Weidenfeld & Nicholson, 1958).

6. For comparative articles, see Seymour Kleinman, "Movement Notation Systems: An Introduction," *Quest Monograph* 23 (1975):33–56; Douglas Turnbaugh, "Dance Notation: Potential and Problems," *Dance Scope* 4 (1970):39–47; responses to Turnbaugh's article, and his reply, in "Dance Notation: A Controversy," *Dance Scope* 5 (1970):39–55.

7. See Martha Davis, *Towards Understanding the Intrinsic in Body Movement* (New York: Arno Press, 1973), for a comparative study of the literature of nonverbal communication research; she discovered that there was a correlation between the choice of movement parameters observed and the conclusions that were drawn about the relationship of movement to social and psychological factors.

8. *Languages of Art*, 198.

9. Margolis, "Autographic Nature of the Dance," this volume, pp. 70–71.

10. Armelagos and Sirridge, "Identity Crisis," 131.

11. Ibid.

12. "Identity Crisis," 135.

13. The distinction between a prescriptive and a descriptive use of notation is that "between a blue-print . . . and a report of . . . a specific performance." Charles Seeger, "Prescriptive and Descriptive Music-Writing," *Musical Quarterly* 44 (1958):184.

All discussion of notational capabilities in this paper refers only to the movement aspects of dance, not to the costumes, lighting, props, and other often essential aspects of the work. Such information is always included in a score, but in verbal or pictographic form.

14. For instance, the International Council of Kinetography Laban (ICKL) meets once every two years to discuss changes in the Laban system. For examples of studies that have necessitated the search for notational solutions, see Gisela Reber, "Movement Notation in Folkloric and Historic Dance Classwork," in *Dance Studies*, vol. 1, ed. Roderyk Lange (Jersey, Channel Islands: Centre for Dance Studies, 1976), 53–64; and Judy Van Zile, "Seeking Notation Solutions, with Reference to Japanese Bon Dances in Hawaii," *Dance Research Journal* 14 (1981–82):53–54.

15. Laban's untranslated writings include *Die Welt des Tänzers* (Stuttgart: Walter Seifert, 1920); *Des Kindes Gymnastik und Tanz* (Oldenburg: Stalling, 1926); *Gymnastik und Tanz* (Oldenburg: Stalling, 1926); *Choreographie* (Jena: Eugen Diederichs, 1926). For translations of sections of these, see Irmgard Bartenieff, "The Root of Laban Theory: Aesthetics and Beyond," in Bartenieff et al., *Four Adaptations of Effort Theory*, 1–27.

16. Albrecht Knust and Ann Hutchinson Guest deserve the most credit for the transformation of Labanotation into the detailed and workable system that it is today. Many others have contributed to its development and to the growth of Effort, Shape, and Space studies. Principal centers for the continuation of Laban's work are, in the United States, Laban/Bartenieff Institute of Movement Studies (New York) and the Dance Notation Bureau (New York and Ohio State University); in the United Kingdom, Laban Centre for Movement and Dance (University of London, Goldsmith's College), Language of Dance Centre (London), and the Centre for Dance Studies (Jersey, Channel Islands). There are also centers in Germany, Eastern Europe, and elsewhere in the world.

17. Valerie Preston-Dunlop, *Readers in Kinetography Laban*, series A, B (London: Macdonald & Evans, 1966–67).

18. Laban, *Language of Movement*, 35.

19. Ibid., originally published as *Choreutics* (London: Macdonald & Evans, 1966).

20. *Choreutics*, 106–8; see also *Choreographie* (1926).

21. For more information on Bartenieff Fundamentals, see Bartenieff, *Body Movement—Coping with the Environment.*

22. Laban Movement Analysis has been used in research, and practical applications have been made, in situations as diverse as movement itself. For an overview of research in the behavioral and social sciences, see Martha Davis, "Laban Analysis of Nonverbal Communication," in *Nonverbal Communication: Readings with Commentary,* 2d ed., ed. Shirley Weitz (New York: Oxford University Press, 1979), 182–206.

23. Marcia B. Siegel, "Training an Audience for Dance," *Arts in Society* 4 (1967): 440.

24. For examples of the use of Labanotation or Laban Movement Analysis in applications other than documentation, see the following studies, in *Essays in Dance Research,* ed. Dianne L. Woodruff (New York: CORD, 1978): Janis Pforsich, "Labananalysis and Dance Style Research: An Historical Survey and Report of the 1976 Ohio State University Research Workshop" (59–74); Elizabeth Kagan, "Towards the Analysis of a Score: A Comparative Study of *Three Epitaphs* by Paul Taylor and *Water Study* by Doris Humphrey" (75–92); Suzanne Youngerman, "The Translation of a Culture into Choreography: A Study of Doris Humphrey's *The Shakers* Based on Labananalysis" (93–110); Jill Gellerman, "The *Mayim* Pattern as an Indicator of Cultural Attitudes in Three Hasidic Communities: A Comparative Approach Based on Labananalysis" (111–44). See also Stephanie Jordan, "Using the Humphrey Scores," *Dance Research Journal* 14 (1981–82):51–53; Martha Ann Davis and Claire Schmais, "An Analysis of the Style and Composition of *Water Study,*" in *Research in Dance: Problems and Possibilities,* ed. Richard Bull (New York: CORD, 1968), 105–13; various articles in *Dance Studies,* ed. Roderyk Lange (Jersey, Channel Islands), especially vol. 1 (1976); International Folk Music Council Study Group for Folk Dance Terminology, "Foundations for the Analysis of the Structure and Form of Folk Dance: A Syllabus," in *1974 Yearbook of the International Folk Music Council* 6 (1975):115–35; Adrienne L. Kaeppler, "Method and Theory in Analyzing Dance Structure with an Analysis of Tongan Dance," *Ethnomusicology* 16 (1972):173–217; Drid Williams, "The Arms and Hands, with Special Reference to an Anglo-Saxon Sign System," *Semiotica* 21 (1977):25–33, and "The Human Action Sign and Semasiology," in *Dance Research Collage,* ed. Patricia A. Rowe and Ernestine Stodelle (New York: CORD, 1979):39–64 (see Judy Van Zile's comments on this article in *Dance Research Journal* 13 [1981]:44–45, and Williams's reply, 46–47), and also her "Note on Human Action and the Language Machine," *Dance Research Journal* 7 (1974–75):8–9.

25. On Benesh, see Brian Street, "A Comment on the Benesh System of Notation," in *The Anthropology of the Body,* ed. John Blacking (New York: Academic Press, 1977):340–42; Colin Roth, "Ballet: A Critical Approach through Notation," *Dancing Times* (1974):574–77, 579.

26. Quoted in Rudolf Sonner, *Music und Tanz,* trans. Irmgard Bartenieff (Leipzig: Quelle & Meyer, 1930). See also the journal published by Laban beginning 1928, *Schrifttanz* (Vienna: Universal-Edition). The journal was later published also in English and French as *Schrifttanz/La Danse Ecrite/Script Dancing* (Vienna: Universal-Edition, 1930).

27. Laban, *Die Welt des Tänzers,* 187, quoted and translated in Ullmann, "What Notated Movement Can Tell," in Lange, *Dance Studies,* 1:19.

28. For information on Wigman's relationship with Laban, see *The Mary Wigman Book,* ed. and trans. Walter Sorell, (Middletown, Conn.: Wesleyan University Press, 1977). On Laban's influence on Jooss, see Anna Markard, "Kurt Jooss and His Work," *Ballet Review* 10 (1982):15–67.

29. See Marcia B. Siegel, *"The Green Table:* Movement Masterpiece," in *At the Vanish-*

ing Point (New York: Saturday Review Press, 1972), 61–65. *The Green Table* is used as an example in Mary Sirridge and Adina Armelagos, "The In's and Out's of Dance: Expression as an Aspect of Style," *Journal of Aesthetics and Art Criticism* 36 (1977):15–24, and in Margolis's paper (this volume). The former authors remarked that this work is based on a "movement code" that is derived from "the use of Laban's projection scheme for correlating emotional values to particular movements." They continue, "There is not much evidence that dancers themselves feel the correlation, and it remains a code of rather an odd kind" (23–24,n.7). Margolis then cites their opinion as evidence of the shortcomings of notation, calling the correlation "awkward and unconvincing" (p. 71). Jooss actually used Laban's eukinetic principles in this choreographic piece to create archetypal characters, using a limited but crystallized constellation of effort and space qualities for each characterization. It is not a "code," but rather a dramatic device; the differentiation of protagonists according to their dynamic qualities is apparent to anyone who sees the work performed according to these principles. The critical acclaim this masterpiece has received from its premiere (winning first prize at the choreographic competition sponsored by Les Archives internationales de la danse in Paris in 1932) until the present day (as a key work in the repertory of the Joffrey Ballet and as frequently restaged by companies around the world) makes the labelling of its expressive foundation as "odd" odd in itself. In fact, in contrast to the statement made by Sirridge and Armelagos concerning the dancers' motivations, consider the following remarks by Robert Joffrey: "Marjorie Mussman, who played the Old Mother in our first performances, feels that it may be even more affecting to dance *The Green Table* than to experience its impact from the audience. Before and after the ballet there is a kind of hush backstage" ("Remembrances of Kurt Jooss," *Ballet News* 1 (1979):29). The impact of *The Green Table* supports rather than challenges the usefulness of Laban movement principles. See Siegel, *"The Green Table:* Movement Masterpiece."

30. Laban, *Language of Movement,* viii.

31. Laban, *Die Welt des Tänzers,* 54, quoted and translated in Bartenieff, "The Roots of Laban Theory: Aesthetics and Beyond," in *Four Adaptations of Effort Theory,* 10.

32. Laban, *Die Welt des Tänzers,* 23, quoted and translated in Bartenieff, "Roots of Laban Theory," 5.

33. For more explanation and applications of space harmony, see Laban, *Language of Movement;* Valerie Preston-Dunlop, "Choreutics: The Study of Logical Spatial Forms in Dance," in *Dance and Dance Theory,* ed. Valerie Preston-Dunlop (London: Laban Centre for Movement and Dance, 1979), 131–54; Marion North, "The Language of Bodily Gesture," *Main Currents* 31 (1974):23–26; Sylvia Bodmer, "Harmonics in Space," *Main Currents* 31 (1981):27–31; H. B. Redfern, "Rudolf Laban and the Aesthetics of Dance," *British Journal of Aesthetics* 16 (1976):61–67.

34. Laban, *Language of Movement,* 27.

35. Ibid., 31.

36. Ibid., 55.

37. Ibid., 27.

38. Ibid., 44.

39. Laban, *Choreographie,* 75, quoted and translated in Bartenieff, "Roots of Laban Theory," 19.

40. Laban, *Die Welt des Tänzers,* 31, quoted and translated in Bartenieff, "Roots of Laban Theory," 24.

41. Goodman, *Languages of Art,* 214.

42. "Identity Crisis in Dance," 131.

43. For information on the process of reconstruction, see Ray Cook, *A Handbook for*

the Dance Director (New York: Ray Cook, 1977), available through the Dance Notation Bureau.

44. For another point of view on the theory and application of notation, see Alan Salter, *Perspectives on Notation:* vol. 1, *Notation and Theory;* vol. 2, *Notation and Dance;* vol. 3, *Notation and Application* (London: Laban Centre for Movement and Dance, 1978).

Phenomenology as a Way of Illuminating Dance

Maxine Sheets-Johnstone

I am going to approach phenomenology as a way of illuminating dance in general terms first. I would like to show how, through a greater or heightened philosophical awareness, we might appraise the knowledge offered us by various writers and researchers in dance on sounder critical grounds. I would like to show, in other words, how we can clarify and deepen our understanding of dance through philosophical inquiry in general. The need for such clarification and deepening is readily apparent in the fact that writings on dance are often permeated by unexamined assumptions or implications. As the following examples will show, these assumptions and implications can lead to genuine philosophical questions.

As a first example, let us consider a particular metaphysical issue that may often lurk hidden or is blatantly evident in a variety of writings on dance: the problem of a division of mind and body or a separation of body from person. Martha Graham was perhaps the first modern dancer to affirm strongly the instrumentality of the body in dance. "Through all times," she wrote some forty years ago, "the acquiring of technique in dance has been for one purpose—so to train the body as to make possible any demand made upon it by that inner self

The first section of this chapter was originally presented as a paper at the conference "Illuminating Dance: Philosophical Inquiry and Aesthetic Criticism," cosponsored by CORD and Temple University at Temple University, Philadelphia, 5 May 1979.

124

which has the vision of what needs to be said."[1] This notion of the body as instrument is still prevalent today. For example, a dance educator writes that "the human body, as the instrument of communication, has to transcend its personal limitations; it must be trained . . . to make neuromuscular discriminations; to sense degrees of action, textures, qualities. . . . It must respond sensitively to the dancer's feelings and needs and to the demands of the choreographer."[2] Yet, it is not simply dance educators who, because of their direct concern with dance training and technique, might be more prone to considering the body as the instrument of a "self" or a mind. For example, a dance historian writes that "all choreographic inventiveness and technical know-how, the agility of mind and body . . . come into play in the Italian *balli* of the fifteenth century"[3]; a neurophysiologically oriented dance researcher, writing on rhythmic perception, states that "sense discrimination refers here to a capacity of man's mind. Mind may be considered a special function of the brain. It is a capacity of man's mind to recognize sensations and to perceive or to 'make sense out of the sensations recognized.'"[4] A dance ethnologist, who writes of the necessity of understanding both the inner and outer aspects of the dancer, speaks of this understanding as a conceptual process that "involves both mind and body in a totality which it is difficult for us to comprehend in our culture, where these two entities stand as a dichotomy, instead of a totality," and she goes on to say that "this [dichotomy] is a barrier that the researcher must recognize and reconcile in order to carry on his work."[5] Were we to take the latter example as paradigmatic of the practice of separating mind and body, we might ask how dance researchers are to "recognize and reconcile" the dichotomy if they are oblivious of perpetuating it in the first place. Clearly, some understanding of philosophy and of how certain philosophical issues are embedded in the very nature of dance would seem vital.

Apart from metaphysical issues that often becloud writings on dance, other philosophical problems may be found. A dance historian, for instance, tacitly expresses an unexamined value system that is unsubstantiated methodologically when she writes that "the ideal historian looks at the past with the eyes of the present interpreting it for our world. You bring history to life by bringing a contemporary point of view to bear on it."[6] Still other examples might be given of writers whose statements, on close inspection, become strangely suggestive or altogether unintelligible. For instance, one researcher writing on body boundaries speaks of "the subjects' unconscious information"[7]; a critic-historian of dance states that "dancers inhabit space and time simultaneously."[8] Finally, an example might be given of those who offer definitions of dance and who thereby suffer from a classically scientific liability: while their definition gives the thing in question the status of reality, the terms used in the definition are either taken for granted—assumed as already given, as already apparent out there in experience—or else the terms themselves necessitate a further definition, and the terms of that definition, a further definition, and so on ad infinitum. Thus a dance anthropologist defines dance as "a cultural, institutional intervention in a psychobiological domain of motor activity which is composed—from the dancer's perspective—of purposeful, intentionally rhythmical, and culturally patterned sequences of nonverbal body movement and gesture which are not ordinary motor activities, the motion having inherent, and 'aesthetic' value."[9]

The questions asked in a philosophical inquiry of dance might be thought of as addressing either metaphysical or aesthetic issues. As examples of the former, one might ask, Where is the dance when it is not being performed? or, If mind and body are separate, where is the mind when the body is dancing? Examples of aesthetic questions might include not only the perennial, What is form? What is style? What is the nature of meaning in dance?, but also such questions as, Does the ephemeral nature of dance pose problems for the dance critic, and if so, what are these? The previously quoted excerpts from the writings of various people on dance show, however, that a very broad range of philosophical issues may be raised, some of which go beyond a strictly metaphysical or aesthetic classification. To get an idea of the scope of the possible issues, let us pose some questions on the basis of the previous examples. We may ask, for instance, What is the ideal or best way to go about doing dance history? Does such an ideal way exist, and if so, why is it considered the best or ideal way? What does it mean to call the human body an instrument, and what are the implications of such a conception of the human body—for example, who or what is directing it? Can an instrument make neuromuscular discriminations? How can a human body transcend its personal limitations? Is there such a thing as information that is unconscious? If so, who or what is sending it, and who or what is receiving it? Are levels of discourse about the body being confused? What can it possibly mean to say that dancers inhabit space and time simultaneously? Are dancers different from normal people in indulging in this curious habit or habitation? If the mind is a special function of the brain, can we expect more from the brain over and beyond its special mind function, and if not now, in the future? What does it mean to speak of an inner dancer and an outer dancer, to divide a dancer into two separate dimensions, one private and one public? Does this separation exacerbate a mind/body distinction rather than aim toward its reconciliation? Is it even logical to speak of two *entities* as comprising a totality? What does "a cultural institutional intervention in a psychobiological domain" mean? And what, for heaven's sakes, is "aesthetic value"?

Any one of these questions might be taken up as a question of genuine philosophical concern, whether a question of value, a question which probes the implications of a certain set of beliefs, a question which examines the grounds of certain attitudes, a question of meaning, or a question of language. A philosophical inquiry into any one of these questions would aim at a clarification of, or a deepening of insight into the issues involved, and thus ultimately provide a sounder understanding of dance itself as well as a sounder critical understanding of writings on dance. The inquiry might proceed from any one of a number of points of view: linguistic, analytic, empirical, phenomenological, semiological, or "eclectic." Before discussing the distinctive nature of a phenomenological inquiry, however, we should look equally at philosophical writings on dance in order to show, from another point of view, how a heightened or greater philosophical awareness on the part of the dancer might provide sounder critical grounds upon which to appraise writings on dance.

This keener awareness is particularly vital because dancers are sometimes all too ready to embrace immediately the views of any philosopher who pays attention to them. The long-awaited recognition of dance is a joy not to be denied in a world where attention has been more usually given over to music, painting, and literature. But the joy of recognition should not dull or blind the dancer's critical faculties. For example, a philosopher who affirms that feelings in dance are learned by

mastering certain movement techniques[10] betrays an orientation to movement in dance as a language, a language that one
might learn as one learns any other language. Similarly, a
philosopher who sees the question of expression in dance as a
question of language[11] betrays an orientation to movement in
dance as a set of counters which function much as words or
predicates function in verbal language, with the result that the
dance becomes in the end merely a label for itself, its "property"—what dancers or critics would call its quality—being
nothing more than the label or predicate one attaches to it.
Such views of dance are logocentric; language is taken as the
measure of all things, and verbal language as the standard of
that measure. Movement in dance is thus *prejudged* to function
as, or to be reducible to, a language that mirrors verbal language. This prejudgment or logocentricity may be exacerbated
at times if the meaningfulness of the presented theory is
thinned out by too many analogical references—to such things
as currant buns and chess games, for example[12]—when reference to actual dances (or to other works of art) might better
serve the theory and sustain its integrity.

In any event, we might say that in the same way that it behooves the dancer to develop a heightened philosophical
awareness, so it behooves the philosopher who would enrich
the world of dance to enter quite literally into the world of
dance. The proverbial armchair of the philosopher needs to be
brought down from its theoretical aerie into the dance studio as
well as into the theater of dance, just as the theater and studio
of dance need to be enlivened by a sense of curiosity and wonder. Thinking and doing are not then polarized but mutually
illuminating; dancers are not then mindless, any more than
philosophers are disembodied.

Now in a phenomenological account of dance, whatever the
particular focus might be, the account begins and ends with the
experience of dance itself. Let me immediately qualify this distinction between phenomenological inquiry and philosophical
inquiry in general by adding four negatives. Phenomenology is
not mere introspection: the descriptive account it offers is not a
mere chronicling of experience, a simple reportorial rendering
of a sequence of events, such as "On raising my eyes I was
aware of an upward movement, and on bending my left knee I
was aware of a downward movement." Secondly, phenomenology is not speculative. The phenomenologist does not contem-

plate, survey, or examine a given experience with the purpose of generating ideas, descriptive or explanatory, about it. Phenomenology is not a reflective *musing*—no matter how deep—over experience. Thirdly, phenomenology is not theoretical: no theories emerge from phenomenological accounts. What does emerge is a description of the essential nature of the phenomenon in question, and that description may always be amplified by further essential insights. Finally, phenomenology, as a method of experiential or existential analysis, is not a point of view on the world, at least not in the sense that it puts a grid upon experience or imposes a theoretical system upon the experience before the experience is had. The phenomenologist does not come to the experience armed with preconceptions or categories to be found or noticed within the experience. Its descriptive account is therefore radically different from what are equally called descriptive accounts in the social sciences or in other kinds of philosophical studies. The focus is wholly on the experience, and the quest is a rendering of the essential features of the experience.

We usually think of science as being the most empirical of disciplines, that is, as being based wholly in observation. Although the meaning of "empirical" in science today has come to be equated with experimentally produced or experimentally gained data, and data that is publicly verifiable, empiricism originally referred to that which is founded in experience, and only in experience. In respect to this original meaning, which may be traced back to Sextus Empiricus, a Greek philosopher and physician living in about 200 A.D., and even earlier to the beginnings of a medical group, the "Empirics," in about 250 B.C., phenomenology may be considered to be the most radical of empiricisms. I am emphasizing this tethering of knowledge to experience because it is peculiar in the extreme to phenomenology. But I am emphasizing it also to bring out the point that we are all closet phenomenologists to the extent that we are all experiencing human beings in the world; regardless of our vocation or predilections—whether we are bent over a microscope, a hot stove, someone's shoulder, or backward, experience is the very core of our being human, the very stuff of our lives, a stuffing with which most of us will not only be ultimately hesitant or reluctant to part, but a stuffing which we would not want to deny here and now. A dance concert, for instance, is taken by each person in the audience as an experi-

ence. For the phenomenologist, that experience might constitute the point of departure for any one of a number of
descriptive accounts of dance: for example, a descriptive account of the power of collaborative choreography. The trick is
to have the experience in the sense of intuiting fully the dance
or dances that are there before us and giving ourselves wholly
to them as they give themselves wholly to us. It is only after that
experience itself is had that one may embark upon a
phenomenological inquiry.

To arrive at a phenomenological analysis, then, requires first
that one come out of the closet. One can then turn one's attention to an understanding of phenomenology as a way of gaining essential insights into the nature of dance, whether in terms
of fathoming the power of collaborative choreography, the
meaning or significance of style, what is meant by a dancer's
projecting himself or herself, and so on. Whatever it is one is
curious about, whatever it is that strikes one and makes one
wonder, such is the point of departure for all philosophical
inquiry.

Now the path to an understanding of phenomenology, as I
see it, is actually forked. There are some philosophers who
devote their lives to an understanding of phenomenology itself
and who are only peripherally concerned with descriptive accounts of lived experiences. Though it may sound paradoxical,
phenomenology may itself be a subject for the phenomenologist. This is because phenomenology is an extremely rich and
complex subject; it is a radically different way of doing philosophy, and it presents a radically different epistemology. It takes
knowledge seriously in the sense of not distancing the knower
from the known. It seeks the ground of all knowledge in experience; that is, in the experiencing subject for whom there is
always a world. To condense and paraphrase the remarks of
one phenomenologist, "Phenomenology reflects on the meaning of the hyphen between subject and object or between subject and world, a hyphen that indicates the primordial moment
at which subject and object have not yet become separate."[13]
While those engaged in the study of phenomenology itself are
concerned with elucidating the structures of that primoridal
moment, those phenomenologists who take up the method of
existential or experiential analysis are concerned with presenting descriptive accounts of lived experiences in such a way that

the essential structures or truths of the experience come to light.

Now I would suggest that the most fruitful way in which a dancer might approach phenomenology is by reading a variety of such descriptive accounts. An understanding of phenomenology is not a matter of following a recipe but of attaining a perspective. In a careful and trenchant reading of these experiential accounts, the phenomenological method comes literally to life: it becomes transparent in the very descriptive renderings themselves. Moreover, as in a fine dance performance, wherein as dancer you are not simply moving through a form but the form is moving through you, so with the practice of phenomenology: "it," in a sense, is doing you. Reflecting back upon the experience, unfettered by preconceptions and prejudgments, you discover that the experience opens up before you. Your work consists in listening acutely to it, being there with it, in the same way that you are not merely doing a movement in the dance but are opening yourself to its dynamics.

But what does it mean to come to an experience unfettered by preconceptions and prejudgments? When I was five or six years old, for example, I thought that to dance was to wear a tutu and to be on a stage. Whatever did not meet those requirements was not dancing. But I knew too that if the tutu on stage were gallumping about, it was not dancing. On the other hand, I also knew that a figure on stage doing *entrechats* was not trying to shake flies off its legs or trying to avoid going to the bathroom. The point is that in a phenomenological description, all such preconceptions and prejudgments are bracketed. They do not color the descriptive account: they are neutralized, deflated; in the technological-political jargon of the day, they are inoperative. This is in part why a phenomenological description is ultimately not merely an individual account of experience but a grasping of the essential nature of the experience. To describe how this essence grasping is accomplished is far too detailed a presentation to consider here. Suffice to say that the method involves first a suspension of belief or judgment, and that through that suspension we are ultimately enabled to describe the thing as it appears without being trapped by our preconceptions about it. On the contrary, our preconceptions are exposed in the very course of the analysis itself.

In describing the thing as it appears, we end up re-languaging the phenomenon: we search out the phrase which captures precisely the quality of the thing *as it is experienced.* For example, suppose we are curious about the nature of movement in dance. Were we to proceed phenomenologically, we would find in the end that the usual mode of speaking about movement in dance is not apt: it lacks descriptive or essential resonance. In the immediate and direct experience of movement in dance, movement does not appear as a change of position; it does not appear as a force in time and space; it does not appear as a medium of expression or a medium of anything else. In the immediate and direct experience of movement in dance, something quite different appears. It is only through an analysis of the visible in dance that one might begin to fathom and describe the essential nature of that experience.[14]

There is not a re-languaging of experience for the sake of developing a new language, however. The re-languaging is prompted by the very nature of the experience itself. As one reflects back upon the experience without the usual preconceptual baggage—that is, as one takes nothing for granted—one thereby gains fresh insights into the nature of the phenomenon. For instance, suppose we *did* believe movement or dance to be a force in time and space. We would espouse a theory, conception, or definiton of movement or dance that is quasi-scientific. We would assme certain items or phenomena as given, as already there—in a word, as self-evident: time and space are *out there.* As we saw earlier, definitions of dance suffer from a false sense of evidential security. To take space and time in dance as self-evident phenomena is to miss the very quiddity of movement and possibly the very essence of most dance: namely, that any movement creates its own time and space, that is, that time and space are not containers which movement fills to varying degrees. It is also to miss the insight that precisely in its very creation of time and space lies the possibility of movement creating different worlds. The discovery that movement creates its own time and space is an open-sesame to a host of fascinating aspects of dance, a discovery that may have repercussions ranging all the way from concerns about teaching technique and composition as well as the vocabulary used in teaching them, to a critical reexamination of customary or usual breakdowns of spatial and temporal aspects of movement into such traditional categories as direction, level, and accent.

It becomes evident then that through the suspension of judgment or belief, one approaches the phenomenon fresh or anew, so that what is usually familiar becomes strange, not in the sense of being foreign and unintelligible but in the sense of being original and untainted. A final example might be given to crystallize even more finely the nature of a phenomenological account. Suppose we wished to gain insight into the nature of the human body in dance. We would not begin by seeing the body within an already imposed framework: the body as a bearer of signs; the body as a thing to be manipulated, trained, or whipped into shape; or the body as the agent of aesthetic behavior. Phenomenologists have elaborated this original, pristine body, this preobjective or preobjectivized body. They call it the lived body. If we wanted to capture the essence of the lived body in the experience of dance, then we would go back to the lived experience of dance itself, for it is there and only there that we might discover the way or ways in which the lived body appears in dance. It is there, in the experience of dance, that we might discover, for example, that there are indeed many ways of being a body in dance: that the lived body for Isadora Duncan is different from the lived body for Martha Graham, that the lived body for Martha Graham is different from the lived body for Steve Paxton, that the lived body for Steve Paxton is different from the lived body for Alvin Ailey or Merce Cunningham.[15] In sum, we might say that the phenomenologist is concerned with ways of being-in-the-world, that is, with experience, prior to any theoretical or objectivating processing of the experience.

While other investigations of, or research into dance have been blossoming along with the current upsurge of enthusiasm for dance, philosophical inquiry into dance has lagged far behind. A cursory glance at the indices of journals of aesthetics in the last five years will quickly substantiate this fact. Perhaps the lack of equal blossoming is the result of people being unaware of the options which are open to them. What I would like to point out is that not only for traditional philosophy, but also for the human sciences, phenomenological studies of dance offer a rich alternative approach and a highly diversified one. Phenomenological hermeneutics, for example, is a totally ignored but trenchant and extremely fertile mode of inquiry for the dance historian particularly, and quite possibly for the psychologist or sociologist of dance as well. For the anthropologist of dance or the dance therapist—for the human or social scientist of dance generally—there is the possibility of utilizing an empirical-phenomenological methodology, a methodology that combines a scientifically ordered gathering of information with an existential analysis. A study utilizing such a methodology does not sacrifice the lived experience of the subject on the altar of neurophysiology or upon the altar of any other reductive system. There are also at the fringe of phenomenology some interesting quasi-phenomenological or phenomenologically spawned pursuits, such as, for example, ethnomethodology in the social sciences.[16] I mention these alternative paths merely to indicate that regardless of one's particular focus—aesthetic, historical, therapeutic, sociological, psychological—if one is interested in illuminating dance with a heightened philosophical awareness, then one does have options: one does not have to commit oneself to a third-person rendering of dance, movement, or bodies; one does not have to commit oneself to a mere compilation of chronologically ordered facts; one does not have to commit oneself to a system that defines in advance the structures that one must discover or notice in the experience; one does not have to commit oneself to particular theoretical stands. One can quite simply commit oneself to descriptive accounts of dance, movement, or bodies, descriptive accounts that begin and end in the very experience itself.

The existential phenomenologist Merleau-Ponty used the phrase "singing the world" in reference to the gestural sense of words, their physiognomic presence or character for us. Singing the world is what my body does as I seek and discover my way in the world of speech. Now if, as Merleau-Ponty goes on to say, "there are several ways for the human body to sing the world's praises and in the last resort to live it,"[17] then surely there are several ways for the human body to dance the world's praises and in the last resort to live it. The task for the phenomenologist is to clarify and to deepen our understanding of how it is the human body dances the world, a task that is as broad and open-ended as dance itself.

I would like to spend the remainder of this essay addressing three oft-raised concerns or issues in order to clarify in advance certain misunderstandings that might otherwise dissuade one from a serious consideration of phenomenology as a bona fide epistemological methodology.

Concerns about access to or difficulties with phenomenology very often center upon the language of phenomenology; to wit, why are many phenomenological accounts so ponderous, so torturous? Particularly in view of the fact that phenomenological accounts are *experiential* accounts, it seems indeed ironic that they are sometimes so difficult to understand. Are we, after all, *that* bedazzled or swamped by our own experiences? It can be readily acknowledged that phenomenologists, like people in other specialized disciplines, certainly indulge in an in-group cant and that, in effect, while one phenomenologist will usually understand another, a beginning reader may often be put off by what appears to be nothing more than specialist jargon. On the other hand, it can also be acknowledged that people are generally much more accustomed, even habituated, to *objective* rather than *essential* descriptions. The common description of movement as change of position, for example, or the common description of movement or dance as a force in time and space are examples of just such objective descriptions. They do not tell us anything essential; they do not get to the heart of the matter. Airplanes and ants, after all, might also as aptly be described as forces in time and space. Objective descriptions, moreover, take for granted the very things we would wish elucidated; for example, What is the nature of time and space in dance? What is "a force" and how, in particular, is movement "a force"? or alternatively, How can movement be a change of position? Does change of position not describe an object in motion rather than movement?

It has been pointed out that if one insists on clinging to the notion of dance or movement as a force in time and space that the description (or perhaps more precisely, the *definition*) might at least be more properly written as timeforcespace, since what is created and what appears is an indissoluble unit.[18] To arrive at essential descriptions one needs to transcend habitual formulations of the object or phenomenon; one must come to grips linguistically with the phenomenon as it gives itself in experience. This means forging a new language that captures precisely the quality—the physiognomy—of the phenomenon in question. In the process of uncovering the phenomenological structures inherent in symbolic forms of dance, movement has been described as a revelation of force, and dance as a form-in-the-making.[19] Both of these descriptive renderings have an essential rather than objective resonance, and both well illustrate the process of re-languaging which is part and parcel of phenomenological accounts.

To say, in addition, that access to phenomenology may be enhanced or that difficulties with phenomenology may be surmounted by getting the "feel" of phenomenology is not some kind of mystical mumbo jumbo, but a testimony to the fact that we do not ordinarily pay attention to our experiences in the sense of fathoming what is actually present, that is, the nature of the thing experienced. Again, it is usually a matter of being satisfied with objective rather than essential knowledge, of not penetrating the very core of the experience itself. In support of the distinction made between objective and essential descriptions and of the common bias toward objective descriptions, one might cite writers in other fields; for example, the psychologist, Ernst Schactel, in his book, *Metamorphosis,*[20] distinguishes two different modes of perception; the customary mode in which one classifies something superficially or recognizes it at a minimal level of attention and pays it no further heed, and the mode in which one reaches into the experience, or, to use a phenomenologically derived metaphor, the mode in which one communes with the object. Clearly, phenomenological research is a rigorous undertaking. It is not a matter of following a simple recipe and coming out not only with a duly risen cake but with a fully frosted one as well. This comment is made not in order to elevate phenomenological research to some lofty plane reserved for an erudite few, but simply to underscore the fact that to come to grips with experience as it is lived is a difficult task; to fathom the essential nature of the experience of dance (rather than the objective nature of movement, for example) is neither a simple matter nor is it an irrevocably conclusive task, something to be set down, sealed, and delivered for all time. True to the open-ended nature of phenomenological research, it is always possible that further refinements and elaborations might be made.

The emphasis upon the rigorous nature of phenomenological studies as disciplined undertakings appears to be quite worthwhile from yet another perspective: that of present-day encroachments upon the term *phenomenology* (which seems to have such a nice, juicy, impressive ring). Not that the meaning of the word is patented by any means, but that its essentially philosophical significance and history is elided and even mocked by certain patently abusive uses of it. Phenomenology is not equivalent to psychological introspection nor is it equivalent to any descriptive rendering whatsoever of experience. To speak of "movement phenomenology," for example, is nonsensical: there are not a number of ways in which movement may be described phenomenologically; there is but a single phenomenology of movement: namely, that particular analysis which may be refined and augmented not by new speculations or new approaches but only by keener and more perspicuous phenomenologically derived insights. One can of course speak of the *phenomenon* of movement as something that might be looked at from different points of view, but not the *phenomenology* of movement. In brief, the term *phenomenology* denotes a method of eidetic analysis invariably associated with the name of Edmund Husserl; beyond this, being a philosophically spawned term to begin with, *phenomenology* has a rich and particular philosophical history that it might be well to recognize.

Finally, it might be noted that questions raised in relation to difficulties with the language of phenomenological descriptions often lead to questions about the best way to approach phenomenology. Obviously a compendium of readings in phenomenology with particular relevance to dance would be worthwhile. Such a book might cover topics ranging from the lived body to the lived experience of dance, from spatiality to aesthetic perception and style. A coherent frame of reference for understanding the quest and focus of phenomenological inquiries into dance might thus be provided. At the same time, the book might also function as a research source by identifying unresolved questions and suggesting new areas for analysis.

Questions about the nature of phenomenological analyses might lead some people to wonder about the possibility of universally valid descriptions. After all, a phenomenological analysis is done by a single person, yet everyone's lived experience is different. How is it, then, that the analysis might be universally valid? Concerns about access to and difficulties with phenomenological analyses are thus not totally unrelated to concerns about the possibility of essence grasping or the gaining of essential insights. In response to this question of essences, mention might be made of the first reduction involved in phenomenological analyses—the suspension of belief—and of what it means in terms of presuppositions. While through a phenomenological analysis one comes to see, for

example, that time and space are not containers of or for movement but are created by movement, it may not be clear just how
one arrives at this insight. In a phenomenological analysis, presuppositions are not removed, as it were, from *actual experiences;*
they are bracketed in respect to *reflected-upon experience.* One
consequently comes to see, in the reflective act, what one has
taken for granted or presupposed in the actual experience. In
other words, it is in the *reflective* act, where belief in the natural
world has been bracketed, where the suspension of belief has
taken place, that one may come ultimately to see what has in
fact been presupposed in the actual experience itself. While
one might later, and from that time on, come to an immediate
experience of the creation of time and space in the very experience of movement or dance, for example, the realization that
movement creates time and space is an insight first grasped in
reflection. In sum, insight into essences via what is termed the
second or eidetic reduction is initially achieved in reflection, not
in actual experience.

The belief that phenomenological investigation cannot lead
to truths appears to be based upon a double misunderstanding
of phenomenology: there is first the misunderstanding, suggested above, that one's actual experience is itself made presuppositionless; that is, that in the immediate experience itself one
performs the epoché—the suspension of belief—so that one
has a presuppositionless experience. As we have seen, it is in
the reflective act that presuppositions within the actual experience come to light. Thus, to insist that there is no such thing as
a passive observer, to insist that observation is always theory-
laden, or to declare by way of example that what one sees
through a microscope before a class in biology and after a class
in biology is radically different offers no sound grounds for
repudiating phenomenological descriptions, for calling essences into question, or for invalidating essence grasping.
Phenomenology is not concerned with *re-making* experience according to a standard of impartiality. Phenomenology is concerned with the experience itself *as it is lived* and with bringing
to light the essential nature of that experience through particular reflective acts that uncover what is actually there in the
experience and that at the same time expose preconceptions
and prejudgments which have, unknown to us, become encrusted onto the experience.

A second confusion might arise in terms of bracketing. It

might be thought that in bracketing one gets rid of intentional-ity—that the meaning aspect of experience is somehow ob-literated. Again, it is a matter of understanding that bracketing takes place in reflection. The meaning of the actual experience is not obliterated in reflecting upon the experience: only worldly beliefs about, or natural attitudes toward the phenome-non are "obliterated." Moreover, it would seem that some con-fusion might exist between an intentional analysis of reflection and a descriptive account of experience through phenomeno-logical reflection. The former would lead to a clear distinction between the brute given and the meaning (between what Hus-serl termed the "hyle" and the "morphe," or the matter and the form, as they are given in the experience of reflection), while a descriptive account of any particular experience, of dance, for example, might or might not involve such a distinction. In or-der to understand intentionality—a meaning-bestowing "act"—vis-à-vis bracketing, that is, vis-à-vis a suspension of belief, or vis-à-vis the grasping of essences, it would be necessary to do an intentional analysis of reflection itself—in effect, to reflect upon the experience of reflection. It might be noted that insofar as an illumination of phenomenological reflection is concerned, an understanding of intentionality would ultimately require an intentional analysis of the reflective *imagination,* since it is in the second epoché or reduction, in the play of free fancy or freely varied forms, that essences come to light.

In general, it would seem that rather than debate the possi-bility of essence grasping or of calling into question the possibil-ity of essences at all, that one might better plunge into phenomenological accounts themselves and let one's experi-ence speak for itself in light of those descriptive accounts. Does a phenomenological account of aesthetic experience, for in-stance, or a phenomenological account of movement or of the body in dance, present foundational insights? Is it understand-able to speak of the lived body of Martha Graham being differ-ent from the lived body of Meredith Monk? The ultimate test or court of appeal so far as phenomenology is concerned is not whether we are biologically capable of bracketing. To say that a suspension of belief is impossible in view of the fact that we can never get outside our biological selves, that is, we cannot un-plug our own neurophysiological circuitry, is to confuse uni-verses of discourse or to jump from one level of discourse to another, at the same time applying the rules or mechanisms of the one to the other, and in such a way that those rules or mechanisms are regarded as basic; in short, it is to be an overly enthusiastic proponent of biological reductionism. On the contrary, for phenomenology, the ultimate court of appeal is our own experience itself. As Husserl said many times over, "Zu den Sachen selbst!": "To the things themselves!"

In consequence, it would seem that unless we are actually phenomenological philosophers engaged in elucidating the very nature of phenomenology itself, we would do best to take a pragmatic approach: our concerns and evaluations would then be with the results of the method, not with the methodological system itself. We are otherwise either talking about the phenomenological method at an abstract level, a level many steps removed from the actual doing of phenomenology, since most probably we have not engaged in phenomenological research or attempted a phenomenological analysis ourselves and have therefore never actually experienced the method; or else we are talking about the method at the level of mere opinion or from the viewpoint of a particular conceptual scheme of the world, such as, for example, that of biological reductionism.

Now in connection with the previous suggestion, it may be pointed out that Merleau-Ponty was quite critical of phenomenology as a method, and though he wrote *Phenomenology of Perception,* he considered his method to be one of "radical reflection" rather than of phenomenological reflection in a Husserlian sense. In view of his actual immersion in philosophy and phenomenological literature, his critical remarks concerning phenomenology are worth most serious consideration. For example, his insistence that Husserlian reflection does not and cannot give us the actual experience in reverse bespeaks not a superficial judgment but a deeply thought-out position in respect to the primordial nature of human existence, that is, that world and humankind cannot be so separated as to yield a distinctly demarcated ground, the one side belonging to that of the subject, the other belonging to that of the world. At the same time that Merleau-Ponty thus calls into question the possibility of essential knowledge, however, he presents us with a foundational insight into the nature of humankind: ambiguity describes the essential character of human existence. How is it that he can renounce essences, one might ask, at the same time that he offers us a foundational description of human reality?

Again, it would seem that unless we are practicing philosophers, i.e., committed to actual philosophical inquiry into the nature of phenomenology, that taking a stance on the one side or the other regarding essences is far less significant and crucial than is coming to grips with phenomenological studies themselves and finding out if and how they are relevant: Are they indeed saying something of fundamental significance to us? Do they jibe with our experience? Whether a question of ambiguity, of the lived body, of a form-in-the-making, or of qualitative presences, what we should seek out is a concordance or discordance of the description at the heart of our own experience of the phenomenon in question. What we should seek out is an answer to the question of what we discover through a phenomenological analysis that we should otherwise not have discovered; and perhaps further, whether we ourselves could augment and crystallize that analysis further.

As for the last of the three oft-raised concerns or issues, it was noted earlier, in connection with the idea that we are all closet phenomenologists, that phenomenology is a frequently overlooked alternative path to knowledge, that more often than not it remains a hidden possibility. If we would only come out of the closet, we would realize that we do have options. We need not lock ourselves into experimentally ordered programs of research; we need not be content with only objective accounts. For example, in respect to psychological studies, particularly in dance therapy, the very thing one should want to elucidate, the very focus of concern is the life-world of the people with whom one is working; in consequence, one cannot divorce oneself from the actual lived experiences of the people who are the core of concern without losing something, and something very critical, in the process. A very interesting doctoral study was in fact done several years ago by a student of clinical psychology.[21] The study utilized an empirical-phenomenological methodology to elucidate the phenomenon of moving together in improvisational dance. The primary concern was to fathom the meanings inherent in the ways in which people spontaneously move together—patients and doctor down a hospital corridor, for example. Improvisational dance was used simply as a well-defined phenomenon in which the nature of moving together spontaneously could be investigated and illuminated. Attention was also called earlier to phenomenological hermeneutics as an

alternative mode of inquiry for historians of dance. An issue
which might be raised here concerns the fact that history is
continually reinterpreted. How then is it possible to view a
phenomenological-hermeneutical account as providing essential insights? On the contrary, is not a phenomenological-
hermeneutical account simply one more interpretation of
history? Again, what is being called into question is the possibility of essential truths. It would seem, however, that in this instance the scepticism is more firmly anchored: it is not merely a
matter of opinion—of "stance taking"—but a question of history itself. Although the question is not the result of having
come to grips with a number of phenomenological-
hermeneutical texts and finding them unenlightening or in-
valid, it is, in effect, a more compelling question. Interestingly
enough, it is a question of which Husserl was not unaware, even
though phenomenological hermeneutics as such was not developed or elaborated by him or, presumably, even known to
him. In *Formal and Transcendental Logic*, in a section partially
titled "The Usual Theories of Evidence Misguided by the Presupposition of Absolute Truth," Husserl speaks of the possibility of absolute *and* relative truths and of the legitimacy of each.
He also goes on to speak in the next section ("Further Criticisms of the Presupposition of Absolute Truth and the Dog-
matistic Theories of Evidence") of "an essentially necessary
relativity"; and finally, in a closing section, he speaks of the
necessity of an ongoing criticism of the evidences that
phenomenological cognition furnishes. In respect to
phenomenological hermeneutics, Husserl might then have
been the first to be concerned with historical relativity; but he
would also have been the first to insist upon an ongoing and
ever-deeper scrutiny of the evidence—that is, an ongoing appraisal and analysis of the historical phenomenon in question—
in the same way that he was always insistent upon further
refinements and more precise elaborations of descriptions of
first-hand experience.

Now it would seem that a phenomenological-hermeneutical
study of dance is valid precisely to the extent that one is able to
uncover the foundational locus of change or development or
that one is able to trace out foundational connections at the
heart of the phenomenon. The very idea of a history of dance
(or a history of anything else, for that matter) *presupposes* beginnings and endings and/or passages. What phenomenological

hermeneutics provides is a unique vantage point upon those presumptive beginnings, endings, and passages; it allows one to come to grips with the very nature of history itself. For example, there is, in the history of dance, what is sometimes referred to as "old dance" and "new dance," the former referring to the works of the early modern dance pioneers in America, the latter referring to the work of Merce Cunningham (after he left Martha Graham's company), the works of artists connected with the Judson Church in New York City in the 1960s, and the works of many contemporary artists. The foundational difference between old dance and new dance is not a matter of saying who choreographed what, when, where—a matter of naming names, places, dates, or even styles—but of illuminating the locus of change in the very making and performing of dances themselves. Earlier mention was made of an essay on old and new dance (see n. 15) that was in part a phenomenological-hermeneutical study: the descriptive analysis was as much anchored in first-hand accounts of dance by dancers, choreographers, and critics of new and old dance as it was anchored in the author's own experiences of the two kinds of dance. To do a phenomenological-hermeneutical study, one must be in touch with actual lived experiences of the phenomenon one is investigating and with the beliefs, attitudes, and values surrounding those experiences; it is through an analysis of first-hand accounts of beliefs, attitudes, values, and experiences that foundational changes in thinking and praxis are revealed.

The relativity of historical accounts, the fact that history is periodically reinterpreted as new historians come on the scene and survey the evidence from a fresh perspective is thus not sufficient grounds for disavowing essential insights gleaned through a phenomenological approach. In the first place, the phenomenological method places the phenomenological-hermeneutical account quite apart from traditional historical accounts or interpretations. As was noted earlier in a different context, it is not a matter of simply new speculations or new approaches. It is a matter of ever-deepening insights into the generative core of the phenomenon. Phenomenology is not *the* way of doing historical, psychological, sociological, or any other kind of research in dance. Phenomenology is, however, *the* way of coming to grips with lived experiences, our own, and in a hermeneutical sense, those of others. As such, phenomenology does provide an alternative method to those commonly used methods of analysis which, for example, impose a schema or prism upon the experience or discount the subject of the experience. In light of this view of phenomenology, it would again seem that what is crucial is taking up phenomenological accounts—reading them, examining them, communing with them—and then assaying them within the crucible of one's own experience; and of equal significance is asking oneself what it is that one discovers through phenomenological accounts that one would otherwise not discover at all. In this way one might develop a solid ground for an appreciation of phenomenology, an appreciation of what it is and what it is not, of what is and what is not possible within its methodology, and perhaps finally, an appreciation of the value of experiential or eidetic analyses.

Notes

1. Martha Graham, "A Modern Dancer's Primer for Action," in *Dance as a Theatre Art,* ed. Selma Jeanne Cohen (New York: Dodd, Mead, 1974), 139.

2. Margery J. Turner, *New Dance, Approaches to Nonliteral Choreography* (Pittsburgh: University of Pittsburgh Press, 1971), 23.

3. Ingrid Brainard, *Court Dances of the Early Renaissance* (New York: Dance Notation Bureau, 1971), vi.

4. F. Mary Fee, "Discovering Rhythm through the Senses: A Theory of Sense Perception," in *Dance Research Monograph One, 1971–1972,* ed. Patricia A. Rowe and Ernestine Stodelle (New York: CORD, 1973), 67.

5. Allegra Fuller Snyder, "The Dance Symbol," in *New Dimensions in Dance Research: Anthropology and Dance—The American Indian,* ed. Tamara Comstock (New York: CORD, 1974), 222.

6. Selma Jeanne Cohen, "How Does the Researcher Organize the Facts?" in *Research in Dance: Problems and Possibilities,* ed. Richard Bull (New York: CORD, 1968), 71.

7. Susan L. Puretz, "Influence of Modern Dance on Body Image," in *Essays in Dance Research,* ed. Dianne L. Woodruff (New York: CORD, 1978), 225.

8. Jack Anderson, *Dance* (New York: Newsweek Books, 1974), 9.

9. Judith Lynn Hanna, report on the Annual Conference of the Association of Social Anthropologists of the Commonwealth (1975) on the theme "The Anthropology of the Body," *Dance Research Journal* 7 (1975):40.

10. David Best, *Expression in Movement and the Arts* (London: Lepus Books, 1974), 173–76.

11. Nelson Goodman, *Languages of Art* (Indianapolis: Hackett, 1976), esp. 57, 88–89. Protestations to the contrary, the "property" of a dance is seen to hang very much on what is said about it. Moreover, the very thing we would like elucidated—metaphorical exemplification as contrasted to literal exemplification—is "unclear" and left as an explanatory task "to the cosmologist" (see 78, 90–91).

12. David Best, "The Aesthetics of Dance," *Dance Research Journal* 7 (1975):13–14.

See also 119–121 and 117, in Best, *Expression in Movement and the Arts,* for the very same comparison.

13. Mikel Dufrenne, "On the Phenomenology and Semiology of Art," in *Phenomenology and Natural Existence: Essays in Honor of Marvin Farber,* ed. Dale Riepe (New York: State University of New York Press, 1973), 93.

14. See Maxine Sheets-Johnstone, "On Movement and Objects in Motion: The Phenomenology of the Visible in Dance," *Journal of Aesthetic Education* 13 (1979):33–46.

15. From Maxine Sheets-Johnstone, "The Passage Rites of the Body: A Phenomenological Account of Change in Dance," unpublished essay. A rigorously abridged version of this essay appeared in *Leonardo* 11 (1978):197–201, under the title "An Account of Recent Changes in Dance in the U.S.A."

16. See, for example, George Psathas, "Ethnomethodology as a Phenomenological Approach in the Social Sciences," in *Interdisciplinary Phenomenology,* ed. Don Ihde and Richard M. Zaner (The Hague: M. Nijhoff, 1977), 79–98. See also John O'Neill, "Mind and Institution," in the same volume, 99–108.

17. Maurice Merleau-Ponty, *Phenomenology of Perception* (New York: Routledge & Kegan Paul, 1962), 187.

18. Maxine Sheets-Johnstone, *The Phenomenology of Dance* (Madison: University of Wisconsin Press, 1966); 2d ed., 1980 (New York: Arno Press; London: Dance Books).

19. Ibid.

20. Ernst Schachtel, *Metamorphosis* (New York: Basic Books, 1959).

21. Bruce Levi, "The Coherence of Gestures in Improvisational Dance: An Empirical Study Informed by Merleau-Ponty's Phenomenological Ontology," Ph.D. diss., Duquesne University, 1978.

Ingarden's Aesthetics and Dance

Sibyl S. Cohen

It is often claimed that the differences among the various art media are so radical that no single approach to describing the different types of works of art is appropriate. It is believed necessary to use different approaches—different models of description—to deal with painting, sculpture, music, literature, and dance. This may very well be the case. Nevertheless, Roman Ingarden's approach to an account of literature works so well that I am intrigued at the prospect of attempting to see just how his frame of reference might apply to dance.

In what follows I shall explore some of the conceptual apparatus that I take to be central in Ingarden's phenomenological description of literature. I will try to discover if his stratified, schematic description can be used for dance. My account will be in terms of the perceiver's experience. The dance performance is to be understood as the work of art that counts as a parallel to the literary work of art.

In his description of literature, Ingarden isolates four strata: (1) phonetic, (2) meaning, (3) portrayed or presented objects, (4) schematized aspects. These strata are seen as partially hierarchical. The phonetic stratum is the founding stratum of literature out of which the meaning stratum is achieved. It is in terms of a meaning stratum that we can then encounter the level of presented objects from one or more points of view (the stratum of schematized aspects).

In suggesting that a work of art is stratified, Roman Ingarden has also claimed that each stratum is schematized. Although only the fourth stratum is specifically called "schematized,"

146

schematic formation is an important characteristic of all the strata. Ingarden's use of the term *schematic* refers to his claim that the literary work of art is not fully determined. There are places of indeterminacy left open by the determinate elements of the work. A reader fills in these places of indeterminacy— these gaps—and thereby achieves a "concretization" of the work. A concretization is the reader's particular experience of the work in which she or he has cocreated by filling the gaps and actualizing potential elements. It becomes an adequate aesthetic concretization—an "aesthetic object"—if the filling out of the schematic structure includes the aesthetic experiencing of the potential aesthetic value of the work of art. The suggestion is that a work of art functions as an intersubjective intentional object that can provide the basis for a monosubjective aesthetic experience of an aesthetic object.

Phonetic Stratum

There is some difficulty in trying to discover the parallel in dance to the phonetic stratum in literature. Ingarden claims that sound is the first essential level in experiencing the literary work of art. Superficially, the visual might be claimed to be the basic stratum in dance. For an audience the dance must be something seen. (At least, as far as I know no one has yet attempted to provide a dance experience to an audience which could not or did not see it.) However, an account of dance as being founded ultimately on a visual experience seems unduly narrow.

One set of constraints occurs by reason of the fact that dance as presented—in most of its performances—is usually "accompanied" by music. I hesitate to allow that the sound that happens in dance is somehow "in addition" to the dance. But dance can also be performed without a musical accompaniment. Even in this case, however, dance cannot occur without relevant sounds. Sound occurs in dance in a number of dimensions. For example, bodily movement generates sound. If sound should be missing altogether, it is a deliberate silence that demands attention and is, perhaps, more significant in that case than the sound of, for example, shuffling feet or slapping hands.

A further complication occurs in locating this basic stratum for dance. Dance is a performing art. The dancer must be

present. (Dance recorded on film may require some amend-
ment to this claim.) There is not the same separation between
author and reader as there is in literature. Granted, there is the
possibility that the choreographer of the dance does not perform in the dance and may therefore be separated from the
experience of the dance in time and space as the author of a
book is separated from the reader. It is, nonetheless, implaus-
ible to suggest that the dancer can ever function (be his or her
dancing ever so rigidly determined by the choreographer) like
marks on a page open to phonetic readings of the reader.

In dance, two levels of "reading" occur (at least). If we focus
on those cases in which the dancer does is set and determined
in specific detail by the choreographer, the dancer "reads" the
choreographer's work in his or her performance of it. The
dancer brings it to sensual life in the performance. And, the
viewer "reads" the interpretation of the dancer. In literature
one reading constitutes the sole performance (except in those
cases where the reader is reading aloud to another). Even in
those cases in which the dancer's "reading" of the dance is
severely limited by the most rigidly set choreography imaginable, there is an important creative enterprise provided in the
dancing that cannot be overlooked. We might consider it a
cocreative activity. But, care must be taken to show that it is not
the same kind of cocreative activity that the audience is engaged in.

In terms of this account, we seem required to isolate three
levels of enterprise: the author (choreographer) of the dance,
the dancer of the dance, and the viewer of the dance. I have
focused on a rigidly determined performance as the limiting
case of creativity on the part of the individual dancer. If it
makes sense in these cases to include the cocreativity of the
dancer, then all contemporary trends in which the individual
creativity of the dancer is encouraged will likewise be accounted
for.

This double reading constitutes an inherent complication in
dance that is not particularly significant in an account of literature. Although I recognize this, I do not intend to do more
than note it and suggest that while the audience's visual reading
of the choreographer's work may be mediated by the dancer,
and the cocreativity on the part of the dancer and choreographer may be seen as complicating the locus of a basic

stratum, neither situation is of itself an obstacle to a determination of that stratum.

If our first attempt to isolate a basic stratum in perceiving dance is to found it in the visual sense, it is because the visual is a particularly important way for us to encounter the lived body of another. If it strikes me as superficial and inadequate, however, to describe the basic stratum of dance as the visual, it is because our encounter with the lived body of another is never "merely" visual.

What is corporeally commonplace is heightened and intensified in the perception of dance. What the dancer may do on stage or "any place at all" in his or her celebration of movement is grasped by the viewer, if at all, in terms of the viewer's lived body. That celebration of motion must occur in the lived body of the viewer as organism. If the viewer merely sees, he or she does not "see." It is possible, I suppose, to analyze and to distinguish the various senses that participate in this experience. For the purpose of discussion about viewer experience, we might isolate subliminal kinesthetic sensations as well as aural sensations. However, the tumult of increasing awareness of one's own body that constitutes the involvement in the dance experience for a viewer makes isolation of separate senses problematic. Consciousness of one's own lived body is the immediate response to seeing dance—a consciousness that seems to internalize the visual "other." My body may not rise out of my seat as the dancer leaps into the air, but I experience a kind of subliminal leap. At times, when I can both experience the leap and experience my experience of the leap, I can notice in myself a variety of bodily feelings: perhaps, a heaving of the chest, contractions of the abdomen, an intake of breath, an elongation of the torso that somehow is still bent into a seated position. The intercorporeal contact is unique and special—a depersonalized but strictly personal consummation. Perhaps this is one reason dance seems to strike so many as sexual. Not only does dance celebrate the living body, but insofar as it involves performance, it celebrates a duality that can achieve consummation.[1]

What painting achieves is for the eyes; what music achieves is for the ears; what dance achieves is for some totality of the senses through the eyes. This is what is meant by focusing on the concept of the lived body as particularly integral to dance.

Not only is it truer to the experience of dance, but it is also more faithful to Ingarden's concept of this first level to focus on the lived body rather than on the visual. Ingarden's first level of literature is phonetic, not visual. Yet reading is normally a visual activity. Ingarden argues,

> The first thing we experience [in reading] is the visual perception of these 'signs'. However, as soon as we 'see' printed signs . . . we perform something more than, or rather something different from, a mere visual perception. . . .
> The auditory apprehension of the phonetic form of the words is so closely related to the visual apprehension of the written form that the intentional correlations of these experiences . . . seem almost to be merely two aspects of the same 'verbal body'.[2]

The "mental act" (Husserl's terminology)[3] of which the dance is the intentional object cannot, therefore, be accounted for in terms of a visual act. The mental act that can count as the basic condition for perceiving dance is difficult to identify because we have no discrete word parallel to "seeing" or "hearing" to describe it. It is a mental act that requires our lived body as organism to function as a totality in the perception of the dance. This is not to say there is a constant use of all of our sensory apparatus in the perception of dance. Rather, because the dance, as intentional object, requires the individual dancer to be his or her lived body with all that that may entail concerning being a body-in-the-world, I too must be able to grasp it in terms of the totality of my lived body—my-body-being-in-the-world. This double corporeal presence seems unique to dance.

With notable exceptions, it seems to be the case that the creator of music must hear in order to provide music that can be made available. To perceive music requires hearing music. But none of this is, of course, a necessary condition of producing music. Obviously, a deaf person can write music; a deaf person could also perform music—these are possibilities, certainly, but strained and carrying with them a high potential for failure. On the other hand, can a mime do his or her miming without having seen, at least at some time or other in his or her life? Can we appreciate miming without seeing? There are some parallels in the other arts to what I am claiming in dance—namely, that the baseline sensory apparatus for creator and perceiver are similar. However, the relations are more tenuous in the other arts.

A caveat: the claim that I am making for the fundamentality of the lived body is limited to an account of what kind of conscious act is elemental in viewing dance—the primary stratum. It would be foolish, even at this level, to indicate that the viewer must experience a mental act identical to that of the choreographer or dancer(s) of a particular dance in order for him or her to count the experience as one of having "seen" the dance. The viewer could, for example, focus on only a single part of the dancer's body. This seems to be what is described in the following remark by Arlene Croce in her comments on the performance of an *Étude* by Struchkova: "On top of her partner's chest in a no-hands lift (but that was unimportant), she drew the whole house to her in a spellbound quiet, and there was nothing left *but her face*" [my emphasis].[4] (What is particularly surprising and suggestive in this comment is that it is the face that is focused upon—and the face in stillness—not a moving part of the body. On the other hand, it is to the face that we more often than not look in everyday life to understand the emotions of another person.) Alternatively, the intentional object might be, not one part of one dancer's body but an entire group of dancers. A brief excerpt from Croce's description of the end of *Deuce Coupe* might illustrate this experience: "The long, slow crescendo of tossing arms, lunges in plié, and backward bourées on point, with here and there a fall to the floor."[5]

I have suggested that the visual may be a necessary but not a sufficient condition for perceiving dance and that the lived body might be a more appropriate parallel to the phonetic stratum in literature. Two additional points require some comment, however, before we move on to the next stratum. First, with regard to the visual as a necessary condition. Although no one may have provided a dance performance that need not be seen, is it impossible? Could a blind person achieve aesthetic appreciation of a dance performance? There are some considerations that tempt me to answer this question with a yes. Blind persons can be taught to dance. They can hear sound as well as sense vibrations that can be carried through flooring surface. Perhaps some additional experience in touching, supplemented by description in words, might work to provide a blind person with enough access to a perceptual experience of a dance performance.

Second, why is the visual not a sufficient condition for view-ing dance? Do not people who merely see the dance also count as viewers of the dance? I cannot deny that seeing provides perceptual access to the dance as a work of art. However, it is difficult to conceive of "merely seeing" a dance performance as truly perceiving the dance. One situation might be that in which I barely see at all—for example, viewing a dance from so far away that intervening sounds and sights interfere, to the extent that I cannot sense clearly in terms of senses other than sight any more than in terms of sight itself. I would suggest that "merely seeing" the dance might be possible only for someone sighted but somatically paralyzed—that is, for someone who was paralyzed from birth and who thus had never experienced corporeal motion. The attempt to imagine an aesthetic experi-ence of moving bodies with no prior experience whatsoever of self-movement appears an impossible task: no *dance* emerges. Thus, even if I were to grant the plausibility of "merely seeing" a dance, at best such an experience would give only limited access to the work of art. The viewer would be totally unable to experience the dance aesthetically if his or her experience of it was limited to "merely seeing." To achieve any aesthetic value— any aesthetic satisfaction—the dance must be perceived through the lived body. The visual sense in itself cannot pro-vide the perceiver with that founding level of experience ade-quate to cocreate an aesthetic object. Using Ingarden's terminology, the perceiver would be incapable of "concretiz-ing" an aesthetic object; he or she could not have an aesthetic experience of this dance.

I have tried to find an analogy in dance of Ingarden's phonetic stratum. My suggestion is that this stratum, in dance, is not a visual stratum at all; rather, it is something that might be called a lived-body stratum.

Meaning Stratum

Ingarden's concern with the meaning level is primarily a con-cern with and an account of language. It would be inappropri-ate here to attempt either to unravel his theory of meaning or to criticize it, since such an enterprise would take us far afield from the scope of this paper. Suffice it to say that Ingarden's theory of meaning is an attempt to deny both the psychologist's view—that meaning of words or sentences is merely a mental experience—and the neopositivist view—that the meaning of a sentence is its verifiability. His theory requires hypostatizing "purely intentional correlates of the sentence"—an extraneous and problematic kind of entity.[6] For our purpose it is sufficient to indicate that there exists a separate stratum intermediate between the basic perceptual level and the level in which portrayed objects (such as fictional events and persons) are experienced from a particular perspective (schematized aspects). Two general issues require discussion in this section. The first one conjoins the question raised by Ingarden, "How do we know that we 'understand' words or sentences?"[7] with the question "What can be said of this understanding in relation to dance?" The second issue is, "How does the meaning stratum operate to found the next two strata?" Let us consider each of these issues in turn.

Ingarden's answer to the question of understanding words and sentences is:

> A living language forms a structured system of meanings which stand in definite formal and material relations to one another and which also exercise various functions in semantic units of greater complexity, particularly sentences.[8]

It is important, therefore, to consider the possibility of a language (or symbol system) for dance. Implicit in the meaning stratum for Ingarden is the concept of meaning units. However difficult it may be to construct an adequate theory of meaning for language (in its more limited reference), easy access to words, sentences, and paragraphs provides some sense of discrete units that is useful. A central problem in identifying this level for dance results from the lack of anything analogous to words. It is in connection with the absence of conventional units in dance that several interesting problems are generated.[9]

If there is a language for dance, presumably it can be captured in a notation. The existence of conventional units seems required for notation in order to provide a "score." The function of a score, according to Nelson Goodman, is "to specify the essential properties a performance must have to belong to the work."[10] There have been different attempts to provide scoring devices for dance. I will consder two quite different approaches that may well represent a number of others: the vocabulary of classical ballet and Labanotation.

There are words for classical ballet movements. Insofar as classical ballet comes to us as a rather rigid, limited form of dance, a vocabulary useful for describing these dances has been received with it. The following description is clear to someone else who is familiar with these terms: "My favorite moment [in *La Bayadère*] comes in the final waltz, when the three principal Shades are doing relevé-passé, relevé-attitude cambré to a rocking rhythm."[11] Classical ballet is in some sense static. The limited vocabulary generated to account for various movements is not sufficient for other forms of dance. Is it enough in classical ballet? Can a score be provided for classical ballet using words alone? How effective a score would such a series of words be, describing the number of *pliés,* by whom, where on the stage, in which direction, and so forth? As a nondancer I can pose these questions, but cannot answer them. However, even if it is possible to claim that words are enough to provide a score for classical ballet, it seems clear that words are not adequate to score other forms of dance. It is as if we attempted to score music with only ordinary words—such as sing "high," "low"—at our disposal.

As to Labanotation, there is nothing inherent in dance that denies the possibility of some kind of atomistic fracturing to allow the capture of significant elements in a notational score. According to Goodman, Labanotation is an attempt to do just that: "Labanotation passes the theoretical tests very well—about as well as does ordinary musical notation, and perhaps as well as is compatible with practicality."[12] As a nondancer, I do not know how well Labanotation functions to identify and reidentify the "same" dance for the dancer. I wonder how important it could be for a viewer of dance in helping to describe, identify, and retain the memory of a dance. Language helps us grasp, identify, and retain experiences not only so that we can talk about or criticize them but also so that we can remember them. Would access to an adequate score or a language of dance provide a viewer with tools to understand and remember a dance better?

One other idea on the subject of scoring might be added parenthetically. The development of holograms might provide a way to score dance that does not require two-dimensional atomistic fracturing. We see three-dimensionally in a hologram—a potentially useful way of capturing more of the multidimensionality of dance. Further, if we could create a continuous hologram of a dance, that continuity from beginning to end might capture in detail what actually occurs in dance and so produce a better dance score.

I have briefly discussed aspects of notation and scoring as belonging within the meaning stratum. These issues do not in any way exhaust what must be included in this level. Insofar as the meaning stratum is understood as grounding the third and fourth strata, some account of what might count as a basis for perceiving presented intentional objects from a schematized aspect must be given. Thus we confront the second issue. In literature the move is from understanding what words, sentences, and paragraphs mean to understanding situations, events, and persons. With respect to literature, knowing the meaning of the words in the text provides the basis for the reader's getting to know the fictional persons, events, and situations. The parallel in dance would be to understand how what is being perceived by the viewer provides the grounds for the viewer's coming to know what the dance is about.

One major difficulty derives from the fact that in everyday encounters with other persons we perceive feelings, emotions, attitudes, moods, as well as actions, without explicit recognition of the factors that ground our perceptions. In an attempt to analyze the basis for our descriptions of our experiences of other persons' actions and feelings, one set of mind–body theorists assumes that there are movements that we take in certain circumstances to be a particular action—for example, the self-propelled lifting of both feet from the floor simultaneously is perceived as jumping.[13] Given various circumstances, we might perceive someone as jumping rope, or trying to dislodge a ball from a high place, or competing in a broad jump contest. Thus the circumstances in which the movement occurs affect the description of the action. Insofar as feelings are presumed to be expressed by motions, no additional movement may be required by these theories to permit us to redescribe a particular action in terms that include the emotions of the doer. The expression of feeling or emotion is presumed to be determined by how the person moves or acts. "He jumped joyfully." Or, more idiomatically, "He jumped for joy." Yet, at the same time that redescription of a particular action can include emotions adverbially, the redescription seems implicitly to presume that the expression of emotion is an addendum to "neutral" bodily motion. In this view, movement and feeling seem implicitly to be understood as separate. Bodily movement in itself has no "color," but it can attain color through the expression of various emotions, recognition of which by another person is determined by sociocultural conventions that affix specific meanings to specific movements. Can these mind–body theorists provide an analysis of those factors that ground emotional distinctions? Where would they look to justify the assertion "He jumped for joy" rather than "He jumped" or "He jumped desperately"? Their view is already a presumptive analysis that, safely ensconced in the acceptance of the dichotomy of mind and body, seeks legitimizing by requiring further analysis. Those who accept this view might proceed by looking for discrete differences in movements, which could then be used to identify jumping for joy as opposed to jumping desperately. Another approach might include giving additional descriptions of the circumstances or situations in which the jumping occurred—all built on the assumption that specifications of the "how" of the jumping might be defined through sociocultural conventions.

If we accept the view, however, that the basic perceptual stratum of the dance is my lived body, the mind–body dichotomy disappears. The following remarks of Merleau-Ponty are suggestive.

> It is through my body that I understand other people.
>
> ·
>
> The sense of the gestures is not given, but understood, that is, recaptured by an act on the spectator's part.
>
> ·
>
> The gesture *does not make me think* of anger, it is anger itself.[14]

Understanding the joy or desperation of another precedes analysis. The body as "a power of natural expression"[15] is in the world and provides my grasp of the world. Insofar as meanings are etched on the world by the lived body, there cannot be a mind–body dichotomy. To paraphrase Merleau-Ponty's claim, "Movement, in the mover, does not translate ready-made meanings, but accomplishes them."[16]

The capacity of the lived body to constitute meaning in the

world can be understood to found the next two strata. This thesis will be tested as we explore these other strata.

Portrayed (Presented) Objects

For Ingarden, this stratum focuses on the claim that literary works of art are about fictional persons, places, events, and states of affairs. There is some parallel in dance that we might explore by focusing on changes in dance over the past forty-odd years.

Some dances—*Swan Lake,* for example—tell a story. The concept of portrayed objects, however, is not limited to stories in classical ballet. When dance was concerned to realize

> total formal cohesion, . . . the dance had to carry meaning . . . it had to be *about* something, the form had to be structured in such a way as to be symbolic—of an event, e.g., Weidman's *Lynchtown,* a drama, e.g., Graham's *Letter to the World,* or of a particular motif or quality, e.g., Humphrey's *Water Study* or Weidman's *Brahm's Waltzes, Opus 39 (PR,* 10).

Insofar as a dance is about something, presumably what it is about counts as a presented intentional object. If the dance is about an event, the dance presents the event as fictional. It is more difficult to show that a motif can count as a portrayed object. Presumably, however, to say that there is a motif in Humphrey's *Water Study* implies that the dance presents certain qualities which are what the dance is about. The dance portrays the rippling of a brook, the twistings and turnings as the brook moves toward the river, the quiet stillness of a pond, the threatening power of the storm-whipped waves of an ocean—the different ways water can appear. This may be called a motif in that all the various objects presented are examples of a unifying theme.

New forms of dance can be distinguished from older forms by the absence of attempts to present packaged meaning. John Cage has said,

> We are not in these dances and music saying something. We are simple-minded enough to think that if we were saying something we would use words. We are rather do-

ing something. The meaning of what we do is determined by each one who sees and hears it (*PR,* 12).

It will be useful to list some of the significant features of new dance before commenting further upon it. They have been described by Maxine Sheets-Johnstone in her paper "The Passage Rites of the Body: A Phenomenological Account of Change in Dance":

[1] Movement was no longer the *medium* of the dance but the dance itself; the body was no longer the *instrument* of dance but the dance itself. To be a human body and to move as humans move were synonymous.

[2] There were no longer any star bodies, bodies to be revered and emulated, special bodies which were always to be center stage.

[3] Props were no longer used in a theatrical sense. . . . Sheer physical presence, whatever its form, fleshly or otherwise, was to be fathomed and celebrated.

[4] The setting of the dance was . . . no longer exclusive. . . . "Any old bodies could dance any old place."

[5] By stripping away all traditional embellishments and ideas which were encrusted on the body of dance, [the new dance artists] ultimately arrived at its source: the unenhanced, pristine human body, a source of wonder, a source of utter conformity, a source to be fathomed, explored and celebrated.

[6] There were several (and more) ways of being a body. . . . [The] body could be simply a moving presence in the world (Cunningham). . . . It could be a collage body, a body which was at once an amalgam of many different styles of moving (Tharp). . . . It could be an environmental body, one which was at every moment engaged in an everyday world of people and things (Monk). . . . It could be a protean body taking on totally different shapes and/or altering its customary form (Nikolais) (*PR,* 14, 19, 22, 23, 25, 29).

The characteristics indicate important changes. Do we account for them by suggesting that the stratum of presented objects is not relevant to new dance? If we eliminate this stratum to accommodate the change, should we also not eliminate the meaning stratum and perhaps the schematized aspect stratum as well? Have we an adequate account of new dance if we suggest only one stratum—that of living-body-perception of living-body-in-motion? I do not think so.

Movements of the living body carry meaning with it. To "fathom, explore, and celebrate" the human body is not to indulge merely in pyrotechnics. Insofar as new dance explores possible ways of being a body-in-the-world, it is exploring the possible ways a body-in-the-world constitutes meaning. One example suggesting that the constitution of meaning by the body is recognized (at least by some) can be drawn from talk about "body language." Spontaneous movements, postures, ways of sitting, positioning arms and legs are understood as ways of reaching toward another, holding back, closing oneself off from another, enjoying, or hating. Psychologists are interested in sociocultural codification of what has always operated as a base level in communication, whether or not those communicating were explicitly aware of it. We might say that new dance, in investigating and celebrating body movements, creates "body language."[17] If moving has meaning and "movement [is] . . . the dance itself," then new dance has meaning. If it has meaning, then, although no deliberate intention to present prepackaged meaning may be involved, meaning is still present.

There are two points to be made on this issue: (1) John Cage suggests not that there is no meaning but that the audience is to determine the meaning; (2) the passages I have quoted from Sheets-Johnstone either explicitly name, or are suggestive, of intentional objects which can count as presented objects, though these objects are different in kind from the ones that older dance forms presented.

First, let us consider the idea that new dance requires the "meaning . . . [to be] determined by each one who sees and hears it." In all strata there are determinate characteristics intersubjectively available, as well as gaps that require the perceiver to fill in—that is, to schematize the stratum. Recognition of this schematic characteristic in both the third and fourth strata can be used to indicate and to understand changes in the form of dance. What seems to be apparent in the new dance is a proportionately high increase of indeterminacy.[18] Elements of determinacy have not been eliminated. Rather, the viewer is given much more opportunity to participate in the creation of the dance experience for him- or her-self—more latitude in envisioning what might count as an adequate, justifiable aesthetic object.

As to the second point, what do the quotations suggest about the form of possible presented objects or name explicitly, as in quotation 6, for example? Certainly, a dance may not be telling a story. Is it the case then that the new form of dance provides a greater variety of objects and that this is an important distinguishing feature? Can we allow that new dance provides presented objects but substantially widens the possibilities as to what might count as a presented object?

The following is Croce's description of Meredith Monk's *16 Millimeter Earrings*.

> This is a solo with films and props, a large-scale theatrical self-portrait for which the audience is delightfully prepared earlier in the evening by a middle-aged woman who crosses the stage and announces, "I'm Meredith's mother." The heroine of *16 Millimeter Earrings* is presented in the multiple manifestations of adolescence. . . . She is (and these are the meanings I see as I watch the piece—for others they may be different) precociously self-enchanted, dreaming on sex, self-expression, heartbreak, mutilation, and suicide. The meanings come from recurrent or parallel images in an interplay of films, objects, sound, and the performer's actions as she moves about the stage—which . . . suggests both a psychic interior and a real place, perhaps the girl's bedroom. The climax comes when, having put on a long, tattered flame-red wig (from a white tabletop there erupts a comet of red streamers, blown upward by a fan), she lowers a white drum onto her shoulders and animated film images of her own face appear on its surface, the hair tormented, one eye hugely distorted through an optical lens. At the end, flames rise again in a color film projected on the backcloth. In the film, a doll seen in silhouette is slowly cremated. As it falls, the heroine on the stage rises nude to take its place in the inferno. Over the sound system, her voice, singing "Greensleeves," breaks on the words "Alas my love—alas my love you do—" and *16 Millimeter Earrings* is over.[19]

In this excellent account there is a description of what is intersubjectively present and verifiable for all who witness the dance—"the long, tattered flame-red wig," "the film images of her own face," and so forth. There are other aspects of Croce's account that may count as either description or interpretation, depending on which aesthetic theory you subscribe to, but that are also intersubjectively present and verifiable—"heroine," "climax," "hair tormented." Further description—"precociously self-enchanted, dreaming on sex"—elicits Croce's comment that these are the meanings she finds and that the elements that support them are open to alternative interpretations. Finally, no additional explanation is given other than that the dance is "a large-scale theatrical self-portrait."

Croce's description of this dance is highly suggestive. Implications for alternative "filling-in" abound. Nonetheless, although the gaps are wide in this dance, there are still determinates which limit it and make it the piece that it is. There are obvious candidates for "objecthood," actual things such as props, for example. But there are other intentional objects as well that are determinates in this dance. There are less obvious candidates, more subtle presences—the fictional female moving through stages of life and then dying, for example, or the places in which she moves ("a psychic interior and a real place"). Granted there may be other dances that may be more difficult to fit into this stratum, yet I think it both possible and valid to incorporate them.

In reference to the first point, then, my suggestion is that new dance is characterized by giving less in the way of determinates and demanding more from the audience. In new dance, movement in many instances is simpler, more ordinary, yet at the same time more open to interpretation by the viewer. The more complicated dance movements tend to cut off alternative interpretations by the audience and have, in effect, fewer gaps. This is not to deny that older dance forms require cocreative endeavors from their audiences. Classical ballet requires "filling-in," but there is a difference. Consider the following remarks by Croce:

> I have often wondered why the greatest classical ballets don't look great but just look natural. And just as you, when you are sitting in the theatre, are just yourself sitting, neither standing nor kneeling, so the dancing is just what it is, something to which we dreamily assent and then go and smoke cigarettes. We don't assent mindlessly, of course, but neither do we, unless we are asses, dissent to the point of questioning those grand ultimates in which classical

dancing deals: Man is, Woman is. Life contains. We don't dissent because we realize that classical style leaves us free to fill in the blanks, and it's nobody's fault if we can't do it.[20]

The rigid form of classical ballet presents a "form of life" through traditional, established, "conventional" portrayed objects. These are possibly ways of body-being-in-the-world that are familiar. Perhaps that is why Croce says they "just look natural."

In reference to the second point, my suggestion is that in new dance there is a very great variety of presented objects possible. The audience, in effect, is given greater responsibility for what it "sees." New forms of dance, for example, may experiment with the seemingly all too familiar ways of body-being-in-the-world. Yet in seeing these ordinary movements actualized in an aesthetic experience we may find ourselves confronted by "strange forms of life": walking is something we have never seen before, walking is a presented object. Clearly possibilities for presented objects abound in dance: they may vary from the formal story elements in classical ballet to the bits and pieces of feelings of a character as in a Monk dance, and from "sheer physical presence, fleshly or otherwise," to the prosaic everyday movements of all of us. The genre of dance does not seem to rule out any of these as presented objects.

Schematized Aspects

The term *voices,* which is in current vogue in literary criticism although not used by Ingarden, may be close enough to help us understand what Ingarden meant by the schematized aspect stratum of literature. In literary works of art, this stratum refers to the point(s) of view from which the story is being told—whose voice(s) is (are) telling the story. The text may provide explicit information as to the point of view, but more often it requires a great deal of input from the reader to determine whose description the text may be providing. (Consider Virginia Wolf's *To The Lighthouse,* for example.) Presumably Ingarden named this stratum "schematized" aspect because the aspect is frequently sketchily offered, and only in skeletal form in the texts. But by "schematized" Ingarden is also again referring to his claim that there are gaps in a work of art—that, although we have been given determinate elements, there is room for the perceiver to fill in. These gaps are present in all strata.

Aspect can be understood as a general term that includes the experience of perspective. Whereas *perspective* is usually limited to objects of perception, *aspect* can be used to cover all conscious experience. That is, whatever we experience, we experience from a certain point of view, from a certain aspect. It is by virtue of our seeing an object from whatever perspective we do see it that we conceive or construe it to be whatever we deem it to be. The object, in terms of its properties, is given in one or more limited number of perspectival views. But we do not need all of the perspectival views, only that total number sufficient to bring to us "the objective properties of a thing."[21]

How is this stratum to be identified in dance? Insofar as a dance may be "telling a story," we may have some concern with identifying which character's point of view is dominant. However, dance is more a spectacle and less a description. The audience is free to focus on the character dancing center stage or the character watching from a position off to the side. Even when it may not be clear that the dance can count as a story of some sort, there will still be some interest in trying to understand from whose point of view presented objects are given. For example, Croce's description of Monk's *16 Millimeter Earrings* suggests that the audience may consider that the portrait is not a self-portrait but rather Meredith's mother's point of view, on the grounds that the dance is introduced by a middle-aged woman claiming to be Meredith's mother. We may not be able to answer the question of whether the dance is or is not presented from Meredith's mother's point of view, but it is a provocative question, and the answer provided by the viewer of the dance must make a difference to that viewer's experience of the dance. Point of view applies even when there is no narrative. Whenever there is a presented object, it must be seen in some aspect or other. Frequently the aspect is implicit and not recognized as such.

The stratum of schematized aspects also concerns technical elements of staging and the affect this can have on an audience. One characteristic of new forms of dance seems to be that there is "no longer any privileged vantage point. . . . Each individual perspective was regarded as an artistically random but fully viable center about which the dance radiated" (*PR*, 23). The elimination of the proscenium arch in some new dance might well be accounted for in terms of this stratum; that is, there may be a deliberate attempt by the choreographer to vary the "distancing" of the audience—for example, by placing the dance in the midst of the audience. The amount of distancing achieved, however, is still part of the perceiver's "filling in" of the givens. In this stratum, as well as the stratum of presented objects, the new forms of dance have not only opened up possibilities for the dancer/choreographer, but they have also provided an opportunity for more cocreative activity by the audience.

Summary

There is that in the dance performance that is available to anyone to view—some intersubjective basis which, without further adumbration, can be assumed to be the work of art. Insofar as it becomes an aesthetic experience for a particular viewer, she or he will have cocreated from this available public work of art an aesthetic object that has aesthetically valuable characteristics.

I have attempted to use the four strata from Roman Ingarden's aesthetic theory in his description of the literary work of art to provide a description of dance. I have claimed that we may understand the primary stratum of dance as the lived-body stratum. Perceiving the dance cannot be an experience exclusive to a single sense, but rather encompasses a congeries of sense that can, perhaps, be summed up as the lived-body stratum. It has seemed particularly useful to employ Merleau-Ponty's concept of the lived body to describe dance, although it does raise the question that if the lived body is to count as the fundamental distinguishing feature of dance, then how is dance to be differentiated from ordinary lived-body experience? In other words, within a phenomenological framework, body-being-in-the-world is understood as the basis for all perceptual experience; how, then, single it out as particularly relevant to dance? Perhaps an answer to this question would tell us something about the dance that is unique to it as an art form. Further, it might tell us something about the centrality of dance to life. However many questions it raises, and whatever those questions might be, the lived body does seem to be an accurate designation of the basic stratum in the viewer's experience of dance.

Notes

1. "A new avenue of relating thus opened up for performer and audience alike in which each was an equal partner in the dance" (Maxine Sheets-Johnstone, "The Passage Rites of the Body: A Phenomenological Account of Change in Dance." A much shorter version of this unpublished paper appeared in *Leonardo* 11 (1978):197–201 under the title "An Account of Recent Changes in Dance in the U.S.A." Hereafter referred to as *PR*. Sheets-Johnstone's comment is about new forms of dance. I am suggesting that although equality may have been achieved only in these new forms of dance, what is available to achieve equality is already present to some degree or other in the perception of any dance.

2. Roman Ingarden, *The Cognition of the Literary Work of Art* (Evanston, Ill.: Northwestern University Press, 1973), 19, 21.

3. See Edmund Husserl's *Logical Investigations*, trans. J. N. Findlay (New York: Humanities Press, 1970). Briefly, Husserl's "mental act" is contrasted with sensation, *not* physical act. Mental acts include judging, perceiving, and imagining. A primary characteristic that distinguishes the mental act from sensation is intentionality. See particularly vol. 2, investigation 5, "On Intentional Experiences and their 'Contents'," 533–658.

4. Arlene Croce, *Afterimages* (New York: Vantage Press, 1977), 8.

5. Ibid., 18.

6. A summary of Ingarden's theory of meaning can be found in his *Cognition of the Literary Work of Art*, 24ff. A full account is in his *Literary Work of Art*. (Evanston: Northwestern University Press, 1973).

7. *Cognition*, 24.

8. Ibid., 29.

9. Nelson Goodman has provided us with interesting criteria for languages of art. Although I am clearly using his ideas, I do not intend any intensive account of his criteria, however provocative and useful they may be.

10. Nelson Goodman, *Languages of Art* (Indianapolis: Bobbs-Merrill, 1968), 212.

11. Croce, *Afterimages*, 72.

12. Goodman, *Languages of Art*, 217.

13. I realize that I have put together a number of discriminable theories that have been and are continuing to be refined in important ways. Some theorists make much of "adverbials" and explicitly deny that their theories reflect a mind–body dichotomy. However, in general these theories seem opposed to a phenomenological view, and it is this gross distinction that I am drawing upon. See, for example, sec. 3, "Body, Mind, and Death," in Paul Edwards and Arthur Pap, *Introduction to Philosophy* (New York: Free Press, 1973), 172–83.

14. Maurice Merleau-Ponty, *Phenomenology of Perception* (London: Routledge & Kegan Paul, 1962), 186, 185, 184.

15. Ibid., 181.

16. Ibid., 178.

17. It might be interesting to consider an analogy with poetry in terms of Merleau-Ponty's notion of poetry as "authentic language" or "first language."

18. I am suggesting something comparable to the notions of "readerly" and "writerly" found in Roland Barthes's *S/Z,* trans. Richard Miller (New York: Farrar, Strauss & Giroux, 1974), 4.

19. *Afterimages,* 341–42.

20. Ibid., 330.

21. Ingarden, *Literary Work of Art,* 263.

Languages and Non-Languages of Dance

Albert A. Johnstone

Is dance a language? A first point needing elucidation is the question itself. For the aesthetician the question is perhaps whether dance should be characterized as the expression of feeling and of views about the world or the human condition. For the anthropologist and the sociologist the emphasis is rather on the extent to which dance reflects and articulates the values and world view of the particular culture or socioeconomic structure in which it arises. For the semiotician and the logician the question is whether dance functions as a symbolic system with a code relating symbols and signified meaning. In what follows we shall be concerned with this third construal of the question.

Our broad task then will be to sift through the wide variety of elements present in dance with a view to determining whether these elements function symbolically. Such a screening process will presuppose some notion as to what is to count as a symbolizing relation. We shall decree a relation to be a symbolizing relation if and only if it is a four-term relation of standing for, where in the eyes of a symbolizer something, the symbol, stands for some other thing, the symbolized, within the context of a particular activity—for example, informing, giving orders, entertaining, or playing. The relation is an intentional rather than a natural one in that it is a relation established or observed by the symbolizer, who may be any conscious being from a honeybee to God. The setting up of the relation is not an end in itself but is preparatory to the playing of some game.

What we shall examine is the dance as it appears to the spectator rather than to the dancer or to the choreographer. This is because we are concerned with theatre dance and not with ritual dance, for instance, or recreational, therapeutic, exhortative, communicational, or courtship dance. Theatre dance is a spectacle—it is created for an audience—and hence what it contains or does not contain is what is there or not there for the spectator. In keeping with this fact, the general approach adopted will be that of experiential description. Since the attitude adopted will be quasi-phenomenological, a word of caution should be inserted with regard to the phenomenological attitude of noninvolvement or detachment. It would be mistaken to assume, as for instance David Best does, that the aim of the phenomenological attitude as applied to dance is to afford an experience of dance free from prejudice and supposition, or, as it were, an untainted view of the dance.[1] Such an experience could only be that of the dance seen through the newly opened eyes of an infant, thus an experience without recognition, without association, without expectation, and consequently bereft of the greater part of its meaning. The end sought by the phenomenological attitude is not a presuppositionless glimpse, but a glimpse at presuppositions.

Somewhat conveniently for the purposes of analysis, three distinct dance forms have appeared successively on the scene of American dance. These are the classical ballet; modern dance, as exemplified by Isadora Duncan, Martha Graham, and Doris Humphrey; and the new modern dance as exemplified by Merce Cunningham, Paul Taylor, and Tricia Brown. The three forms suggest the possibility of a division into three distinct types of dance, termed respectively narrative dance, expressive or depictive dance, and nonthematic or formal dance. These types of dance, in turn, suggest three types of movement, briefly describable as follows: *narrative movement* is movement essential to the unfolding of a narrative; *expressive* or *depictive movement* is movement which portrays feeling, nature, or atmosphere; *nonthematic* or *formal movement* is any dance movement which cannot be classed under either of the two preceding headings. At first glance the evolution of dance forms from narrative to expressive to formal might seem to be a process of successive elimination, but it would be more accurately described as a shift in emphasis. The three types of movement are commonly found in a single dance, and in certain dances are so blended as to make any labelling of the dance tenuous. Furthermore, it would be a mistake to require that individual dance movements each fall into only one of the three types of movement. Narrative movements, for instance, are almost invariably modulated with expressive and/or formal overtones: a movement of flight, while essential to the unfolding of a plot, may also be both expressive and formal. Thus to speak of a movement as being of a certain type is in reality to speak of a certain aspect or function of the movement. In the discussion which follows, the three types of movement will be examined in turn with a view to determining to what extent each of them involves symbolization.

Narrative Movement

On a cursory view it might seem that since the dance narrative relies little if at all on the spoken or printed word, the multiplicity of movements constituting the dance must play the role that language plays in literature; the tale is told in movement, just as it might have been told in English or in some other language. It is fairly obvious that there must be some truth in this summation of the situation, although it is much less obvious what the correct account of that truth is. A dance narrative turns out, on scrutiny, to be a somewhat complex affair. It contains three structurally distinct levels at which some form of symbolism or "telling" might occur. First of all, there is the relation of the dancers to the characters personified. Secondly, there is the relation of these characters to particular individuals in the actual world. Finally, on a different level again, there are the possible relations of symbolization within the narrative itself; for instance, relations between the various movements and what these movements indicate of a character's intentions, attitudes, and personality. We shall look briefly at each of these three levels in turn.

Dancer-to-Narrative Symbolism

The question of whether the relation of the dancer to the character in the narrative is a symbolizing relation seems straightforward enough. Yet the most casual pecking at the matter soon uncovers mildly puzzling complications. The dancer must be identical with the character in the dance narrative, since the one individual on the stage during the dance is both the dancer and the character, e.g., Martha Graham and Jocasta. And yet the relation between the two cannot simply be a relation of identity, for then the two would not be two but one. How is such a situation possible?

Let us begin with the concrete: a dancer enters bounding exuberantly across the stage, halts abruptly on noticing a hunched figure, and, as astonishment turns to compassion, half approaches, hesitates, then steals softly out. The first point to be noted is that what is seen is not to be described as a body in motion, or as limbs going through movements, or even as an organism, but as a living human person. A turning of the head is seen as a noticing; faltering steps as an internal debate; while a sequential infolding of face, neck, and torso is seen as a wave of tenderness. The exuberance, surprise, compassion, and misgivings are visible there in the movements and postures. It follows, of course, that the individual seen is the character in the narrative. The latter is the person who is surprised and hesitant, exuberant, and perplexed.

Yet if the individual seen is the character in the narrative, then what has become of the dancer? The dancer is surely the one who bounds exuberantly and holds the transfixed stance. This is undeniable. But it is equally undeniable that the dancer feels no surprise on seeing the hunched figure; the same figure has been there at each rehearsal for weeks. In point of fact the dancer feels no compassion, no doubts, and little exuberance; only the character feels these things. The person, there, quite visible to the spectators, is admittedly the dancer, but the dancer shrouded in a sentient aura conjured by his or her movements. What is seen is the illusion he or she creates, helped along to be sure by costumes, props, lighting, and sound, the illusion of such and such a character in such and such a setting living through certain incidents and experiences.

The illusion created by the dancer is not an optical illusion in the usual sense. The character's legs are after all the dancer's legs, and the movements the character makes are those the dancer makes. The illusion is not a change of shape or substance, as when straight lines look bent or some non-red thing appears red. It is closer in nature to a mistake in judgement. It consists of expectations or assumptions created by a certain spectacle, assumptions rather like one's assumption that the print on a page in the newspaper continues under the thumb holding the page. The dancer executes certain movements and is attributed certain attitudes, feelings, and beliefs. The latter are illusory. The movement, of course, remains what it is, a very real movement in its least modulations.

Let us step back a moment to see if we have uncovered a symbolizing relation. The dancer–character illusion is certainly a relation involving two terms, the dancer's movements and the character's movements, but is this relation a symbolizing one? It would seem not. To produce an illusion is not ipso facto to symbolize anything. Moreover, in the situation as described, there is nothing to make the dancer's movements *stand for* the character's movements. If they are to do so, this can only be in the context of some activity, but the only activity encountered thus far is that of the producing of illusions. This latter activity is at best the mere setting up of a correlation. With a correlation established, a game might begin, but the game itself must be some further activity.

A point we have thus far neglected is the fact that the illusion is known to be an illusion. Not only is there a prior awareness that the events taking place are sham, but the character's manner of moving, the scenery, costumes, stage props, lighting, and sound all concur to belie a realistic interpretation of the apparent sequence of events. The discrepancy between fact and fiction necessitates some element of complicity in a game of narrative pretense. At the very least, obvious incongruities must be discounted. In Balanchine's *The Prodigal Son,* for instance, one must pretend with the afflicted youth that the emptiness cupped in his eager hands is water and that the floor boards over which he is dragging himself are the road back to his father's house. Without such pretense the narrative would dissolve, relinquishing the stage to an array of curiously costumed dancers.

The element of pretense transforms the relation of dancer to narrative-character quite beyond that found in mere illusion. The situation in narrative dance indeed becomes analogous to that in make-believe practiced by children. In the latter activity there are good grounds for speaking of a symbol and a symbolized. The little boy pushing a line of blocks and making puffing noises is pretending that the blocks are a train. In this game the line of blocks may be said to be a symbol for the train, the puffing to stand for the noise of a train, and the matchsticks lying on the blocks to go proxy for the passengers. Symbolism of this kind might be termed *ludic symbolism*. That dance narrative involves a system of ludic symbolism is suggested by the presence of props, the function of which is to stand for various elements in the narrative. In this function the props are joined by the backdrop and stage, and sometimes by lighting and sound doing duty for daylight or a storm or some cosmic force. Once it is granted that the setting functions symbolically, it is difficult to avoid adding that the dancer stands for the character in the narrative.

In systems of ludic symbolism generally, the meta-semantic rules are somewhat strict on the matter of what qualifies as a symbol. In the train game mentioned earlier, no normal child would willingly change the respective roles of the blocks, matches, and puffing. Similarly, a dance would not have a drinking cup symbolized by two Siamese cats or a dagger symbolized by a handful of feathers. The symbol must resemble the symbolized object closely enough in its geometric characteristics to be identifiable as the sort of thing it is meant to symbolize.

Resemblance plays an equally important role in the symbolizing of the narrative events. Western theater dance contains no narrative movement peculiar to dance. Unlike expressive and nonthematic movement, which may take on forms to be found nowhere except in dance, the comprehension of narrative events requires little knowledge or skill beyond that necessary for interpreting everyday behavior and commerce in the Western world. The narrative unfolds with activities, meetings, manifestations of surprise, curiosity, and affection, behavior appropriate to attack or flight, and so on. No specialized training is required in spectating or in interpreting movement codes, so that in the main there is little difficulty in following the plot. In certain historical narratives or in tales transposed from literature, some prior acquaintance is nevertheless often useful. A comprehension of the plot of *Giselle*, in particular, is considerably enhanced by the services of a guide. Generally speaking, however, the narrative is self-explanatory. As Balanchine is reputed to have stated, "There are no mothers-in-law in ballet,"[2] which is to say, whoever the characters and whatever the relationships among them, the characters and relationships are clear in purely visual terms. Most contemporary choreographers would agree: whatever the situation, it must be immediately apparent. Thus, in ludic symbolism as found in a dance narrative, close resemblance between symbol and sym-bolized would seem to be a de facto necessary condition. It is not a sufficient condition, since, in addition, an attitude of pre-tense is necessary.

There would seem to be a quite defendable sense, then, albeit a broad one, in which narrative dance may be said to be a language. A narrative is told in movement in the sense that it is acted out. The acting out is pretense supported essentially by resemblance and helped along by illusory effects.

Narrative-to-World Symbolism

Let us now turn our attention to the second relation: the possibility that the character personified by the dancer sym-bolizes an actual historical personnage. By the most liberal stan-dards of computation, only a surprisingly small number of narrative dances may be aptly described as the reenactment of some historical event. In the vast majority of cases both the characters and incidents of the narrative are fictional, in the sense that there are no historical personnages or occurrences which they might be said to represent or depict. Among the rare exceptions to this general trend are Lester Horton's *Salome (The Face of Violence),* possibly Maud Allan's *Vision of Salome,* Martha Graham's *Seraphic Dialogue,* and Doris Humphrey's *La-ment for Ignacio Sanchez Mejías.*

A type of dance more frequently encountered is one contain-ing what might be termed a sociohistorical narrative. Here the dancer plays a character typical of a certain period, historical situation, or social class, rather than some particular individual such as Joan of Arc or Diogenes. This is the case notably for dance having a message to convey, or as it might be termed, enunciative dance. Examples are legion. The dancers in Mur-ray Louis's *Junk Dances* might be said to represent modern ur-ban couples of modest income, those in Lester Horton's *The Beloved* to represent the model of a Victorian couple. Donald McKayle's *Rainbow 'Round My Shoulder* centers on convicts in a southern chain gang, while Alvin Ailey's *Masekela Language* portrays blacks in contemporary South Africa. Daniel Nagrin, in his dance *The Peloponnesian War,* might be said to portray successively people of various eras, types, and classes caught up in war. The dancers in Alwin Nikolais's *Sanctum* might some-what tenuously be seen to represent living creatures playing their absurd roles on the cosmic stage. In all of these dances some fairly clear sense can be given to the notion of a symbol and a symbolized.

In both types of biographical narrative dance—sociohistorical and nonsociohistorical—conventional devices for designation play a quite minor role in the spectator's grasping of the symbolizing relation. The general tendency is to let the dance tell its own story without help from extraneous sources such as titles, program blurbs, or placards paraded on the stage. Generally the spectator is expected to take his or her cues from costumes, setting, and the plot itself to establish whatever connection the choreographer may have wished the spectator to make. The relation of symbol to symbolized is again one of depiction through resemblance. In modern dance, denotation is iconic; that is, it relies on recognition and identification through the quite natural device of the seeing of resemblance. If dancers are to portray Harlem blacks, they will not appear as Nordic blonds decked in the ceremonial regalia of Plains Indians; they must bear some close resemblance to the characters they are playing, sufficiently close for the average spectator to identify them in the given setting. Generally speaking, the sole denotative convention operative in the identification process is the spectator's assumption that the characters will possibly symbolize some historical personnage or type of person.

Conversely, where the degree of similarity is insufficient, the narrative dance is not biographical. In Merce Cunningham's *Squaregame*, the characters, dressed like players in training, move about four piles of duffle bags in a setting representing a gymnasium, but it would be quite unwarranted to see the characters as symbolizing athletes. Their behavior and interactions are not particularly typical of athletes. The movement patterns into which their activity meshes are loosely suggestive of a game, but the notion that the game played is symbolic of games in general or of certain types of games has a distinct flavor of gratuity. Similarly, in Alwin Nikolais's *Tent* and Paul Taylor's *Insects and Heroes,* although the dancers play the roles of human beings there is no serious suggestion of a message about human nature or the human condition. The resemblance between a particular feature of the narrative and some feature of reality is too fugitive and unsystematic for the former to be seen as illustrative or typical of the latter. Once again resemblance or degree of resemblance plays the crucial role. Nelson Goodman's curious remark regarding representational art, "Resemblance disappears as a criterion of representation,"[3] flies in the face of denotative practices in contemporary narrative dance.

Biographical dance obviously adds a dimension over and above simple narrative dance. Resemblance plays a key role in determining whether a narrative dance is biographical. In any narrative dance attention naturally focuses on the make-believe character strutting and fretting his hour upon the stage. However, the biographical character evokes an additional retinue of expectations, recognitions, and empathies. Phenomenologically speaking, the relation between character and world essential to biographical dance may take a variety of forms. In the minimal case, the character triggers a mere intermittent labelling of him- or her-self as so-and-so, while at the opposite extreme the character colors the events with dramatic intensity. Whatever the mode of presence of the character's relation to the world, it is an added dimension over and above that of ludic symbolism.

Movement-to-Narrative Symbolism

Movement can be highly informative. It may reveal the mover's feelings and intentions and, indeed, his or her beliefs, character, and personality. From this there arises a certain temptation to speak of such movement as a language. Do we have here, then, a further form of symbolization, one in which the symbol and the symbolized are elements within the narrative itself?

A first obvious point to be made is that whatever the value of the movement for the revelation of character or feeling, it does not follow that an analogous symbolizing relation exists between the movement and each aspect of the narrative. Movement might be a language in which certain aspects of the tale are told, but it is not a language in which the whole tale is told. The dancer's (or rather, the character's) buoyant entrance, in the example mentioned earlier, may be indicative of good spirits, the silent huddle indicative of brooding concentration, and perhaps the abrupt halt indicative of normal visual acuity and commendable environmental responsivity. However, the soaring leap is not *indicative* of a soaring leap—it *is* a soaring leap. If narrative dance contained a comprehensive indicative language with movements playing a role analogous to that of words, then it would require a vastly expanded system of indicators to symbolize each of the various narrative events: the leaps, huddlings, and so on.

It seems indisputable that at least some movement may rightly be said to symbolize the disposition or sentiments of the person moving. Consider, for instance, a mimed mopping of the brow, or a look of puzzlement thrown to a third party in the context of everyday life. In view of their conventional nature, both qualify as instances of gesture language, but they share a further interesting feature: they are strongly imitative of behavior appropriate to the actual situation. The person who pretends to mop his or her brow is feeling hot, and the person throwing a puzzled look is actually puzzled. Both are communicating actual feelings by imitating the relevant appropriate behavior. The situation is essentially the same when a person leaps for joy to show appreciation, or ostensibly shuffles papers to communicate that he or she is busy. Feigned performance has been seen as a first important step toward communication—by Englefield, for example, who gives as an instance a dog's fruitless scratchng at a door handle with the apparent aim of soliciting assistance.[4] Whatever one's evaluation of the thesis, it must be acknowledged that such feigned behavior appears to involve a symbolizing relation: the feigned activity on one hand, and an actual feeling or desire on the other, the first serving to communicate the second.

Unfeigned behavior apparently admits of no such construal. It can be quite revealing of some intimate inner life, but not symbolic of it. A brooder's fixed gaze, for instance, may be highly indicative of his or her preoccupation with some future plans, but it is symbolic neither of that preoccupation nor of the brooder's plans. It is a facet of a complex activity and cannot be aptly construed as standing for, or going proxy for, some other, perhaps private, facet of that activity. Similar observations hold, *mutatis mutandis,* for unfeigned emotion: a genuine gasp of surprise, cringe of fear, or scream of rage are each indicative of feelings and perhaps intentions or beliefs, but they are not symbolic of them. To express feelings, as opposed to repressing them, is not to symbolize them but to give them free rein. Strictly speaking, the expression "body language," in present vogue, involves a misuse of the term *language.* Behavior reveals feelings and attitudes in much the same way that handwriting reveals personality. The former are operative in any human activity, and are plainly visible if one cares to look. This does not make the activity a language expressing those attitudes, except in a tenuously metaphorical sense.

Narrative dance does of course contain an intranarrative language insofar as the characters use gestures to communicate. Bereft of speech, they might employ any means at hand: beckonings, dismissals, or a Gallic shrug. They may also on occasion resort to the symbolism of feigned behavior, as when a feigned mopping of the brow is used to communicate a real state of discomfort. The presence of such language is, however, of somewhat marginal interest in the present context.

Expressive/Depictive Movement

Now that a jogging path of sorts has been roughly cut through the intricacies of the dance narrative, the moment is perhaps opportune to observe that the narrative is an essentially subsidiary aspect of dance. Admittedly, in many dances the focus of the spectacle is the narrative, but in no dance is it in virtue of the narrative that the spectacle is a dance. If the spectacle consisted exclusively of those movements necessary to the enacting of the narrative, it would be more aptly characterized as mime. To declare it to be a dance would be as little justified as to declare it to be opera without music or theater without dialogue. The spectacle is termed a dance in virtue of the features it contains other than the narrative ones, which features may be guardedly characterized as *nonfunctional* or *nonnarrative movement*. This kind of movement is the subject of the two remaining sections of this paper.

One nonnarrative feature of dance, expressive/depictive movement, is distinguished by the fact that its function is to portray or to express some aspect of the world. Since some expressive/depictive movement is a natural extension of a practice found in narrative movement, we might do well to consider it first.

Simulation is already operative in ludic symbolism as the means of setting up the resemblance of symbol to symbolized. To play an angry character, the dancer simulates the movements and manner of moving characteristic of a person who is angry. In like fashion, to play a swan the dancer simulates swan movements (with the possible exception of movements characteristic of death throes). The extension of the procedure is natural enough. For example, from the lacustrine swan and the firebird, it is but a short step to the living eagle with its aloof stance and soaring flight. The latter become the material of a portrait in Edwin Strawbridge's *The Eagle*. Again, it is but a short additional step to the simulation of the movement in some natural phenomenon. The sinuous convolutions of rising smoke animate the dancer in Ruth St. Denis's *Incense,* while in Doris Humphrey's *Water Study* the combined movements of the dancers evoke the movements of water, its breaking, sloshing, and quiet undulations. It is difficult to conceive of instances of movement for which such simulation is precluded; simulation might in fact be undertaken of any natural movement phenomenon which catches the choreographer's fancy.

Dance has a widespread reputation as being expressive of feeling or of the human psyche, so much so that kinetic expressiveness is sometimes taken to be its distinguishing trait. In its minimal form, this expressiveness is to be found in narrative movement, where a dancer playing a given character is led to simulate certain moods and emotions, that is, to act as would a person having those feelings. The expressiveness which concerns us is that over and above what would be required for the strictly factual details of the narrative. In what does this expressiveness consist, and how, if at all, does it relate to depiction?

At this juncture an illustration might be helpful. Martha Graham's dance, *Lamentation,* is a paradigm for the symbolization of emotion. A dancer swathed in an enveloping, clinging black shroud sits on a low platform, feet askew, faceless, body twisted, contorting, writhing, the tubular line of the arms alternately rising diagonally and collapsing into an inward churning of forearms cradled by a rocking, heaving torso. As a portrayal of grief, the dance is overwhelmingly successful; the question that concerns us is why this should be so.

One answer that has been put forth is that there is no real question. The argument runs as follows: the dance may be said to exemplify the predicate "grief," and since the dancer feels no actual grief the exemplification is metaphorical. Moreover, the answer runs, the question why the predicate applies metaphorically has as little answer as the question of why it applies literally. Such would seem to be a fair statement of Goodman's position,[5] a position that is singularly unilluminating. It leaves unexplained, and declares inexplicable, the quite evident fact that *Lamentation* is superior as a metaphorical exemplification of grief to other dances—for instance, to St. Denis's *Incense* or to Nikolais's *Gallery*—and that it is a rather poor metaphorical exemplification of certain other predicates—for instance, "eternal femininity." Metaphor generally would seem grounded in aspectical similarity,[6] and the determination of the nature of the similarity is a matter for empirical inquiry.

If we ask in what way expressive movements differ from movements of mere simulation, perhaps the first response to come to mind is that they differ through accentuation or exaggeration. The twisted contortions of the body seized with pain, the huddled misery cradled in a monotonous rocking, are all exaggerated versions of everyday behavior. The technique used here is similar in nature to that of caricature. Such a technique is quite prevalent in narrative dance: supplication is represented by wildly outstretched arms, interest by a gaping stare, rumination by a belabored brow and an accentuated stroking of the chin. A substantial part of expressive movement is just such caricaturizing.

The term *caricature,* however, is inappropriate for much of the movement to be found in *Lamentation:* the movement of the arms is symbolic, symbolic of an inward churning which periodically, through an upward surge of the crooked tubular spout, finds an outlet in a grotesque wail; the long diagonal folds reflect the tense angularity of the limbs; the shrouded head, the disarray of the feet, the constricting swaths about arms and legs, are symbolic of the absence of opening toward the world, of a total absorption in the turmoil of pain. The movement of the dance is symbolic of the feeling of grief through being dynamically and vectorially congruent with the movement constitutive of the feeling. The dance is an instance to which Maxine Sheets-Johnstone's more general statement of the matter applies:

> When we look at a dance we see a form which, because of its very organization, its very dynamic flow—the way forces are released, attenuated, checked, solidified, diffused—is symbolically expressive of a feeling. The very specific dynamic flow of the dance, the very specific qualitative or-

ganization of force, makes the dance in and of itself "gloomy" or "joyful."[7]

The notion of dynamic and vectorial congruence requires perhaps some further elaboration. The issue is beclouded considerably by a somewhat prevalent confusion as to the relation of feeling to bodily movement. Commentators on the question, for example, those as widely divergent in their approaches as Monroe Beardsley and David Best, agree that feeling and movement are only contingently related. This assessment leads Beardsley to say, "Slow cheerfulness and fast solemnity are not logical contradictions, they are just very unlikely or empirically impossible."[8] It leads Best to entertain the following strange supposition: "If human beings were very different and, for example, made quick, light, vivacious movements, with smiling faces, when they were thoroughly miserable. . . ."[9] There is something quite seriously amiss in suppositions of this kind. Not only can the dancer in *Lamentation* not make light, vivacious steps, but no human being, not even one endowed with a different nature, can be overwhelmed with grief and make such steps. The impossibility here is a *logical* impossibility. Grief is, among other things, a quite specific state of muscular tension and energy flow, convulsion alternating with listlessness, and this state (whether as felt or as seen) is logically incompatible with the energy flow and tension dynamics of lightness and vivacity. To make movements involving the latter, whether spontaneously or with obstinate determination, is no longer to be in the specific state of tension called "grief." It is to be either in some state of emotion other than grief or to be in a state of quelled grief.

Suppose for a moment that, unconvinced by the above reflections, we should set out to make the acquaintance of a pure feeling or emotion in order to determine in what relationship it stands to body movement. Our first introspective finding would be that nowhere is there to be found anything that might be appropriately termed a mental state. What is found is a quasi–three-dimensionality, a bodily complex of interrelated feelings, strains, tensions, and pressures of various sorts, the whole organized around some task or center of attention or interest. This is the entity which Edmund Husserl calls *der Leib,* the lived body, and analyzes at length in the second volume of his *Ideas.*[10]

A second finding would be that the emotion suffuses the

entire body. While attention might center first on bubblings or constrictions of the chest and throat, it is only by arbitrary decree that the location of the feeling could be restricted to these two regions. A lightness of the head, limpness of the back, or agitation of the fingers have every right to be included as ingredients of the feeling. No part of the body is uninvolved. A thrill, a surge of joy, a wave of regret permeate everywhere.

Thirdly, and most importantly for our present purpose, the feeling is not a pure quality, like tomato juice in a glass. It is a certain complex of tactual strains, stresses, and energies. Each emotion has its own specific set of tensions, its own dynamics, and any movement made is made with the tensions and dynamics peculiar to that emotion. The topographical congruence of the body as felt with the body as seen makes for a visual tension corresponding to each tactual tension. Body "language," the reading of feeling in visible movement, is elementary solid geometry.

On the question of the relation of feeling to movement, a great deal is often made of the apparent conventionality of much typical feeling behavior. A smile, a leap, or a shout are claimed to be in a quite contingent relation to joy. The view is doubly simplistic. First, the parting of lips, the leaping, and the shouting are each done with a specific degree of tension constitutive of joy. The same actions done in fear or in anger have a distinguishably different tension structure. Secondly, a hopping about or a cry are outlets for energy under pressure and are thus not totally artificial. What might be construed as conventional is an individual's proclivity toward one outlet rather than another—stamping, for example, rather than shouting—and also any further elaboration of the kind whereby a bouncing shuffle becomes a raucous leap. Generally speaking, however, the role of convention in feeling behavior has been overemphasized. The impressive display of rage of which a newly born infant is capable is not imputable to the proficiency of pedagogical methods. Feelings are not taught. It is possible to teach what to fear, when to fear, what to do in a frightening situation, how to overcome fear, or how to make it pass, for example, but the trembling hands, constricted throat, and petrification are not the carefully fashioned products of some acquired technique.

To sum up, a feeling or emotion is a complex organic structure of interrelated and changing tensions and bodily dynam-

ics. This fact is crucial to the question of expression in dance.
Since any emotion is a certain structure of tensions, it may be
symbolized in dance by movements similar in structure vectorially and dynamically. Hence a succession of joyful leaps given
by a dancer are not aptly construed merely as a conventional act
or as a caricature of such an act. The lightness and buoyancy
are symbolic of the light, soaring dynamics of the feeling of joy.
A taut, backward leap embodies the felt surge of alarm; and
ripples of gaiety are echoed in a flurry of light little steps.
Dances such as *Lamentation,* which are built mainly on natural
dynamics, are susceptible of having cross-cultural appeal. Admittedly in some sense requiring elucidation, they will be "culturally emergent," to borrow Joseph Margolis's phrase,[11] but
they could be culturally relative only in the impossible case
where the natural species-specific dynamics of feeling varied
while remaining what they were.

The similarity of the dynamics of the dance to the dynamics
of the emotion place this type of expressive dance in one family
with the expressive dances considered earlier. One and the
same operation is central throughout—that is, kinetic simulation—and one line of successive abstraction runs from the depiction of an eagle, to that of smoke or water, to that of feeling.
Among the more distant descendants of the line are Helen
Tamiris's *Walt Whitman Suite,* reflecting the poet's optimism and
open, enthusiastic approach to life, and *The Lark Ascending,*
Alvin Ailey's paean to the human spirit.

If movement dynamically and vectorially congruent with the
movement of water is depictive of water, then movements
standing in an analogous relation to the dynamics of feeling
should be considered depictive of feeling. Since caricature is
also clearly depictive, all of the types of expressive movement
that we have considered may be classed as types of depictive
movement. It should be noted, however, that kinetic resemblance does not of itself constitute a symbolizing relation.
Kinetic imitation, that is, the mere producing of kinetic resemblance—is an activity in which young children engage, but in its
initial forms it clearly fails to qualify as symbolization. For the
latter, what is required is some activity in which the resembling
term goes proxy for the resembled. The requisite activity is the
game of kinetic depiction, a variant of the game of acting out
narratives. There is a whole array of activities between kinetic
simulation and kinetic depiction. In view of the gradual shad-

ing of the one into the other, the decision as to where to fix the line of demarcation between nonsymbolic and symbolic must be largely an arbitrary matter.

What the above analysis brings out, *contra* Goodman, is the pervasiveness of resemblance as modus operandi of symbolization in dance, not only in narrative dance with ludic and biographical symbolism but in expressive dance with kinetic depiction. Metaphorical exemplification, as we have just seen, turns out on examination to be a form of depiction, a point that Goodman misses when he turns the matter over to the cosmologist. By the same token, his remark, "No degree of resemblance is a necessary or sufficient condition for representation,"[12] turns out to be irrelevant to contemporary Western theater dance. The remark is defensible only if taken to affirm that dance, in some singularly bizarre culture, could conceivably be ruled by conventions of so arbitrary a nature that anything might go proxy for anything.

Nonthematic/Formal Movement

Narrative dance is generally permeated with nonthematic or formal movement. A particular sequence of *glissades* or *pirouettes,* when appropriately situated in a narrative dance, will necessarily have some narrative function, if only that of displacing the dancer or dancers to some other part of the stage. It will also, through the tempo of the sequence, the amplitude of the movements, or the propulsive texture help to depict the feelings of certain of the personnages. The import of the sequence, however, manifestly exceeds these two functions. The elegance, lightness, and patterns of movement are worthy of interest in their own right. It may be protested that these qualities of the movement contribute to the creation of a fantasy world peopled with ethereal beings. While such is undoubtedly the case, it is difficult to agree that the role of the movements is limited to this function. They are worth watching for what they are, regardless of any further role they play.

Corroboration of this estimate is to be found in the fact that many modern ballets dispense with narrative altogether, as also with the depiction of feeling or character. Frederick Ashton's *Symphonic Variations* adheres rather strictly to the repertoire of steps of classical balletic technique, while Balanchine's *Violin*

Concerto takes greater liberties. Yet in both, interest centers upon movement alone—on line, pattern, and dynamic flow. When asked whether dance reflects life, Balanchine's response indicates his priorities: "It has nothing to do with life . . . we're like flowers. A flower doesn't tell you a story. It's in itself a beautiful thing."[13]

Balanchine would seem to be right in his assessment. A graceful leap is not symbolic. When present in a narrative dance, it is incorporated in the ludic symbolism whereby the dancer's graceful leap stands for the character's leap. Yet such symbolism does not make the perceived grace, that is, the character's grace, symbolic. Neither a graceful movement nor a harmonious pattern of such movement is symbolic of anything. Neither one represents, nor depicts, nor expresses, nor metaphorically exemplifies. In a word, insofar as dance movement enchants, it is in no sense a language.

Types and combinations of movement other than graceful balletic patterns may very well appear in dance as worthy of interest in their own right. The animal ease and swiftness of Cunningham's movements, for instance, are not symbolic in themselves; they are qualities of the movement, and their fascination is quite independent of any possible symbolic use to which they might be put. The intensity characteristic of movements of Cunningham dancers is equally a real feature of the movement as opposed to a simulated one, a feature which is interesting independently of any use as a symbol. Similarly, the more complex effects of the dance, the animated architecture and visual counterpoint, do not need to be construed as symbols.

Furthermore, there would seem to be no reason why such movement could not be made the focus of a dance. Certainly such a dance is possible in principle. Just as it is possible to have a narrative dance devoid of a biographical dimension, so it should also be possible to have a dance focusing on dynamic flow but devoid of any depictive relationship to natural phenomena. Instances of such dances abound. One nonballetic equivalent of Balanchine's *Violin Concerto* is Charles Weidman's *Opus 51,* which equally contains no narrative and has no subject in the traditional sense. The movements have a more varied origin, being drawn in part from classical dance but also from mime, acrobatics, and the wealth of task-oriented everyday movements. Kinetic continuity provides the link in otherwise madly incongruous juxtapositionings. Here it is the wild flow of movement which gives the spectacle its reason for being. As McDonagh states the matter, the concern of the dance is not "social betterment or any elevated feeling other than the sheer joy of dance movement."[14]

The latter remark is in fact applicable to a number of dances. One such is Merce Cunningham's *Sounddance,* a dance quite devoid of narrative continuity, in spite of a wealth of movement suggestive of narrative movements: impatience, perplexity, interest, exuberance, bustle, frenzy, affection, even an image of a fastidious old schoolmaster passing his charges in review. These narrative touches remain, however, evanescent and unrelated, failing to coagulate into a coherent, storylike sequence. The general effect is that of a human kaleidoscope of movement, coming apart and reuniting, the activity peaking at times in a frenzy driven along by the outrageous din. It is possible to discern parallels between certain aspects of the dance and certain features of the actual world, but these are insufficiently traced for the dance to be seen as symbolic of those features. What appears is an exhilarating movement spectacle.

Cunningham dances generally are not symbolic. This is most obviously the case with the more abstract, starker dances—*Suite for Five in Space and Time, Canfield, Torse, Walkaround Time,* or *Scramble*—which, although not totally devoid of atmosphere, are more obviously focused on form and dynamics. Yet even in the case of less abstract dances, such as the sensuously lyrical *Summerspace,* there is no theme, no underlying idea to be portrayed or communicated, to the service of which the movement is bent. *Winterbranch* might be seen as an exception to this claim. The heavy gloom, pierced with screeches, has been variously seen as depictive of modern city life, of the condition of the American black, or of some natural catastrophe. Yet such differing interpretations can be proposed only because the dance is in fact committed to none and is being forced into a mold which is alien to it. As Sheets-Johnstone has put it, for Merce Cunningham, "to dance is to live the human body in movement . . . and let the chips of meaning fall where they may."[15]

It is perhaps interesting to note that the nonthematic nature of Cunningham dance generally is a reflection of Cunningham's method of choreographing. In an interview, Cunningham states that in choreographing he does not begin with an idea to be translated into movement but with a movement itself, which is then developed and allowed to take on its own momentum, to go where it will. Applying this remark to *Rainforest,* one might say that the dance did not originate choreographically in a decision to depict a certain period in the life of early man but grew out of the capricious, noiseless movements of helium-filled cushions, perhaps initially suggestive of stealth, and in turn calling for alertness, and ultimately creating the atmosphere of unexpectedness and primitiveness of the finished dance. This choreographic development by internal association, fitting adjunctions, and interactions explains the reluctance one feels to classify *Rainforest* as a depictive dance. Equally significant in this regard is the account of a rehearsal by Carolyn Brown, long one of Cunningham's leading dancers: "And so goes the afternoon. No talk about meanings or quality. No images given. No attempts made to nurture expressivity in any particular dancer. The dances are treated more as puzzles than works of art; the pieces are space and time, shape and rhythm."[16] Cunningham dance, then, reflects what Cunningham characterizes as an "appetite for motion," or an interest in "motion for its own sake."[17] Thus when John Cage remarks, "We are simple-minded enough to think that if we were saying something we would use words",[18] he is echoing Balanchine's phrase quoted earlier, "We are like flowers." Where Cunningham differs from Balanchine is in his choice of diet.

The conclusion to be drawn is that much of Western theater dance is formal or nonthematic in nature and has no inherent connection with symbolism. A study in depth of aesthetic interest and delight might conceivably bring to light the workings of some system of symbolism—thus contradicting the above conclusion—a delectic symbolism analogous in function to the symbolism Sarte purports to find in personal likes and dislikes of particular qualities—the taste of pea soup, oysters, or tomato, for example.[19] For the present, in the absence of any convincing psychoanalysis of aesthetic taste, nonthematic dance must be concluded not to be symbolic and hence not to be a language. Dance may be likened to a language only insofar as it unfolds a narrative through a system of ludic symbolism, or insofar as it is related to the world, either in being biographical or in being depictive of some aspect of reality. The language of dance in each case is iconic, firmly rooted in resemblance.

Notes

1. David Best, *Philosophy and Human Movement* (London: George Allen & Unwin, 1978), 68–69.

2. Arlene Croce, *Afterimages* (New York: Random House, 1977), 99.

3. Nelson Goodman, *Languages of Art* (Indianapolis: Hackett, 1976), 231.

4. F. R. H. Englefield, *Language: Its Origin and Relation to Thought* (New York: Charles Scribner's Sons, 1977), 14–18

5. *Languages of Art*, 78.

6. This view is implicit in the subtle analysis of metaphor by Joseph Margolis in his *Language of Art and Art Criticism* (Detroit: Wayne State University, 1965), 174–75.

7. Maxine Sheets-Johnstone, *The Phenomenology of Dance*, 2d ed. (London: Dance Books, 1979), 83.

8. Monroe C. Beardsley, *Aesthetics* (New York: Harcourt, Brace, 1958), 331.

9. David Best, *Expression in Movement and the Arts* (London: Lepus Books, 1974), 187.

10. Edmund Husserl, *Ideen zu einer reinen Phänomenolgie und phänomenologischen Philosophie*, vol. 2 (The Hague: Martinus Nijhoff, 1952).

11. Joseph Margolis, "Works of Art Are Physically Embodied and Culturally Emergent Entities," in *Culture and Art,* ed. Lars Aagaard-Morgensen (Atlantic Highlands, N.J.: Humanities Press, 1976).

12. *Languages of Art*, 5, 40.

13. George Balanchine, "Work in Progress," in *Dance as a Theatre Art,* ed. Selma Jeanne Cohen (New York: Dodd, Mead, 1974), 190–91.

14. Don McDonagh, *Complete Guide to Modern Dance* (New York: Popular Library, 1977), 143.

15. Maxine Sheets-Johnstone, "An Account of Recent Changes in Dance in the U. S. A.," *Leonardo* 11 (1978):198. The statement is also made in an unpublished paper, "The Passage Rites of the Body: A Phenomenological Account of Change in Dance," of which the *Leonardo* article is an abridgment.

16. Carolyn Brown, untitled article in *Merce Cunningham,* ed. James Klosty (New York: Saturday Review Press, 1975), 24.

17. Calvin Tomkins, *The Bride and the Bachelors* (New York: Viking Press, 1965), 251–52.

18. Erica Abeel, "The New New Dance," in *The Dance Experience,* ed. M. H. Nadel and C. G. Nadel (New York: Praeger, 1970), 117.

19. Jean-Paul Sartre, *L'être et le néant* (Paris: Gallimard, 1943), 690 ff.; *Being and Nothingness,* trans. Hazel E. Barnes (New York: Philosophical Library, 1956), 595.

The Dancing Body:
Divisions on a Sartrian Ground

Francis Sparshott

I

Jean-Paul Sartre's phenomenological ontology, in his *Being and Nothingness,* incorporates a phenomenology of corporeality. The "second dimension" of the body is that aspect of our awareness of ourselves as embodied that is derived from our awareness of other people as alive.[1] We do not perceive them as masses of flesh in which a consciousness lurks, but as wholly vital: the moving form of the body is not distinguished from the consciousness and character of the embodied person. Yet we can also be aware of the other, and derivatively of ourselves, as *flesh,* a body not infused with life but dragged around by a living agency.

"Nothing can be less *in the flesh* than a dancer, even when she is nude," Sartre writes.[2] But dancers, we observe, are seldom nude. The dancer's body, when most exposed, is usually sheathed in some fabric that unites to the mass of the body those ineluctably flopping and dangling parts with which the bodies even of dancers are likely to be equipped. Parts of the dancer are not so much concealed as *held in,* not to hide the dancer's body but to nullify the fleshiness of her, and even more of his, flesh.

Sartre is thinking of dance, evidently, as celebration of the second dimension of the body. He invokes the old-fashioned concept of gracefulness as a basic value in dance, gracefulness being traditionally thought of as a class of forms derived from, and taking their meaning from, the unforced movements in which a well-formed and healthy animal most easily manifests its vitality. But if we are more attentive to the inner impulse of his thought, we may prefer to say that such a dance as he has in mind, or should have in mind, is one in which not movement but aliveness is made visible and complete and all-pervasive.

Visibility, completeness, and *all-pervasiveness* here take the place of the three conditions of beauty specified by the old scholastic definitions of beauty. Philosophers nowadays seldom use such formulae, but in such a context as ours they retain their use, because it was in order to capture the obvious aspects of exactly the sort of phenomenon that now concerns us that they were formulated. Visibility, then, answers to the scholastics' brightness, *claritas,* the immediate sensed quality of what is perceived: the "radiance of the form," however imagined or achieved or imparted. Completeness is the scholastic *unitas,* the body's manifestation and celebration of a single life: an integrated organicity. And the all-pervasiveness is *integritas,* wholeness: nothing is missing, and nothing fails to be integrated. The body is not only radiantly alive, and alive with a single life, but is so in every part.

Having said that, we recall our mention of the tights and codpieces that habitually cancel the swag of flesh. In most dances, the participants are more extensively and extravagantly clad than that; costume and body paint in their customary elaboration are surely part of the dance, though not of every dance. And in terms of the present argument, we must say that the costume and paint can be experienced in two ways, or perhaps in three. The possible third way has to do with visibility: the sequins and the paint serve simply to identify the dancer as a dancer, as a displayer of the body. The other two ways concern our argument more closely. "Clothes make the man": when one is considering widespread practices, clichés must be taken seriously. By painting and clothing our bodies, we claim them for humanity, even if the clothes we wear symbolize deity. The lily of the field is not arrayed like Solomon in all his glory. Any costume complements the animal identity of the limbs with a social identity. And as an alternative to that we may conceive of the costume as a screen, concealing the parts of the dancer that are not actively involved in the dance. In a stiffly brocaded costume and an elaborate mask, it may be that only the eyes and the hands are alive, the life of the dancer concentrated in them. For the term *all-pervasiveness* is an incomplete expression: it does not specify what the "all" is that is to pervade or be pervaded. By familiarity with tradition or by the cues of costume and concealment, the spectator may know what character, or type of being, is dancing.

The dance of some part of the body—toe-dance, tap-dance, finger-dance, belly-dance—if it aspires to the art of dance considered as we are now considering it, is never simply the dance of the part of the body: it is a dance in which the dancer is revealed in that part of the body, the whole person is there. So costume may convey recognition of where the energy of dance is channelled, functioning as an elaborately worked screen. But, as I hinted just now, such a screen is not necessary: the mutual understanding of dancer and spectator may be enough to channel the attention, so that we effectively see only those movements of only those bodily parts that constitute the entirety of this dancer of this dance. Such understandings are often recognized as governing our awareness of arts of all kinds, and theater arts especially.

The second dimension of the body is the body of the other; it is by imagining ourselves as the other's other that we are aware of our own corporeal presence in this mode. One would suppose, then, that the value of such a dance as we have described or imagined would be a value *for the spectator,* who in his or her awareness of the perfected freedom made visible in the dancer's movements or sheer presence becomes aware of, and sustained in, the consciousness of his or her own corporeal puissance.

II

Sartre's mention of dance, casual as it is, relates it to the second dimension of the body. But the awareness of the lived body has two other "dimensions," corresponding to the third and first persons in conjugated verbs. The second dimension corresponds to my awareness of *your* body; the third dimension answers to my awareness of *everyone's* body, the human body in general. But the first dimension of the body is my immediate experience of (or rather, *in*) my *own* corporeality. Before there can be a body for others, I must be a body for myself. This immediate corporeality is, for Sartre, simply my awareness of the world as one in which I am situated at a particular place (on which I have a unique perspective) and on which I operate—into which my being extends instrumentally. I am in my world by being located in it and by being active in and on it; this is the original meaning of my body, my basic way of being embodied. In living this out unself-consciously I become a body for another's consciousness and therefore make available to the other the awareness of being objectively embodied.

Can there be a dance of the first bodily dimension, as there is of the second? It seems at first that there could not—the first dimension is unself-consciously lived, and the dance is a display. But then we reflect that my awareness of the body-for-others is at first my conscious awareness of a life unself-consciously lived, and not of anything that could reasonably be called a dance.[3] The dance is art and artificial, whatever its basis. So nothing stops us from saying that there is a dance of the first bodily dimension—if we can say what it is, and if we can win acceptance for our characterization of it.

The dance of the first bodily dimension would be a dance of pure thereness and pure instrumentality—a thereness without actual location and an instrumentality without actual operation. Those words have a paradoxical or silly look, but one hardly knows what words would serve better: the intention is simply to find a rough description for what a dance would be that celebrated the general aspects of living of which Sartre's full and not at all fanciful account of the first bodily dimension is meant to evoke the realization. I do not know that such dances actually exist, or that any actual dances lend themselves to this description. But there is a common *myth* of dance that seems to fill the bill. This postulates a dance in which a mythical creator brings a world into being by his mere proximity: the creator dances (analogously to the way in which the Aristotelian "unmoved mover" thinks), and the world comes into active being around or before him in recognition of his compelling presence and by the power of (but not in any literal sense as the *effect* of) his dancing. Such a dance is analogous in one way to the music of Orpheus. According to a rather different mode of imagining, the world dances before or around the creative figure of its god; in this mode, the god dances, and the world exists. Such a dance needs no spectators, for it is a dance in which the worldliness or embeddedness of living is given imaginative force. It plays no part, presumably, in any art of dance, for such an art depends on the body as it could be for others before (logically before, not before in time) it is one's own body for oneself. But it may well be that those who feel compelled to dance but not to display themselves in dancing are responding to an urge for which this metaphor is better than any other.

Perhaps, though, it is excessive to suppose that dances of the first bodily dimension are necessarily or typically related to such myths of divine or heroic, and in any case *magical,* efficacy. (I use the word *magical* here in Sartre's sense, to denote a facile, supposed efficacy that is less than causal though it purports to be more than causal.) It is enough to say that if I dance simply to celebrate my presence in the world, my dance is a dance of the first dimension, and the more properly so the more the actual way I dance can be related in some specific way to this its animating impulse. Perhaps many dances in which I dance as music makes me—in which I am moved to dance by an impulse from music, and what I dance is the meaning I find in the music—are really of this sort. That is likely to be the case if what I do is take from the music a new sense both of my presence and of the quality of my presence which I express in the way I actualize my sense of stance and motion.

III

What sort of dance would be properly assigned to the third bodily dimension? It is not easy to be sure. One supposes that the dances of the third dimension would be social dances, whether ritual and religious dances that belong to the community as such or the fashionable dances (from waltz and before to disco and after) of popular recreation. The third bodily dimension in Sartre, the dimension in which the body is lived as everyman's body, the body that can be subjected to medical and gymnastic regimes and for which institutions can share our responsibility, is the least personal, the least vital, but as a "third dimension" (the verbal felicity is more than a pun) confers solidity, factuality, closes the circle by providing a reifying context in which the more immediate first and second dimensions are eventually grounded. So, one supposes, the solitary dancer of the first dimension (and I must admit that the figure of the solitary dancer, to me enigmatic, is one to which my thought obsessively returns) and the dance artist of the second dimension, of which the first dances for and to him- or her-self but not for others and the second dances for others but not for him- or her-self, are both of them anchored in, and culturally take their rise from, the social dancer, who shares the experience of his or her own and others' dancing, with others who are dancing in the same way that he or she dances or who, breathless, await or imagine their turn to take a place in the dance.

IV

Are we to say that Sartre's three dimensions of the body have afforded an exhaustive triadic classification of possible or imaginable dances? Certainly not. The phenomena which Sartre calls "the body" are only part of the phenomenology of human experience; the proper basis for any classification of dance would be looked for elsewhere, in the very different domain of "free action." If we are to use Sartre's phenomenology at all (and there is, of course, no reason why we should), we should use the whole of it and pay attention to the system of interpretation that its creator builds on it or into it. Anyone who reads *Being and Nothingness* in that way can easily see how dancing and dances are to be thought of: dancing, and any particular way of dancing, and any particular person's dancing, and any particular dance are to be thought of as ways of symbolically possessing the world and ways of symbolizing the failed dream of being the self-founding founder of a world.[4] To spin out a way of interpreting dances in these terms would be easy for someone with the fertile literary imagination of Sartre. In fact, it would be too easy to be worth doing: one would undertake it only in some specific case that imposed a limit on one's ingenuity.

The reference to the dancer's body in the Sartrian discussion we have been exploiting is casual and incidental. What we have built on it is, at best, a three-way analysis of an aspect of dance or a possible sort of dance: the dance of pure bodily presence. But dance is usually taken to be an art (or several arts), not of presence, but of movement. No doubt there can be for a human being no presence without movement, as there can be no consciousness without freedom; but we should not make too much of that.

The tendency of the preceding paragraph is countered by an

article written by Jacques Rivière in 1913 in which he contrasted Nijinsky's choreography in *Le Sacre du printemps* with
Fokine's in *Le Spectre de la rose* (1911).[5] Rivière begins with the
perception that in Stravinsky's score (by contrast with such im-
pressionist music as that of Debussy) each theme is isolated and
attacked head-on, not woven into a seamless and shimmering
web of sound. Nijinsky's choreography, he says, has the same
character: dances, movements, groupings of the corps, are
sharply outlined and juxtaposed, so that the unity of the whole
is built by contrasts and not by reducing the components to
members in a single unity. In Fokine's choreography, the dance
celebrates the movement of life, but in this celebration the body
is lost in the created world of the dance itself. Such a dance then
becomes false to the original impulse of the dance, which was to
idealize the meaningful movement of the body as a body.
Rivière claims to have already sensed in Nijinsky's dancing of
Fokine's dances something that was false, an unsatisfactory tension between Nijinsky's dance as an integral part of a ballet and
Nijinsky's dance as the dance of Nijinsky himself. In Nijinsky's
own choreography, this tension vanishes. Every movement now
is true to the dance as an expression of the dancer's individual
body; it is a dance in which the body as a person's body reasserts
its rights against the dissolving claims of the dance as movement.

Sartre's contrast between body and flesh puts the value of
humanity on the side of the body, and in so doing exalts graceful movement as the sign of the perfection of embodiment. But
for Rivière that same graceful movement takes us away from
the human body into a world in which the only present humanity is furnished by the choreographer's imagination—although
that is not Rivière's way of putting the matter, nor is it one that
he would have liked. If, however, we decline to follow Rivière
and insist instead on staying with Sartre's valuation, we shall
need a new way of posing the contrast. What Sartre (and probably Fokine) had in mind was a dance in which every movement
is reconstructed to reveal the vitality of the body and cancel its
dead weight. What Rivière valued in Nijinsky's choreography
was a dance in which vitality, being that of a body as a body and
not as symbol of a soul, incorporated awkwardness, weight, the
intransigence of bone, as elements in a whole in which the
intractability of the parts was not denied.

Rivière's description of Nijinsky's choreography is incomplete—or rather, his comparison of it with that of Fokine does not take into account everything that his description recognizes. Nijinsky's dance, by renouncing the harmonizing plasticity of Fokine, restores to the body its rights, its pathos and weakness as inseparable from its strength and joy. But a body can retain its eloquence in these regards only by being the body through which an individual lives a life. The counterweight to a dance expressing the body as vehicle of life is a dance expressing the body as lived humanity.

In the ideology of twentieth-century dance, this is familiar to us as the dance of Martha Graham. It is a dance in which pain, sadness, and constraint prevail, because it is in these that the contrast between truth and grace becomes evident. Neither the dance of Graham nor that of Fokine is a dance of pure bodily presence: each represents one pole in the possibility of expressing and celebrating the bodily life of the double-natured creature that the mythology of our civilization has always taken man to be.

V

According to Rivière, in Fokine's choreography the dancer loses him- or her-self in the dance, but in Nijinsky's the dancer's body retains its integrity, and the spectator is not rendered uneasy by something akin to a lie. But both are choreographies, ways of creating dances. The difference lies in the nature of the artifact, not in the presence or absence of artifice. And in the dance of the second bodily dimension, as I pointed out at the time, the dancer is creating in his or her body a dance for the other: the spontaneous dance would be that of the first bodily dimension, and that would have no place in dance as art.

There is, however, a venerable and powerful tradition that resists the exclusion of spontaneity from art. John Dewey is followed by some pragmatists of the present day in distinguishing two kinds of art, or aspects of art, or modes of art. On the one hand, the work of art may be a work of artifice, involving the learning and execution of movements (such as the manipulation of an engraver's burin) discontinuous with those of everyday and inexpert life. On the other hand, the work of art may be the aesthetically weighted performance of movements and exercise of skills that all human beings use in their daily lives. All human beings move, and are sometimes called on to move, elegantly or decorously or precisely: the extension and concentration of such movements is already dance.[6] Everyone talks, and we sometimes have to talk with care and precision, persuasively or amusingly: such talk, when carried to a certain indeterminate point, is already literature.[7]

John Dewey liked to think of art as experience and experience as art, and thus assimilated all art to the kind that merely extends in an aesthetic direction the things that we all do. But we do not want to forget that there is such a thing as the making of a dance, and of a play or a poem. Are we then to say that literature leads a double life, so that natural and unnatural ways of writing may both be artistic but represent art of radically different origin and tendency? Is the sense in which anyone may become a dancer by emphasizing and refining what is dancelike in natural movement quite different from the sense in which a dancer must begin in childhood the painful exercise of transforming the body into a dancer's body capable of performing the exacting movements of the dance? Should we even, perhaps, recognize this difference by acknowledging the distinction that our language already seems to acknowledge, between the art of *dancing* and the art of *the dance*? Dancing is what we do; dances are what we make.

From any practical point of view, the contrast we have suggested is altogether too strong. We must recall that Sartre's contrast between the dimensions of the body belongs to a phenomenology, an attempt to isolate for philosophical attention the essential components of our world. Actually, however, we live one life in one world, and the dimensions are dimensions of one body. The second dimension, though essentially that of the body for others and of the other's body for us, becomes a lived aspect of our own corporeality, and the first dimension of corporeal living is something we can recognize in others, since we accept them as beings like ourselves. In practice, accordingly, we would not expect the two kinds of art that the pragmatists differentiate to be sharply distinct from each other. There is artful spontaneity, and there is spontaneous artifice. Yet the distinction remains, and may serve as a device for sorting out some of the interwoven ambiguities and complexities of practice.

It is a favorite pastime of writers, something halfway between a literary trope and a heuristic device, to use one of the fine arts to illuminate another. Painting and poetry have most often been used in this way; music and architecture are another favored pair. It came naturally to us just now to compare dance with literature, viewing both as arts in which one might achieve art by simply emphasizing values already necessarily inherent in everyday practice. But many writers take for granted a much closer connection between dance and music. Some even appear to believe that dance is basically the transposition into bodily movement of a musical experience. What is intended is not that music must occasion and accompany every movement that can be called dance, but rather that the arts of dance are in each case systems of transposing musical forms and dynamisms into physical terms or replacing them by physical analogs.

One reason alleged for saying that dance depends on music makes use of the pragmatist thesis that dancing is a natural extension of natural movement. But the thesis is used in a way that the pragmatists would never accept. Dance, it is said, being thus natural, cannot sustain itself without some such external means of organization as musical rhythm supplies—just as literature, which we coupled with dance in this regard, could never rise to the dignity of art unless it were controlled by musical rhythm and transformed into poetry.

The argument of the preceding paragraph is not very persuasive. Why should we not just turn the tables and retort that music itself is natural in exactly the same way, an extension of song, which is itself an extension of excited speech, and hence equally amorphous and equally incapable of sustaining itself as art without some separate structuring principle? There is no reason why we should not, and the whole argument falls to the ground. I introduced it not for its inherent merit but because music has a traditional answer which dance also might give, and which proves to be an alternative version of that transformation of the body into an instrument, a body-for-the-dance, that we derived from the Sartrian idea of the body-for-others.

Musicians often say that everything that is properly called music is distinguished from natural sound by being based on a system of tones, sounds precisely pitched and tuned in relation to each other: a gamut, a system, of modes or tonality. That is, the sounds from which music proper is built are themselves the outcome of musical thought, defined by their place within a musical system. This is certainly the way music in our Western tradition has to be understood. I once heard a phenomenologist tell his audience that each of them might on any day "hear a sound that will be a tone *for you*." By that he meant, of course, a sound that for the hearer would play the part in his or her life that the sounds of music play, and the burden of his discourse was to tell us what that part was. But many musicians would say that he spoke improperly, because a sound is defined as a "tone" not by its effect, an effect that any sound might have at the right time, but by its being properly perceived as, and actually functioning as, an element defined in relation to a determinate system of possible sounds. The phenomenology of music would have to be the phenomenology of *musical hearing*, of the experience of such systems in all their relatedness.

But now, suppose that we accept these musicians' view of music, and suppose that we also take seriously the idea that analogies between dance and music are likely to prove fruitful. We should then entertain the thesis that there is no true dance, no artistic dance, no art of dance, that does not rely on a repertoire of positions, poses, steps, that are artificially cultivated and defined in relation to each other. We cannot say, as we could with music, that the elements are defined *by* their relation to each other, because the absoluteness of the body prevents us from doing anything that really corresponds to the common practice of raising or lowering a piece of music from one pitch to another without really changing it (I do not say transposing it from one *key* to another, because that may alter the relationships). The process of modifying a dance to adapt it to a dancer of different bodily size and shape is not at all the same as such raising or lowering, even if it bears some faint analogy to it—a matter in which I defer to whatever choreographers and dancers may find. But despite this failure of fit, the modified thesis might be sustained. It is in fact often argued that in our Western civilization ballet is the only true art of dance, precisely because its repertory of positions, steps, exercises, and procedures has developed and maintained itself as a system, whereas all other ways of dancing merely reflect the bodily habit, predilection, and capacity of this or that seminal dancer and cannot maintain their integrity for more than a generation or two after that originating personal presence is removed.[8]

The doctrine that artistic dance must have a repertory of steps and positions answering to the musical repertory of inter-related tones and associated procedures does not require that there should be only one such repertory in the world, or even within a single culture. It used to be argued that the traditional tonal system was the only possible one, guaranteed by the facts of mathematics and physiology, but few people would argue that way now, and we are accustomed to the idea that any number of alternative musics are possible in principle, even if in practice we confine ourselves to one or two. So in the matter of dance we may recognize, here and there in the world, systems of dance with quite different repertory and syntax from those of ballet and allow them artistic integrity on the basis of the clarity and consistency, the completeness and expressive capacity, of the systems they embody.

We are thus left with the simple thesis that a true dance, or a truly artistic dance, is a reconstruction of human movement as other than natural movement, just as artistic music is a reconstruction of sound as other than natural sound. But this thesis will tend perpetually to evoke its antithesis. It took the place, we recall, of the doctrine that artful dance is dance based on a remaking of the dancer's body. And the antithesis now will take the place of the former contention that there is an art of dancing (if not of dance) that is an enhancement of the quality of natural movement. The antithesis will take the form of a demand for, and development or recovery of, a free music, a free dance, in which all sounds and all movements are allowed their proper place. Exactly this demand and claim are familiar to us in the utterance and example of John Cage and Merce Cunningham, and it is of interest from our present point of view that we associate this pair with a revolution in which dance and music are united, even though we all know which of the pair is the musician and which is the dance-maker.

Given a thesis and an antithesis, we know what to expect. Some will say that only what is based on a gamut or system can be taken seriously as art. Others will say that only liberated art is art, the old formalities being not art but a horrid perversion of art into mere artifice. Others will say that both are equally art in their own ways, given a proper understanding of art. Others will say that both await combination in a new synthesis.[9] Others will say that all such sayings and denyings are inconsequential, that people will continue to do what they want to do or have to do, regardless of whether it is to be called dance or art or anything else; and other people will call what those people do whatever they please to call it, for any reason or for no reason at all.

VI

We have just witnessed the distinction between a dance of the natural body and a dance of the transfigured body transform itself, with the help of an analogy from music, into a contrast between a dance of free movement and a dance of formal movement. This last contrast comes very close to a distinction with which Nelson Goodman has intrigued the philosophical community: the distinction between arts that are susceptible of notation and arts that are not.[10] Only what can be recognized as a distinct feature can be captured in a notation. And a dance of free movement may be free just because its features are not thus distinct. The very existence of a notation may therefore favor formal methods over informal ones, and may alter the balance between formal and informal elements in an art. Consider what must have happened when music began to be written down, and when a complete notation was at last achieved. Notation could begin only when there was agreement as to what was essential to the form of an art work and what was not essential, because not everything can be notated; and this agreement had to incorporate an understanding as to what distinctions had to be observed within what the notation sought to capture. I will not attempt to recapitulate any part of Goodman's beautiful and succinct presentation. I will only point out here that Goodman contends that once an art is notated, a work comes to be much more closely identified with what the notation captures: notation accelerates the analytical process on which it initially depends and in the end must transform the way we think of such an art.[11] Goodman wonders what will become of our ways of thinking about dance if a system of notation ever becomes accepted in anything like the way staff notation was so long accepted as part of the normal experience of music making. However, Goodman's views of the relation between score and performance have not been so widely accepted that we could build much on them here.

VII

We have derived from our authors a series of contrasts bespeaking different convictions about what is central to dance and to the art of dance. The kinds of dance that can be related to the three "dimensions" of corporeality as Sartre conceived it have significances that can be neither eliminated nor reduced to each other. And all dances of corporeality can be contrasted with dances of free movement in terms of Sartrian phenomenology. Dances of the body in its movement are contrasted with dances of the movement the body engenders, and this is close to, but not the same as, a contrast between dances of weight and dances of lightness. And all dances that emphasize bodily movement of any quality or kind can be contrasted with dances in which the movement is a symbol of *Erlebnis,* of lived experience. (Within the latter, by the way, we may contrast introvert dances with extravert ones, those in which the "experience" is all in the mind with those in which the experience is that of interacting with the world.)[12] Dances of life-movement enhanced are contrasted with dances in which movement is remade, and dances that embrace all movement are contrasted with dances that develop and depend on a system of dance movement; and both of these fail to coincide with a possible contrast between dance as direct expression of the creative idea and dance as essentially susceptible of notation.

Little more can be claimed for this set of related oppositions than that they give us something to think with and something to think about. Those who present them usually think of them as describing different ways of dancing, but in most cases they seem rather to represent different reasons for thinking dance important, or different excuses for preferring one practice to another. My reason for presenting them is that the Sartrian analysis at least raises fundamental issues and these issues seem to be related to some of the things people arguing about dancing have wanted to say.

Notes

1. Jean-Paul Sartre, *Being and Nothingness* (New York: Washington Square Press, 1966), 401–70.

2. Ibid., 506.

3. Compare Mary Wigman's apothegm: "First demand on a dancer: To establish the conception of the body as a rhythmic instrument rather than a mere physical torso" (*The Mary Wigman Book,* ed. and trans. Walter Sorell [Middletown, Conn.: Wesleyan University Press, 1975], 87).

4. See *Being and Nothingness,* 734–65.

5. Jacques Rivière, "Le Sacre du printemps," in his *Ideal Reader* (New York: Meridian

Books, 1960), 125–47. I am obliged to Dr. Selma Odom for directing my attention to this article.

6. Mary Wigman said "A human being who begins to dance, actuated by an inner impulse, does so perhaps from a festive feeling, from an inner acceleration which transforms his everyday movement into dance-movement, even if he does not notice it himself" (Sorell, *Mary Wigman Book,* 142).

7. This argument is implicit in John Dewey, *Art As Experience* (New York: Minton, Balch, 1934).

8. Cf. Lincoln Kirstein, *Movement and Metaphor: Four Centuries of Ballet* (New York: Praeger, 1970), 4.

9. Mary Wigman, after decades of the usual polemic waged by modern dancers against ballet, decided at the end of her life that the overall effect of the German *Ausdruckstanz* had after all been to effect a reform in German ballet, ballet retaining "in principle" its position as the traditional dance of Europe: "Everything has become modern ballet" (Sorell, *Mary Wigman Book,* 198). This convergence has become a commonplace, but the effect of the synthesis has been to evoke a new antithesis, "contemporary" or "postmodern" dance.

10. Nelson Goodman, *Languages of Art* (Indianapolis: Bobbs-Merrill, 1968), chaps. 4–5; dance is considered on pp. 211–18.

11. Mary Wigman says of Rudolf Laban that the roots of his dance notation grew from the need to develop a new style of dancing, and that "it took him years and years of never ceasing work to tame the freed and wild-growing movement, to lead the overflowing waters into the controllable channel of a consciously limited harmony—so it might become a speakable, legible, and *writable* language of its own" (Sorell, *Mary Wigman Book,* 32, my emphasis). The use of notation here is to emancipate a new style of dance from that subordination to a particular teacher's personality and body to which Kirstein refers (n. 8) and which is implicit in Wigman's apothegm (n. 3): compare her reference to "the most fascinating expedition existing for a dancer: to discover *his own* body and *its* metamorphosis from body into instrument" (Sorell, *Mary Wigman Book,* 52, my emphasis).

12. Mary Wigman found that the American girls in her Dresden classes "were different from the European girls who danced with such deadly seriousness and who analyzed their emotions, turned their minds so deeply inward that they lost spontaneity. The American students gave themselves to the dance freely, instinctively, yet not thoughtlessly" (Sorell, *Mary Wigman Book,* 133).